Jim Haynes is a first-generation Aussie whose mother migrated from the UK as a child during the Depression. His father arrived on a British warship at the end of WWII, met his mother and stayed. 'My parents always insisted we were Australian, not British,' says Jim.

Educated at Sydney Boys High and Sydney Teachers College, he taught for six years at Menindee, on the Darling River, and later at high schools in Northern New South Wales and in London. He has also worked in radio and as a nurse, cleaner and sapphire salesman, and has two degrees in literature from the University of New England and a master's degree from the University of Wales in the UK.

Jim formed the Bandy Bill & Co Bush Band in Inverell in 1978. He also worked in commercial radio and on the popular ABC *Australia All Over* program. In 1988 he signed as a solo recording artist with Festival Records, began touring and had a minor hit with 'Mow Ya Lawn'. Other record deals followed, along with hits like 'Since Cheryl Went Feral' and 'Don't Call Wagga Wagga Wagga'.

Having written and compiled 24 books, released many albums of songs, verse and humour and broadcast his weekly Australiana segment on Radio 2UE for fifteen years, Jim was awarded the Order of Australia Medal in 2016 'for service to the performing arts as an entertainer, author, broadcaster and historian'. He lives at Moore Park in Sydney with his wife, Robyn.

## ALSO BY JIM HAYNES

# The Best Australian Racing Stories

## From Archer to Makybe Diva

### JIM HAYNES

**ALLEN&UNWIN**
SYDNEY · MELBOURNE · AUCKLAND · LONDON

This edition published in 2018
First published in 2010

Copyright © Jim Haynes 2010

All rights reserved. No part of this book may be reproduced or transmitted in
any form or by any means, electronic or mechanical, including photocopying,
recording or by any information storage and retrieval system, without prior
permission in writing from the publisher. The Australian *Copyright Act 1968*
(the Act) allows a maximum of one chapter or 10 per cent of this book, whichever
is the greater, to be photocopied by any educational institution for its educational
purposes provided that the educational institution (or body that administers it) has
given a remuneration notice to the Copyright Agency (Australia) under the Act.

Allen & Unwin
83 Alexander Street
Crows Nest NSW 2065
Australia
Phone: (61 2) 8425 0100
Email: info@allenandunwin.com
Web: www.allenandunwin.com

 A catalogue record for this
book is available from the
National Library of Australia

ISBN 978 1 76063 331 8

Set in Bembo by Post Pre-press Group, Australia
Front cover images: (top) Gunsynd; (middle, L to R) Bernborough; Bart Cummings
with Think Big; Phar Lap; (bottom) Birdsville Races, 2009 (all Newspix/News Limited).

Printed and bound in Australia by SOS Print + Media Group

10 9 8 7 6 5 4 3 2

The paper in this book is FSC® certified.
FSC® promotes environmentally responsible,
socially beneficial and economically viable
management of the world's forests.

MIX
Paper from
responsible sources
FSC® C001695
www.fsc.org

*This book is for Robyn, who allows me
to indulge my racing obsession and knows
I really go to Randwick for the steak
and kidney pie in the Members'.*

# Contents

## Part 1    Champions All

## Part 2    The Humour of the Track

# Part 3   The Cup is More Than a Horse Race

# Part 4   The Good Old Days

# PART 1

# Champions All

# Our first champions: 1810–1924

## JIM HAYNES

No NATION IN THE world has venerated its champion racehorses as
Australia has. Every few years we seem to find a new thoroughbred
to admire. It is a part of our culture to have a champion to follow as
each racing year unfolds. This tradition was established quite early
in colonial times.

Australians have a particular obsession with racing, which is
probably due to the importance of horses in the development of
the colonies in the 19th century. The horse was the main mode of
transport until the industrial age, and without the horse this vast
country could not have been settled.

Apart from the convicts, the first settlers were mostly military
men and most of them owned horses—and, when given a chance
and a holiday, they enjoyed racing them.

As settlements spread out into the bush, horses became even
more essential. Entertainment was limited and race meetings
became the most common way to let one's hair down after a
spell of hard work and socialise after living in isolation for weeks
or even months. Along with this came the love of a long weekend or a holiday, the belief that handicapping the more talented

performers makes things 'more interesting', and the Australian love of gambling.

General public involvement in racing is far greater in Australia than anywhere else in the world. It is amusing to speculate that the percentage of Australians who actually attended Spring Carnival racing in Melbourne in the 1890s, if translated into similar figures in Britain, would have seen four million people attending the Derby meeting at Epsom!

Australian racing officially began in the colony of New South Wales in 1810, when the first three-day meeting was held at Hyde Park in Sydney. The winning post was approximately where Market Street meets Elizabeth Street today, and the meeting established the tradition for right-handed racing in New South Wales, that being the most convenient way of going as the sun set to the west.

Both Arab and thoroughbred horses had been imported into the colony from the time of the first European settlement, and match races had been popular prior to that first meeting in 1810.

When the 73rd Regiment was transferred to Ceylon in 1814, the colony lost its race committee and racing became uncontrolled and was banned for a time by Governor Macquarie.

The original Sydney Turf Club* was formed in 1825 and began racing at Captain Piper's racecourse at Bellevue Hill under the patronage of Governor Brisbane, who had banned unofficial meetings and dangerous races around the now dilapidated course at Hyde Park.

Colonial politics and a public insult at an STC dinner led to the next governor, Governor Darling, withdrawing his patronage from the STC in 1927. Twenty-nine members resigned in support of the governor and formed the Australian Racing and Jockey Club.

The STC raced at Camperdown and the ARJC raced at Parramatta, and from 1832 to 1841 racing was conducted on cleared scrubland at Randwick, which was known as 'The Sandy Track'.

---

*This is *not* the STC we have today, which was formed by the NSW Government in 1944 to run what had been 'proprietory' or privately owned racetracks.

Racing in Sydney suffered from the poor condition of tracks until 1840, when the Australian Race Committee was formed to set up a decent racetrack at Homebush. This group then decided to form a permanent race club, and the Australian Jockey Club was officially born in 1842. The Homebush track was used until the completion of the 'new' Randwick in 1860.

In Melbourne, racing started at Flemington in 1840. In 1848, 350 acres were officially designated to be a public racecourse, and a committee, which became the Port Phillip Racing Club, was set up to regulate racing. In the 1850s this club disbanded and two new clubs, the Victoria Turf Club and the Victoria Jockey Club, became bitter rivals.

It was the VTC which instituted the Melbourne Cup in 1861. The third Cup, however, was a disaster: only seven horses started after all intercolonial trainers boycotted the event when the committee refused to accept Archer's entry on technical grounds. Politics and intercolonial rivalry threatened to ruin the event until the clearer heads of both the VTC and VJC came together to form the Victorian Racing Club in 1864, and Flemington and the Cup became the property of the VRC.

Australia's first popular champion racehorse was a gelding called Jorrocks, who raced in the 1840s.

## Jorrocks (foaled 1833)

Jorrocks was the first horse to attain popularity and champion status in Australia. His sire, Whisker, was by the English Derby winner of the same name and had been the colony's best racehorse, winning the Governor's Cup at the very first Randwick meeting in 1833. Jorrocks' dam, Matilda, had been the colony's best race mare and the mating between the two contemporary champions produced Jorrocks. Both his parents traced their lineage back to the mighty Eclipse, and his bloodline on his dam side contained a fair dose of Arab as well as English thoroughbred.

What is odd is that, despite his excellent racing pedigree, Jorrocks didn't race until he was five. This was probably due to the sale of the property where he was bred at South Creek and his transfer to another farm near Mudgee, where Jorrocks was used as a stock horse until winning a sweepstakes at Coolah at the age of five, when he was sent to be trained at Windsor by noted trainer Joseph Brown.

His ownership changed hands many times over the years but Richard Rouse, who saw him in Joseph Brown's stables before his career had properly begun, famously bought him. The price paid by Rouse was eight heifers, valued at £40.

Jorrocks clearly had strong legs and a steely constitution and became known as the 'Iron Gelding'. He was the first racehorse in Australia to have his picture in the newspaper and poems written about him. He stood 14.2 hands—tiny by today's standards—and was a long, low animal with an amazingly deep girth and fine Arab head.

Jorrocks raced in an era when most events were decided on the best of three heats, often over 2 or 3 miles each. He probably started more than 100 times; the true figure is hard to estimate due to the three-heat system of races. We do know that he won the AJC Australian Plate five times and the Bathurst Town Plate four times. He was also victorious twice in such races as the Homebush Champion Cup, Cumberland Cup, Metropolitan Stakes, Hawkesbury Members' Purse and Town Plate.

Jorrocks began racing seriously as an eight-year-old, and at the age of 17 he started eight times for four wins. His last hurrah came at the grand old age of 19.

The Australian Jockey Club had abandoned Randwick in 1842 for the Homebush course, which became Sydney's headquarters of racing until the AJC returned to the improved Randwick course in 1860. So it was at Homebush that Jorrocks won his major victories and ran his final race, finishing tailed off last in the Metropolitan Stakes of 1852.

Jorrocks was finally retired to live out his days on a farm at Richmond, about an hour northwest of Sydney. His grave is marked by a plaque and is situated on what is today the Richmond Airbase.

He set the trend for champion racehorses becoming much-loved 'public figures' with the Australian press and general population.

Racing during Jorrocks' time was a very different affair to the racing we know today. Races were started by a man on a pony whose job it was to attempt to muster the contestants into a reasonably straight line before dropping a large white flag. Races were most commonly run over the best of three heats and the winner was the horse with the best overall result. There was a large pole situated on each racecourse, sometimes about a furlong from the winning post or near the turn. This was known as the 'distance' and horses that did not 'make the distance' in a heat were 'out of the running' and could not compete in the subsequent heats.

If the judges considered a finish too close to call, the heat was declared 'dead' and the horses that figured in the close finish would 'run off' over the same distance again to decide the winner. So, in those days, a 'dead heat' was not a result, but a 'non result' which required another heat to be run.

There were no saddlecloth numbers until the 1870s and official colours were not compulsory for jockeys until the AJC introduced that rule in 1842. After each race the contestants would line up in front of the judges' box. The judges then looked at each horse and rider and checked the horses' looks and jockeys' colours against the 'official entries' list. The judges then announced the place-getters, who returned to scale to be weighed-in.

By the 1860s a new era of racing had dawned. Racing clubs had begun to regulate racing in the colonies, with the AJC taking the lead, and the famous Admiral Rous had standardised the rules of racing in Britain and established the weight-for-age system where horses of each sex carry a set weight at a certain age over certain distances. His close personal friend, Captain Standish, had left England following a rather disastrous betting plunge in the Derby, to become Chief Commissioner of Police in the colony of Victoria.

Standish has two claims to fame in Australian history. He led the rather inept hunt for the Kelly gang and, as chairman of the

Victoria Turf Club, he is credited as being the man who 'invented' the Melbourne Cup.

The Cup began in 1861, the same year that the AJC introduced the Australian Derby, and a new era of racing developed around it.

The rival clubs of Victoria put aside their differences and merged into the VRC in 1864. Meanwhile, in Sydney, the AJC, having returned to a new and improved Randwick in 1860, soon attempted to emulate the success of their Melbourne counterparts.

In 1866 the AJC introduced four new races, the Metropolitan Handicap, the first official Sydney Cup, the Champagne Stakes and the Doncaster Handicap. And along with the new races came a new champion.

## The Barb (foaled 1863)

The Barb was a small jet-black horse who became known in the press as 'The Black Demon'. Bred by the pioneering Lee family at Bathurst, he was famously stolen by bushrangers as a foal at foot.

A large group of valuable horses was taken by the bushrangers from the Lees' farm and driven south. One of the family, Henry Lee, followed the bushrangers to Monaro, where police apprehended them and all the horses except one were recovered.

The missing horse was a black colt foal that the kindly, horse-loving bushrangers had left with a farmer at Caloola when it went lame and could not travel. The loss was reported in the press and the farmer returned the foal to its rightful owners a few weeks later. The foal grew up to be The Barb.

The year that the new races were introduced at Randwick, 1866, saw The Barb winning the AJC Derby. His sire, Sir Hercules, also sired the winner of the first Sydney Cup, the mighty Yattendon, and Bylong, who won the first Metropolitan Handicap.

In the true spirit of intercolonial rivalry the Victorian colt, Fish-hook, was purchased for a record sum at the dispersal of Hurtle Fisher's Maribyrnong Stud by his brother, C.B. Fisher, and sent to Sydney to win the Derby.

Fishhook was from the last crop of the great English sire Fisherman, imported into Victoria to ensure that colony's superiority in the racing game. He finished a poor third to The Barb, giving the colonial-bred New South Wales champion sire, Sir Hercules, a major victory over Victoria's imported bloodlines.

Having accounted for the Victorian colt in the Derby, The Barb's trainer, 'Honest' John Tait, decided to take him to Melbourne and rub salt into the wounds by winning the Melbourne Cup.

The Barb would go on to win the Sydney Cup twice, as well as the AJC St Leger, the AJC Queen's Plate and the other 'new classic' race, the AJC Metropolitan Handicap. He travelled successfully to win the Melbourne Cup aged three, and took out the VRC Port Phillip Stakes and the Launceston Town Plate in Tasmania as a four-year-old.

The Barb's Melbourne Cup victory, as a three-year-old, in 1866 was the first of Tait's four Cup victories. It was a controversial Cup. There were two horses named Falcon engaged. One of them, also trained by Tait, finished third behind The Barb but the judge would not declare a third place, as the colours carried by the 'Sydney Falcon'—yellow jacket and red cap—did not match any of the entries given to the judges on the official race card.

Tait had substituted a red cap on his second runner to differentiate the colours from those carried by The Barb, but evidently he didn't notify the judge officially. The following day at 4 p.m. the stewards declared 'Sydney Falcon' had been placed third, but many bookmakers refused to pay out on the horse, arguing that only the judge had the power to 'place' horses officially.

Before the registration of names was properly controlled, different horses often raced with the same names. There were three Tim Whifflers in the Australian colonies in the 1860s: one was an imported stallion who sired the 1876 Melbourne Cup winner Briseis, and the other two Tim Whifflers both raced in the Melbourne Cup of 1867. 'Sydney Tim', trained by Etienne de Mestre, won the Cup and 'Melbourne Tim' ran fifth!

After his Melbourne Cup victory as a three-year-old The Barb went on to win 16 of his 23 starts. In one of his Sydney Cup wins he carried the biggest winning weight in the race's history: 10 st 8 lb (67 kg). He was virtually unbeatable at weight for age and was unbeaten as a five-year-old. One of his defeats was actually a win. He defeated de Mestre's Tim Whiffler in the Queen's Plate but weighed in 2 lb light.

When entered for the Melbourne Cup of 1868, The Barb was given the biggest weight ever allotted—11 st 7 lb (73 kg)—so John Tait decided to retire him to stud. He stood at stud until his death in 1889 and produced some useful horses, but no champions.

John Tait was given his nickname, 'Honest John', because he only ever protested once, when his horse Falcon was blatantly 'hocked' in the Sydney Cup of 1866. Even then he protested out of a sense of justice, not to gain the race, which was won by Yattendon. When The Barb weighed in light in the Queen's Plate of 1868, he offered £100 reward to anyone who could prove foul play.

Tait was born near Edinburgh and trained as a jeweller before deciding on a new life in Tasmania and emigrating in 1837 with his young wife and daughter at the age of 24. He found Hobart rather slow and moved to New South Wales in 1843, where he ran hotels at Hartley and Bathurst. Tait then moved to Sydney in 1851 to train horses and become licensee of the Commercial Hotel on Castlereagh Street. His skill in the art of boxing and his sense of fair play helped him to run pubs successfully.

Tait and Etienne de Mestre dominated racing in New South Wales for two decades, being the first trainers to bring commercial principles and good management practices to the sport of racing.

In 1847 Tait had won the New South Wales St Leger at Homebush with a horse named Whalebone. After a few very successful seasons he sold his horses and visited England to choose breeding stock. On his return he set up stables at Randwick and a stud at Mount Druitt, west of Sydney, and changed his racing colours from black jacket and red cap to the famous yellow jacket and black cap. Perhaps his colours were too close to those of his rival Etienne de Mestre whose horses, including the famous Archer, raced in all black.

Between 1861 and 1878 the two great Sydney trainers won half of the Melbourne Cups contested, with de Mestre taking the Cup five times and John Tait four times.

Australian racing had been through a stage of incredible growth in the 1860s, and the 1870s saw a series of unsavoury scandals involving trainers hiding horses' true abilities.

Two of the worst of these incidents involved horses from St Albans stud near Geelong. A protest was entered the day after the 1873 Melbourne Cup over the uncertain ownership, age and identity of winner Don Juan. A tale of disguised ownership emerged, and the public image of racing suffered even more when a huge Melbourne Cup plunge on the lightly raced Savanaka occurred in 1877.

Savanaka lost the Cup to the Sydney champ Chester, but the unsavoury link between betting and training was damaging the image of racing. The tragic loss in a storm of nine Sydney horses bound for the 1876 Melbourne Spring Carnival on board the steamer *City of Melbourne* was made worse by the celebrations initiated by Melbourne's bookmakers on hearing the news.

Things were on the improve by the 1880s. The decade began with the Melbourne Cup win of one of my favourite champions of the Australian turf.

## Grand Flaneur (foaled 1877)

Grand Flaneur holds a unique place in racing history—he is the only Melbourne Cup winner who was never defeated on a racetrack. Added to this is the fact that he was a very successful and influential sire.

Grand Flaneur was by the great colonial sire Yattendon, out of an imported mare, First Lady, a daughter of the great British sire St Albans. Owned by AJC committeeman Mr W.A. Long, he won at Flemington over 5 furlongs as a two-year-old and then was rested until the Sydney Spring Carnival of 1880. He duly took out the AJC Derby and Mares Produce Stakes, and then returned to Melbourne to win the Victoria Derby, Melbourne Cup and Mares

Produce Stakes within a week. The Melbourne champion colt, Progress, finished second every time.

Grand Flaneur was also the horse who finally gave the greatest jockey of his time, Tom Hales, his one and only Melbourne Cup win. He defeated Progress again in the 1881 VRC Champion Stakes and VRC St Leger Stakes and ended his career by winning the 1881 VRC Town Plate. Taken back to Sydney for the AJC Autumn Carnival he broke down and was retired to stand at stud. Bravo, the 1891 Melbourne Cup winner, was from his first crop; Grand Flaneur also sired the 1894 Cup winner Patron and was the leading Australian sire in 1894–95.

Grand Flaneur's son Merman won the Williamstown Cup in 1896 and then went to race in Britain. Owned by actress Lillie Langtry, Merman won the Goodwood Cup in 1899 and the Ascot Gold Cup in 1900, the same year that his sire Grand Flaneur died, aged 22, at the Chipping Norton Stud near Liverpool, southwest of Sydney.

The AJC had taken firm control of New South Wales racing by the 1880s, and the VRC established the Official Racing Calendar in 1882 and declared that all race meetings throughout Victoria had to run in accordance with the VRC rules. Horses competing on racetracks that did not comply were banned from racing at Flemington.

Racing was entering a golden era as the 1890s rolled around. The skulduggery and shonky practices of the 1860s and 1870s had receded to a large degree. 'Pony' or unregistered racing was growing in popularity in Sydney and Melbourne, and that form of racing would remain popular until the 1930s and perhaps provided an outlet for the less savoury elements of the racing industry.

So the scene was set for the greatest champion of them all to appear and take Australia and New Zealand on the ride of a lifetime. The time was ripe for the appearance of the greatest racehorse that ever breathed.

## Carbine (foaled 1885)

Carbine was foaled at Sylvia Park Stud near Auckland and had multiple crosses on both sides of his pedigree back to two great

18th century horses, Eclipse and Herod. His dam was the unraced imported mare Mersey, and he was the last foal of the good sire Musket, who won the Ascot Stakes and eight other races before being sent to stand at stud in New Zealand.

Musket, who died at age 18 after siring Carbine, was a very successful sire of stayers; his son Martini-Henri won the 1883 Melbourne Cup.

Carbine won 33 of his 43 starts and was unplaced only once, when suffering from a cracked hoof. He won 15 races in succession, and 17 of his last 18 races.

After five wins in New Zealand he was sent to Melbourne for the VRC Derby in 1888. Carbine finished second in the Derby; his jockey, New Zealander Bob Derret, dropped a rein in the tight finish and Carbine was beaten a head by Sydney-trained horse Ensign, carrying the famous blue and white colours of Mr James White and ridden brilliantly by Tom Hales.

Carbine's owner, Dan O'Brien, lost heavily on the Derby and decided to sell Carbine, who had won the Flying Stakes over 7 furlongs and the Foal Stakes over 10 furlongs in the week following his narrow defeat in the Derby.

At the auction at the end of the carnival VRC committeeman Donald Wallace, urged on by Melbourne trainer Walter Hickenbotham, reluctantly paid 3000 guineas for him, having failed to secure the horse he really wanted to buy at the sale.

Being the under-bidder on that previous lot—a now long-forgotten horse called Tradition, which sold that day for 3050 guineas—was to be the best piece of luck in Donald Wallace's life.

Walter Hickenbotham now took over training Carbine and prepared him to run third in the Newmarket Handicap and second in the Australian Cup to the champion Lochiel. He then went on a winning spree, taking first place seven times from his next eight starts as a three-year-old, at distances from 7 furlongs to 3 miles, including the Sydney Cup in which he carried 12 pounds over weight for age.

As a three-year-old Carbine won four races in four days during the Sydney Autumn Carnival in 1890, including the Sydney Cup on the second day. The next day he won the All-Aged Stakes over a mile and the Cumberland Stakes over 2 miles, and two days later he won the AJC Plate over 3 miles.

While in training for his four-year-old season Carbine cracked a heel so badly that he could not race that season without a special binding of beeswax and cloth and a special bar shoe. This accounts for his poor start to the season, second in the Caulfield Stakes, third in the Melbourne (now the Mackinnon) Stakes and a brave second to Bravo in the Melbourne Cup. Carrying 10 st (63.5 kg) to Bravo's 8 st 7 lb (54 kg), Carbine's hoof opened during the race and he was beaten a length by a son of Grand Flaneur.

Two days later, with his hoof repaired, he won the Flying Stakes over 7 furlongs but, two days after that, he ran last in the Canterbury Plate over 2 miles when the binding on his hoof completely fell apart. It was the only unplaced run of his career.

With a good rest and his hoof patched up again, Carbine returned to racing in March 1891 and won three of his four starts in Melbourne before heading to Sydney for the Autumn Carnival.

As a four-year-old Carbine went one better than the previous year. This time he won five races at distances from 1 mile to 3 miles in seven days: the Autumn Stakes, on 5 April; the Sydney Cup, carrying 9 st 9 lb (61.5 kg), on 7 April; the All-Aged Stakes and the Cumberland Stakes on 10 April; and the AJC Plate on 12 April.

Carbine had now won seven races in succession, and would go on to win another eight before the sequence ended a year later, when he ran second in the All-Aged Stakes.

Victories in the Spring Stakes and Craven Plate came after a five-month spell; then the horse the public called 'Old Jack' travelled back to Melbourne to win the Melbourne Stakes and race into immortality in the Melbourne Cup of 1890, carrying the biggest winning weight in history, 10 st 5 lb (66.5 kg).

The great racing writer and novelist Nat Gould gave an eyewitness account of the amazing scenes at Flemington that day:

When the saddling bell rang before the Cup race there was intense excitement, and Carbine held his position as favourite firm as a rock, and 'Old Jack' was fairly mobbed as he was being saddled, but as usual he took no notice of the crowd. When he came on to the track there was a terrific burst of cheering. Carbine stood still and looked round, and then declined to go to the post.

His trainer, Mr. Hickenbotham, gave him a push behind, and Carbine moved a few paces. This was a slow process. At last Ramage threw the reins over the horse's head, and Mr. Hickenbotham fairly dragged him up the course.

I shall never forget that race.

Carbine held a good position throughout, but did not get well to the front until they were in the straight. At the home turn Highborn looked to have a chance second to none . . . No sooner, however, did Carbine see an opening than he shot through, and after that it was a case of hare and hounds. On came 'Old Jack', with his 10st.5lb., and at the distance he had the race won.

Cheer after cheer rent the air, and people went almost frantic with excitement. It was a wild scene. For months the public had backed Carbine, and at last the suspense was over. It was a glorious victory, and everyone knew it.

Carbine raced seven more times, in the autumn of 1891, for six victories. His narrow defeat came in the All-Aged Stakes at Randwick. His hoof was so bad that day that shoes could not be fitted, so he raced without shoes and ran second to Marvel on a slippery wet track. Unperturbed, Walter Hickenbotham took Carbine back to his stall, persevered and finally managed to get shoes on the champion, who promptly went out a few races later and beat Marvel easily over 2 miles in the Cumberland Stakes.

Carbine then went for a spell with the intention of being trained for the 1891 Melbourne Cup, in spite of being given 11 st (70 kg) by the VRC handicapper.

In early training Carbine injured his hoof again and suffered ligament damage, so it was decided he would stand a season at stud and perhaps return to racing in the autumn. However, the stud fee of 200 guineas was more than three times that of any other horse in Australia, and there was a stock market crash and a Depression looming; consequently Carbine served just three mares in 1891. Two foals survived to race and one of them, from a mare named Melodious, was Wallace, who would prove to be Carbine's best-performed Australian son and a huge success at stud.

It became apparent that Carbine's racing days were over and a lucrative offer—reputed to be more than £20,000—was made for him to stand at stud in America. Donald Wallace wanted him to stay in Australia, however, and he stood four seasons at Wallace's Stud near Bacchus Marsh, northwest of Melbourne, and sired the winners of 208 races, including: 12 stakes winners including dual Derby winner Amberite; La Carabine, winner of an Australian Cup, Sydney Cup and two AJC Plates; and Wallace, who won the VRC Derby, Sydney Cup, Caulfield Guineas, AJC St Leger and four other stakes races before going on to be a great sire of champions, including Melbourne Cup winners Kingsborough and Patrobus.

As the Depression hit and the drought worsened in the early 1890s, Donald Wallace's fortunes slumped drastically and he decided to sell all his horses in a dispersal sale in 1895.

The Duke of Portland, who was looking for a stallion with a quiet temperament as an outcross to mares from his brilliant but fiery champion stallion St Simon, bought Carbine for 13,000 guineas to stand at Welbeck Stud in England.

Ten thousand people came to the docks to say goodbye to 'Old Jack' as the steamship *Orizaba* pulled out of Port Melbourne.

Carbine survived the trip, and an emergency stomach operation in Colombo, and was able to live in his new home, with its soft English ground, without wearing shoes. A special device was sent with the great horse to England. It was a special 'umbrella hat' to keep the rain and snow off his ears. 'Old Jack' hated rain on his ears and would run and hide from rain. Walter Hickenbotham often had to take his umbrella to the races and cover Carbine's ears as he went onto the track. He also used the umbrella to get the lethargic stallion moving towards the barrier by opening and closing it rapidly in his face until he broke into a trot.

In spite of being only 'second fiddle' sire at Welbeck, Carbine finished fourth on the list of successful sires in the UK in 1902 and 1906, and sired 138 winners and 253 second placegetters there.

Carbine's son Spearmint won the 1906 Epsom Derby and was a great success at stud. Spearmint's progeny won 93 races and included Derby winner and great sire Spion Kop. Spearmint also sired the broodmares Catnip and Plucky Liege, which means that all horses with Nearco, Nasrullah and Northern Dancer lines trace back to Carbine, as do all progeny of Sir Gallahad III, the champion son of Plucky Liege.

Sir Gallahad III raced with great success in France and was the sire of three Kentucky Derby winners. He was the most influential stallion in the USA in the 20th century, being leading sire in 1930, 1933, 1934 and 1940, and leading broodmare sire in North America in 1939, then from 1943 to 1952 and again in 1955.

Also out of Plucky Liege was the great Epsom Derby winner Bois Roussel, who started only three times for two wins and a third; his son, Delville Wood, was five times champion sire of Australia.

Carbine died in 1914 at the ripe old age of 29 and his skeleton is on display at the Australian Racing Museum at Caulfield. His blood has been present in the pedigrees of more than 50 Melbourne Cup winners, including Makybe Diva.

Phar Lap was Carbine's great-great-grandson and had Musket on both sides of his pedigree. Sunline had Carbine on both sides of her pedigree, and Kingston Town had multiple Carbine and St Simon bloodlines.

## Wakeful (foaled 1896)

A new century saw Australia become a nation, and our first truly national champion racehorse was the first female thoroughbred to achieve the position of 'public hero number one'. Her name was Wakeful.

It is true that two fillies, Briseis and Auraria, had won the Melbourne Cup in its first four decades and been much admired by the racing public, but neither of them achieved the true champion status and public adoration that was to be the lot of the mighty Wakeful. Indeed, the phrase 'best since Wakeful' was used by racing men all through the 20th century to describe great racing mares and fillies. The phrase 'better than Wakeful', however, was one you would never have heard used in that time, except in jest.

Briseis and Auraria were champion three-year-old fillies whose careers were finished at four. Wakeful, on the other hand, did not race at all until her fifth year, when she won the Oakleigh Plate as a maiden at her third start.

Wakeful's story is a fascinating one, full of coincidence, good luck, victory in adversity and strange twists of fate, some of which occurred long before she was even foaled.

Wakeful's dam, Insomnia, was by the champion Robinson Crusoe, a great racehorse and a great sire. Winner of the 1876 AJC Derby, Robinson Crusoe, by Angler out of Chrysolite, was a grandson of the great imported sire Fisherman. He was owned by C.B. Fisher, who had neglected to name the horse before he won the Derby.

It was not entirely unknown for horses to race unnamed in those days. The registration process was somewhat slower then and horses having their first few starts, or never racing at all, were often referred to merely by their breeding. Many pedigrees contain nameless unraced mares if you look back far enough. Robinson Crusoe would have appeared in the race book, or race card as it was then, as 'brown colt by Angler from Chrysolite'.

Having won the Derby, the colt was then sent to Melbourne for the Cup aboard the steamship *City of Melbourne*. This was the vessel from which nine horses, travelling to the Spring Carnival, were lost in a great storm; among them was Robin Hood, Etienne de Mestre's champion and favourite for the Cup.

Only two horses travelling on the deck of the *City of Melbourne* survived the storm; the other nine were washed overboard or killed when thrown around the deck by the mighty waves. The captain sought shelter at Jervis Bay and luckily no human lives were lost that day, although 17 people died when the steamship *Dandenong* was disabled in the same storm.

One of the two horses to survive was the unnamed Derby-winning colt. Although desperately ill and weak from his ordeal, he recovered to become not only a great champion on the racetrack, but one of the most influential sires in Australian racing history. Having survived the tragic voyage, his owner finally found a name for him—Robinson Crusoe.

It was indeed the hand of fate that enabled Wakeful's grandsire to survive, and it was another series of coincidences which led to the great mare having any sort of career on the track at all.

Wakeful was bred at St Albans Stud in Geelong by Mr W. Wilson. Her sire was Trenton, a son of Musket, who was also sire of the mighty Carbine.

Wakeful was trialled as a two-year-old and showed ability before a track accident caused her to be returned to the paddock. She suffered from lameness through her two-year-old and three-year-old seasons and remained almost forgotten in the paddock at St Albans.

The great mare would almost certainly have never raced but for the death of her owner early in 1900. At the dispersal sale after Wilson's death she was described in the catalogue as 'a nice little mare by Trenton that should be worth a place in any Stud'. Although she was still a three-year-old filly at the time, it is obvious that all and sundry considered her only value to be as a broodmare, not on the racetrack.

Luckily, however, there was one man who knew better. Les MacDonald was a former manager of St Albans and he obviously knew a few things about the filly that others bidding at the sale didn't. He commissioned Mr Neil Campbell to make the purchase for him at 310 guineas, which was a fair amount for an unraced though well-bred filly. In hindsight it was the bargain of a lifetime.

Wakeful was a powerfully built bay mare. She stood 15.2 hands, a good size for a mare in those days, and her near-perfect action was marred slightly by some awkwardness in her forelegs. She suffered from bouts of lameness all her life, which may account for the odd anomalies in consistency in her career and her occasional, uncharacteristic minor placings.

Trained at Mordialloc in Victoria by Hugh Munro, father of great jockeys Jim and Darby, Wakeful began her racing career as a four-year-old, running second over 5 furlongs at Caulfield. At her second start she raced poorly over 6 furlongs at Flemington, finishing 20th and pulling up lame once again. She was immediately sent back to the paddock.

Four months later many things had changed. Australia had become a nation on 1 January 1901, and Wakeful had recovered from her lameness and was back at Munro's stables and running amazing times on the training track.

What occurred next must be considered one of the most amazing racing feats, not to mention betting coups, of all time. Wakeful, a maiden galloper rising five, won the Oakleigh Plate and took half a second off the race record. Not only did she win one of the nation's premier sprint races, she started at 4 to 1 favourite following a huge betting plunge by her owner Les MacDonald.

The mare was then given the maximum penalty of 10 lb for the VRC Newmarket Handicap. Even with this penalty she carried the relatively light weight of 7 st 6 lb (47 kg) and won easily, once again backed in to start favourite at 5 to 2.

In those days the weights for the AJC Autumn Carnival were issued in January, and Wakeful, even with the maximum penalty, was thrown into the Doncaster Handicap with 7 st 10 lb (49 kg). She won the famous mile race easily and, with really no preparation as a stayer, ran a gallant third in the Sydney Cup two days later. The AJC immediately rescheduled weight declarations to prevent such a thing happening again.

In the spring Wakeful returned to racing by winning the Caulfield Stakes. She then started favourite in the Caulfield Cup. After stumbling and almost falling in the straight, she recovered to catch Hymettus and the crowd thought she had won. The judge, however, gave the race to Hymettus on the bob of the head—they had taken one and a half seconds off the race record.

Wakeful then won the first of her three consecutive Melbourne Stakes, defeating Hymettus who could only manage fourth placing. She had not been trained for the Melbourne Cup and tired to run fifth in the big race after contesting the lead in the straight with the eventual winner, her stablemate Revenue, who carried 1 stone less. MacDonald, who also owned Revenue, did not expect her to run out the 2 miles, and she started at 10 to 1.

When Wakeful returned to racing in the autumn of 1902, she had been trained and conditioned to stay, her target being the Sydney Cup. She opened her campaign by winning the mile and a half Essendon Stakes, but on her second outing, over 3 miles, she ran second to Carbine's daughter La Carabine. In what was perhaps an attempt to toughen up the mare, two days after her second placing Munro started her twice in one day at Flemington. She easily won the All-Aged Stakes over a mile, but could only manage third over 14 furlongs later the same day.

Munro then took the mare to Sydney where, after a three-week break, she proceeded to 'do a Carbine' by winning four major races in seven days at the Autumn Carnival. She won the Autumn Stakes over a mile and a half on the first day and, two days later, recorded what was perhaps her greatest victory. Carrying a record weight for a mare of 9 st 7 lb (60.5 kg) she won the Sydney Cup by 2 lengths, taking an amazing three seconds off the race record held by, among others, the mighty Carbine and his champion son Wallace. Three days later she won the All-Aged Stakes over a mile, and two days after that the AJC Plate over 3 miles.

As a six-year-old Wakeful started 15 times for ten wins, four seconds and a third. Trained to stay, her wins came at distances from 9 furlongs to 3 miles and her placings, all except one at 10 furlongs, were in shorter races. The great mare bypassed the Melbourne Cup that year to concentrate on weight-for-age races. In winning her second Melbourne Stakes, however, she easily defeated The Victory, who won the Melbourne Cup at his next start.

In the twilight of her career, as a seven-year-old, Wakeful raced eight times for three wins, three seconds and a third. It is strange that, considering her amazing record and all her great wins, racing historians consider her best efforts to be two second placings. The first of these was the Caulfield Cup of 1901 when she stumbled only to recover and be unluckily placed second to Hymettus in that dubious judge's decision, which could only have been guesswork. The second, and most incredible effort of all, came in the champion mare's final race, the Melbourne Cup of 1903.

The most weight carried by a female horse to win the Cup prior to 1903 was the 7 st 4 lb (46.5 kg) carried to victory by Auraria in 1895. The most weight carried to victory by a mare in the Cup's entire history was 9 st 1 lb (58 kg), when Makybe Diva won her third Cup in 2005. Wakeful was given 10 st (63.5 kg), still the biggest weight ever allotted to the female sex in the great race's history, and it is likely to remain so for all time.

The gallant mare raced to the lead half a mile before the finish and led into the straight by 2 lengths, only to be run down by the good stayer Lord Cardigan, carrying 6 st 8 lb (42 kg)—a massive 21.5 kg less than Wakeful. Lord Cardigan, whose connections had successfully 'cheated' the handicapper to get the tough young stayer into the race with a featherweight, won by less than a length. Many experts considered that Wakeful could have beaten Lord Cardigan if jockey Frank Dunn had waited another furlong before going for home on the champion mare.

Wakeful was a very successful broodmare. She produced five winning sons, including Night Watch who won a Melbourne Cup, and the great sprinter Blairgour, who won an Oakleigh Plate and a Futurity Stakes. Her daughters were not successful on the track but two, San Repos and Camilla, became great broodmares, producing many good horses and passing Wakeful's genes down to later generations of good stayers like Frill Prince and Yarramba.

The year after Wakeful's gallant Cup defeat, the fairer sex had revenge when the aged mare, Acrasia, defeated Lord Cardigan by exactly the same margin as he had beaten Wakeful. The difference was that Acrasia carried 7 st 6 lb (48 kg) and Lord Cardigan carried 9 st 6 lb (60 kg), a 'turnaround' in the weights of 33.5 kg in favour of the mares.

Lord Cardigan was generally acknowledged as Australia's best racehorse when Wakeful retired. By the imported champion son of St Simon, Positano, out of the good Trenton mare Lady Trenton, Lord Cardigan won the Sydney Cup as well as the Melbourne Cup, but his effort in running second to Acrasia caused him to rupture and he died several days after the Cup, at the age of four. Acrasia was owned by Sydney bookmaker Humphrey Oxenham, who lost her in a card game to Lord Cardigan's owner, John Mayo, on the eve of the Caulfield Cup, but bought her back the next day for 2000 guineas.

After Wakeful's retirement and the premature death of Lord Cardigan, the racing public didn't have to wait long to find another great champion to adore and follow—and 1906 saw the arrival of perhaps the greatest three-year-old in our racing history, who happened to be another son of Positano.

## Poseidon (foaled 1903)

In 1904 the Moses family, from the famous Arrowfield Stud in the Hunter Valley, purchased the Martini-Henry mare Jacinth, with a colt foal at foot, at the dispersal of Neotsfield Stud, also in the Hunter. They paid 400 guineas and decided to sell the colt at the Sydney Easter Yearling Sales of 1905. The colt, Poseidon, sold to Sir Hugh Denison for 500 guineas, which looked like a very good result for the Moses family when he managed to win only one race from six starts as a two-year-old. Poseidon's amazing three-year-old season, however, made the 500 guineas look like petty cash.

Poseidon started 14 times as a three-year-old for 11 wins and three seconds. The wins included the VRC and AJC Derbies and St Legers, the Eclipse Stakes, and the Caulfield and Melbourne Cups. He remains the only horse to ever achieve that sequence of wins.

He returned as a four-year-old to win seven from 12 starts. His weight-for-age victories that year included the AJC Spring Stakes,

Cumberland Stakes and AJC Plate, as well as the Eclipse Stakes for a second time, the Melbourne Stakes, and the Rawson Stakes. He carried the 9 st 3 lb (58.5 kg) to become the first horse to ever win consecutive Caulfield Cups; and he finished 11th, carrying a massive 10 st 3 lb (65 kg), behind Apologue in the Melbourne Cup of 1907.

Poseidon lived to the age of 26 and stood at stud at Eumerella, in Gulgong, New South Wales. He was a moderately successful sire; his son Rascasse won the Queensland Derby and another son, Telecles, won the Moonee Valley Cup.

Poseidon not only made a fortune for his big-betting owner, but also famously made a fortune for a Chinese market gardener from Bankstown named Jimmy Ah Poon, who had an uncanny knack of backing Poseidon only when he won. Jimmy backed him on every occasion that he won, but never when he ran second or worse.

Jimmy was known as 'Louis the Possum' by bookmakers because he could not pronounce 'Poseidon' and called the horse on which he won his fortune 'Possumum'. Evidently Jimmy returned to China and lived out his days in luxury with the estimated £35,000 fortune he acquired backing 'Possumum'.

Between Federation in 1901 and the outbreak of war in 1914, Australia enjoyed a period of growth and prosperity. The drought and Depression years of the 1890s were merely a memory. The economy was booming and so was racing, and the public had some outstanding horses to follow and admire.

Following the retirement of Poseidon, great stayers continued to dominate the racing scene as far as public popularity was concerned. Three of the greatest stayers ever bred to race in Australia dominated this era, and they were three very different horses—Trafalgar, Prince Foote and Comedy King.

Of the three, Trafalgar was undoubtedly the most popular, although the other two were more brilliant, more versatile and better performed overall. Firstly, though, let's take a look at Prince Foote, who was probably the best of the three in terms of sheer talent.

# Prince Foote (foaled 1906)

A small bay horse trained by the master trainer of stayers, Frank McGrath, Prince Foote was the product of all English bloodlines, being by the imported stallion Sir Foote from the imported mare Petrushka, and so had the great 1875 Epsom Derby winner Galopin on both sides of his pedigree. Galopin started 11 times for ten wins and a second, and was the leading sire in Britain in 1888, 1889 and 1898.

As a two-year-old Prince Foote won the AJC Sires' Produce Stakes in what was a moral victory for non-colonially bred horses, but he was considered by many to be too small to be a good stayer. Frank McGrath proved the doubters wrong when the horse took out the AJC and VRC Derbies, both St Legers, the Champion Stakes and the Melbourne Cup as a three-year-old. In that year Prince Foote started 11 times for nine wins.

His greatest victories were in the AJC Derby where he was badly checked twice, fell back through the field, was forced to race wide and went around every other horse to win by a length and a half; and the Melbourne Cup, where he came late and flew past Trafalgar and Alawa to win by 3 lengths.

Owned by the Newcastle coal baron and shipowner, John Brown, Prince Foote was a great success at stud, being the sire of dual Derby winner Richmond Main, Craven Plate winner Prince Viridis, and 1922 Sydney Cup winner Prince Charles. He was also a good sire of broodmares and his daughter, Princess Berry, was the dam of Rosehill Guineas winner, Balloon King.

# Trafalgar (foaled 1905)

Trafalgar was a son of Wallace, which of course makes him a grandson of the great Carbine. He was a light chestnut with a flaxen mane and tail, so his colouring was identical to the great stayer Peter Pan, who was to grace the racetracks of Australia three decades later.

Trafalgar was a more solid horse than the later champion, and his popularity with the racing public was based as much upon his courage and dour staying ability as it was on his good looks. He started 59 times for 24 wins, 11 seconds and six thirds. His best wins were in the Sydney Cup, the AJC Plate and the Melbourne Stakes. His greatest run came in the Melbourne Cup of 1910, when, carrying 9 st 2 lb (58 kg), he unwound a mighty finish to come from near last and just failed to catch Comedy King, carrying 7 st 8 lb (48 kg). The margin was half a head.

Trafalgar was one of the most loved horses to ever race in Australia. He ran in three consecutive Melbourne Cups carrying huge weights—more than 9 st each time—and finished fourth, second and 11th, but he was always the crowd favourite. Some idea of his popularity can be gained by looking at the events surrounding the running of the Melbourne Stakes of 1911, three days before Trafalgar's final Melbourne Cup run.

Most punters considered the 10 furlongs of this race far too short for a dour stayer like Trafalgar. His old nemesis, Comedy King, was red-hot favourite at 5 to 4 on, while Trafalgar was unwanted in the ring at 15 to 1. The great stayer was to finish behind Comedy King eight times in his career but that day, when he produced another of his great finishing runs to defeat the imported champion, the Flemington crowd cheered him all the way back to scale—a show of affection rarely seen for a horse that had just defeated an odds-on favourite.

## Comedy King (foaled 1907)

Comedy King went on to win the Melbourne Cup of 1910 and was the first imported horse ever to do so. He was bred at King Edward's stud and purchased and imported by the popular Melbourne bookmaker Sol Green as a foal at foot with his dam, Tragedy Queen. His sire, Persimmon, a son of St Simon, started only nine times for seven wins, a second and a third, but those wins included the Epsom Derby, the St Leger, the Eclipse Stakes and the Ascot Gold Cup twice.

Sol Green was born into a poor Jewish family in London and was apprenticed to the royal upholsterer as a lad. When he discovered how little his master made, he decided there had to be more to aim for in life and he set off for Australia at 15, travelling fourth class to Melbourne with sixpence in his pocket. He slept in old boilers on the docks and bought and sold anything he could get his hands on. Eventually he became the biggest bookmaker in Victoria and one of Australia's wealthiest men, with massive real estate holdings in Melbourne and rural areas.

Sol Green never forgot his humble origins. He gave enormous amounts of money to charities, established a housing estate for ex-servicemen and a children's playground in South Melbourne, and constantly donated large sums to Melbourne's public hospitals.

Green's popularity was one reason for the public support of his imported champion, Comedy King. The handsome black galloper won the Caulfield Futurity as a three-year-old before going on to win six times from 12 starts at four, including the AJC Spring Stakes and Autumn Stakes in Sydney and the St George Stakes, Essendon Stakes, All-Aged Stakes and Melbourne Cup in his home town. He returned at five to win the Eclipse Stakes before finishing a gallant fifth in his second Melbourne Cup, lumping a massive 9 st 7 lb (60.5 kg).

At stud Comedy King continued to make his mark in Australian racing history. He sired two Melbourne Cup winners, King Ingoda and Artilleryman, and many other useful stayers, like the immortal Shadow King who started in six Melbourne Cups for two seconds, two thirds, a fourth and a sixth. His grand-daughter Witty Maid was the mother of Comic Court, who won the Melbourne Cup for Jim Cummings in 1950, and his son Artilleryman was perhaps the best racehorse ever foaled in Australia.

## Artilleryman (foaled 1916)

Bred by legendary bookmaker Sol Green at Shipley Stud in Victoria, Artilleryman was purchased for 1000 guineas at the stud dispersal sale by well-known grazier and businessman Sir Samuel Horden.

His dam was the well-bred New Zealand mare Cross Battery, who had Carbine's sire Musket and the great imported sire Fisherman on her sire's side and was a great-grand-daughter of the unbeaten Melbourne Cup winner Grand Flaneur on her dam side.

Reputed to be the best-looking horse ever to race in Australia, the headstrong brown colt's wins at three years old included the 1919 AJC Derby, Caulfield Guineas, Memsie Stakes, CB Fisher Stakes and Melbourne Cup. He dead-heated in the AJC Derby with Richmond Main, a son of his sire's contemporary Prince Foote, and ran second to that colt in the VRC Derby after pulling fiercely throughout the race. In the Melbourne Cup, however, Artilleryman settled the matter of who was the superior racehorse by defeating Richmond Main by 6 lengths at equal weights. He then completed his three-year-old season by taking out the 1920 St George Stakes, Governors' Stakes, King's Plate and St Leger Stakes in Melbourne and the Rawson Stakes in Sydney.

While being spelled, Artilleryman developed a growth on a hind leg and thickening of his veins, but he was still sent out as a 12 to 1 on favourite for the St Leger in Sydney. In a boil-over he ran second to Millieme and then failed in the Sydney Cup and the All-Aged Stakes. It was obvious to vets that the horse had an enormous growth or cancer internally, and this proved to be true when he suddenly haemorrhaged and died in January 1921.

## Poitrel (foaled 1914)

The year after Artilleryman's Melbourne Cup win the great race was won by another popular champion in Poitrel, carrying 10 st (63.5 kg), which places him behind Carbine and Archer as the third-greatest Cup-winning weight carrier. Poitrel was bred and owned by the Moses brothers of Arrowfield Stud, who had sold Poseidon to Sir Hugh Denison. Luckily for the brothers Poitrel failed to reach his reserve at the 1916 Easter Sales and the brothers reluctantly decided to race him themselves. He went on to win 17 of 37 starts, although his career was blighted by brittle hooves.

Poitrel was sired by St Alwyne, a son of the English champion performer and sire, St Frusquin, who was by St Simon. St Alwyne was imported by the Moses brothers and brought more of the wonderful St Simon blood into Australia.

Poitrel failed in three races as a two-year-old but managed three wins from just five starts at three. It was as a four- and five-year-old that he claimed a unique record in Australasian racing history—when he beat the great New Zealand mare Desert Gold in record time in the Spring Stakes and, in winning the same race again at five, he defeated Gloaming, who jointly held the Australasian record of 19 consecutive wins with Desert Gold. Poitrel also won the Cumberland Stakes and AJC Plate at four, real staying races.

Poitrel then won a string of weight-for-age races and ran a close second to Kennaquhair in the Sydney Cup with 9 st 9 lb (61 kg) in an Australasian record time for 2 miles of 3 minutes 22.75 seconds. The two horses dead-heated in the AJC Spring Stakes that year, giving Poitrel his third win in that race, and he also won the AJC Plate again before heading for Melbourne for the first time, as a six-year-old, to take on the great Western Australian champion Eurythmic in the Melbourne Stakes and Melbourne Cup.

Eurythmic had arrived in Melbourne from Western Australia and won the Memsie Stakes, October Stakes, Caulfield Stakes and Caulfield Cup, all in a row! He made it five in a row in Victoria, and nine straight wins, in the Melbourne Stakes, with Poitrel finishing third behind Greenstead. Poitrel also finished behind Eurythmic again later, running second to him in the CB Fisher Plate. Between the two defeats, however, Poitrel won the one that mattered, outstaying Erasmus, Comedy Queen and Eurythmic to win the Melbourne Cup with 10 st (63.5 kg).

Poitrel's last start was another dead heat for first, this time with John Brown's good stayer Richmond Main, in the Rawson Stakes at Rosehill. At stud Poitrel was a moderate success, the best of his sons being Belgamba, who won three St Legers.

Apart from his great record as a dour stayer, Poitrel is remembered as being the conqueror of three absolute champions of his era—Desert Gold, Gloaming and Eurythmic.

The Melbourne and Sydney spring and autumn racing carnivals had been attracting 'raiders' from New Zealand, as well as the neighbouring colonies or states of Tasmania and Queensland, for decades.

In the 1880s the amazingly versatile Malua had arrived from Tasmania to win not only the Melbourne Cup at 2 miles, but also the Newmarket Handicap at 6 furlongs and the Grand National Hurdle over 3 miles! The great Queenslander Le Grand, winner of 13 races from 21 starts, raced successfully in Sydney and Melbourne, winning the AJC Derby in 1883 and the VRC Champion Stakes in 1884.

New Zealand horses had been making the trip across the Tasman for many decades, and prizemoney was much better in Australia. New Zealand's rich limestone soil and cooler climate produced great horses, notably stayers. We need look no further than the two greatest of all time, Carbine and Phar Lap, to prove the point. But one of the first Kiwi raiders to storm our shores was a flying filly who won hearts wherever she went.

## Desert Gold (foaled 1912)

Desert Gold, the first horse to string together a remarkable 19 victories in Australasia, was New Zealand bred, owned and trained.

At two she won at her first four, starts in the Great Northern Foal Stakes, Royal Stakes, Manawatu Sires Produce Stakes and the North Island Challenge Stakes, but ran second in the Great Northern Champagne Stakes.

It was her last start as a two-year-old, the Hawke's Bay Stakes of May 1915, which began her amazing sequence of 19 successive wins. As a three-year-old, Desert Gold won 14 races and she remained unbeaten until age four, when she came up against a two-year-old named Kilflinn in the North Island Challenge Stakes of April 1917. At three she won the Hawke's Bay Guineas, New Zealand Derby and Oaks, Great Northern Derby, Oaks and St Leger.

When she came to Australia at five she defeated the best Australian horses at weight for age. She suffered her first defeat in Australia at the hands of Poitrel in the Spring Stakes over a mile and a half. She won the All-Aged Stakes in Sydney and the St George Stakes in Melbourne and carried top weight of 9 st 6 lb (60 kg) in the 1918 Melbourne Cup, finishing eighth behind Wakeful's son Night Watch, carrying 6 st 9 lb (42 kg).

Back in New Zealand, when she was a six-year-old, she defeated the three-year-old Gloaming—who was later to equal her record of 19 straight wins—when he missed the start in the Taranaki Stakes in 1919. However, the two later met four times and each time Gloaming won.

Desert Gold retired to the Okawa Stud, where she had been bred, and her daughters and grand-daughters produced many winners, among them the brilliant Gold Rod, a champion sprinter-miler in New Zealand in the 1930s, who also won the Epsom and Doncaster Miles at Randwick in Sydney.

Desert Gold raced through the dark days of World War I and brought some joy into the gloomy war years for New Zealanders and Australians. Her amazing sequence of wins was followed eagerly in the press by two nations for whom anything but war news was a blessed relief.

With an overall record of 36 wins, 13 seconds and four thirds from 59 starts, Desert Gold's win rate stands at 61 per cent, and her amazing place rate at 90 per cent. Both of these strike rates are very close to those of another legendary New Zealand mare of a later era, Sunline.

While Desert Gold was New Zealand bred, her sire, All Black, was imported from Britain, and her dam, Aurarius, was Australian bred, being a daughter of the great sire Maltster and a grand-daughter of Wallace. This meant that Desert Gold had both Carbine and St Simon on her dam side and Galopin on both sides of her pedigree.

In the case of Gloaming, who took over her mantle as New Zealand's favourite horse, Australia can claim the honour of having at least bred the champion. He was owned and trained in New Zealand, however, and returned to plunder the rich races in the land of his birth.

## Gloaming (foaled 1915)

Gloaming was bred at the Melton Stud in Victoria but his bloodlines were all British—both sire, The Welkin, and dam, Light, were imported. His pedigree is interesting as he was inbred, to the great Galopin, on his sire side, and to no less than three good horses—Sterling, Rosebery and Bend Or—on the dam side.

He was purchased for a mere 230 guineas by New Zealander George Greenwood and shipped over to New Zealand to be trained by Dick Mason. He became shin sore at two, so he was gelded and turned out. At three he showed enough promise to be shipped back across the Tasman to begin his racing career in the Chelmsford Stakes in Sydney. He won the race by 8 lengths in record time and then won the AJC Derby at his second start.

In a truly remarkable career, Gloaming raced from age three until he was nine—even today that would be outstanding but in the 1920s it was unheard of. He started 67 times, won 57 times and ran second nine times. His only unplaced result came in the North Island Challenge Stakes at three, when he managed to get his head tangled in the starting wires and fell, taking no part in the race. So, it is true to say that Gloaming ran first or second in every race he ever contested.

The accident probably occurred in an attempt to anticipate the rise of the barrier wires. The horse had done the same thing several starts previously in the Taranaki Stakes over 6 furlongs, but had untangled himself and chased down the field to run second. Unfortunately for Gloaming's connections two factors stopped him winning a remarkable victory that day. Firstly the race was over the short sprint distance of 6 furlongs, giving Gloaming little time to catch the field, and secondly he was racing against the great mare Desert Gold, in the twilight of her career, and she held on to win by a neck. Gloaming defeated the great mare on four subsequent occasions.

Gloaming returned to Sydney every year (he reputedly crossed the Tasman 15 times!) but bled as a five-year-old, became too sick to train at six, and suffered a minor injury in training at eight, so he only raced in Australia at three, four, seven and nine. His record on this side of the Tasman was 14 starts for nine wins and five seconds, and it took great horses like Poitrel, Heroic and Beauford to deny him more victories. On the occasions when he was fit enough to race in Sydney, he not only won the AJC Derby, Chelmsford Stakes and Hill Stakes, he also won the Craven Stakes three times, defeating his old rival Beauford on the last occasion. He started once only in his birthplace state of Victoria, winning the 1924 Melbourne Stakes, at the age of nine, at his last start in Australia, but he did an exhibition gallop before the Cox Plate and was paraded before the 1924 Melbourne Cup.

The gallant bay gelding began his amazing run of 19 straight victories with the first of his three Craven Stakes wins in Sydney at age four; the other 18 wins were all in New Zealand, and the sequence ended when he ran second at his attempt to win a fourth successive Islington Plate at age six. Gloaming was defeated that day by the good young miler Thespian, who broke the race record in winning and was beaten out of a place behind Gloaming at his next start. The 19 wins were over distances ranging from 4 furlongs to 12 furlongs. Distance didn't mean a lot to Gloaming: he was as effective over a mile and a half as he was over half a mile.

In what would be considered a completely 'upside down' racing career today, he had begun racing at three by winning over 9 furlongs and then at a mile and a half, and then won twice over 4 furlongs at age five!

It is easy to disparage Gloaming's record by saying that New Zealand racing provided easy pickings for the talented galloper. Perhaps the depth of racing was not great on the Shaky Isles during his career, but the truth is that he had to race against two of the greatest New Zealand gallopers of all time in Desert Gold and The Hawk, as well as good younger horses like Thespian, and great Australian champions like Poitrel and Eurythmic, in what was a golden age of racing.

The Hawk, another legendary New Zealand galloper, started 136 times for a record of 32 wins, 18 seconds and 20 thirds. He was by the locally bred New Zealand sire Martian from an imported mare, Sparrow Hawk. Ironically, however, Martian carried all English bloodlines while Sparrow Hawk was a great-grand-daughter of New Zealand bred Carbine, as well as the great St Simon.

The Hawk raced until he was 13 years old and successfully 'raided' the lucrative Australian carnivals as a five- and six-year-old, winning the Hill Stakes, All-Aged Stakes, Futurity Stakes, Lloyd Stakes, Caulfield Stakes, Challenge Stakes and Rawson Stakes, and the St George and Essendon Stakes twice each.

It was in a memorable clash with The Hawk, aged six, in the Ormonde Gold Cup over a mile at Hastings in May 1925, that Gloaming ended his career at the age of nine. The only two other acceptors were scratched, so the two champions were involved in a match race at equal weights, both carrying 9 st 10 lb (62.5 kg).

The Hawk led to the halfway mark and then the two raced head to head until Gloaming pulled away to win by a length. It was his eighth win in succession as a nine-year-old.

Gloaming lived out his days on his owner's property near Canterbury and was buried there—at a place now called Gloaming's Hill—when he died in 1932. In one of those 'spooky coincidences' his trainer Dick Mason died the following week, and his owner, George Greenwood, several weeks later.

## Eurythmic (foaled 1916)

While Desert Gold and Gloaming had 'attacked' the rich racing carnivals of Sydney and Melbourne from the east, the great champion Eurythmic made his attack from the west. Many old-timers still believe he is the best horse to ever be trained and owned in Western Australia, although Fred Kearsley, trainer of the great Northerly, would probably disagree.

Eurythmic was bred at the Camyr Allyn Stud at Scone in New South Wales, and purchased as a yearling by Mr Lee-Steere, chairman of the West Australian Turf Club. His sire was the imported stallion Eudorus, a great-grandson of St Simon, and his dam was the Australian-bred mare Bob Cherry. Bob Cherry was a daughter of Bobadil, the champion three-year-old of his day and a grandson of St Simon. The mare was also a grand-daughter of Wallace on her dam side, and had Musket on both sides of her pedigree.

No doubt the presence of St Simon, Musket and Carbine in Eurythmic's pedigree was a big factor in Mr Lee-Steere's decision not only to purchase the horse to race in Western Australia, but also to leave him ungelded. Eurythmic was to prove a remarkable champion, winning 31 of his 47 starts and being placed a further ten times. He also became the first horse to pass the stake-winning record set by his great-great-grandfather, Carbine.

Sadly, Eurythmic failed to pass on his ability or that of his ancestors when retired to stud. On the racetrack, however, he was a champion of the highest order, being unplaced only six times, two of which were in the Melbourne Cup when he finished a gallant fourth at his first attempt and broke down at his second.

In an odd way Mr Lee-Steere's plan backfired. He purchased the colt to race in his home state of Western Australia. Eurythmic was so good, however, that he ran out of competition in the west and had to be brought back east to fulfil his potential.

Trained by John Kelly, Eurythmic won ten of his 14 starts in Western Australia, including the WATC Derby, St Leger, Perth Cup and Osborne Stakes. He was then sent back east, to be trained by Jack Holt in Melbourne.

Little attention was paid to the horse at first by Melbourne racing men, who considered Western Australian racing well below par. Eurythmic slipped under the radar and won the Memsie Stakes at 20 to 1. By the time he had easily won the October Stakes and Caulfield Stakes, however, it was a different matter and he was sent out, as the shortest-priced favourite ever, at 6 to 4, to win the Caulfield Cup. He then won the Melbourne Stakes before finishing fourth in the Melbourne Cup, behind Poitrel.

He then won eight races in a row, starting with the CB Fisher Plate, in which he defeated Melbourne Cup winner Poitrel. His wins in Sydney included the Autumn Stakes, Cumberland Stakes and Sydney Cup, carrying a massive 9 st 8 lb (61 kg), and his champion status was confirmed when the VRC handicapper gave him 10 st 5 lb (66.5 kg) for the 1921 Melbourne Cup. This was the same weight carried to victory in 1890 by his illustrious forebear, the mighty Carbine.

Eurythmic's victories since coming east had been so emphatic and impressive that he was sent out as 5 to 1 favourite for the Cup, despite having to equal a weight-carrying record to win the big race.

In racing there are days when your luck simply runs out, and it is doubly unfortunate if that day happens to be Melbourne Cup Day, as it was for the horse many called 'the best from the West'.

Eurythmic's troubles began at the start when a strand of wire from the starting barrier caught his mouth, causing him to miss the start. Even so, he was galloping well and cruising into the race at the half-mile mark when he suffered severe interference, causing him to pull a muscle in his pastern. The champion limped home in last place as the three-year-old filly, Sister Olive, whose only other win had been as a two-year-old, led the field home to become only the fourth of her sex to win the mighty race in its 60-year history.

Eurythmic's jockey, W. McLachlan, always swore the horse would have won that day. When the interference occured McLachlan said that Eurythmic was 'only cantering, and could have gone to the front at any time'.

While this claim can be dismissed as mere speculation, there is no doubting Eurythmic's ability to carry weight and to stay. His win in the Sydney Cup is regarded as his greatest ever achievement, and he returned to racing in the autumn of 1922 and carried a massive 10 st 7 lb (67 kg) to victory in the Futurity Stakes. So who is to say that he might not have equalled Carbine's record that day, had his luck not run out?

Eurythmic's record speaks for itself. He won quality races against great horses, including the Caulfield Stakes three years in a row, before retiring to stud aged six. He was, indeed, 'the best from the West'.

## Heroic (foaled 1921)

The mid-1920s was an age of great stayers. There were champions like Gloaming, Windbag, Spearfelt, The Hawk and Manfred racing over distance, as well as good horses like Lilypond, Pilliewinkle, Purser and the tough old stayer David.

These last two horses were part of the supporting cast in the curtain raiser to this great era. It began at the Sydney Autumn Carnival, Easter 1923, the day that David won the Sydney Cup.

The final race that day was the Highweight Handicap and one of the runners was the Melbourne horse Purser. The well-named gelding, by Sea Prince out of Paper Money, had won the Moonee Valley Cup and the Warrnambool Cup and had twice been placed in the Caulfield Cup. His chances at Randwick that day, however, seemed rather forlorn. In a field of 29 runners he had to carry the huge top weight of 11 st 3 lb (71 kg), his best days appeared to be behind him and he had not won a race for over six months.

His trainer, Cecil Godby, and his big-betting owner, Jack Corteen, knew better and the betting ring was hammered in a well-planned coup as Purser was backed in from 20 to 1 to 5 to 1 within seconds of betting opening on the race. He won by a length and a half.

The Easter Yearling Sales began the following day at Inglis Saleyards and the money won by Corteen the previous day was used to purchase a chestnut colt from the second crop of the imported stallion Valais, out of imported mare Chersonese.

Valais raced only seven times for a win in the Windsor Stakes and two placings in top-class races in England, but he carried the blood of Bend Or on both sides of his pedigree.

The Bend Or bloodline was the most popular and successful in the world at that time, producing stallions which topped the sires lists in Britain, France, USA and Australia. In fact there was so much of the bloodline available in Britain that the Moses brothers, of Arrowfield Stud, had been able to purchase Valais for 2000 guineas after he had stood for one season in England. They also purchased Chersonese, who had the Bend Or bloodline through her grandsire Cyllene, who was also the grandsire of Valais.

This close in-breeding to Bend Or produced the colt that Corteen and Godby were so keen to purchase. They were cashed up and kept bidding until the colt was knocked down to them for 1800 guineas, the highest price paid at the sale. They named him Heroic.

Few horses in turf history have had a more sensational career than Heroic. The powerful chestnut was rarely out of the headlines for all the wrong reasons.

A docile animal at home, he was a barrier rogue with shocking manners on the racetrack. At two years of age he overcame a nasty eye infection which almost ended his career before it began by threatening to permanently blind him. The problem was solved by veterinary persistence and he won the Breeder's Plate easily at his first start and, in spite of his shocking performances at the barrier, won six of ten starts to establish a new stakes-winning record for a two-year-old in Australia. In doing so Heroic humped weights that are unimaginable for a two-year-old today. In carrying 10 st 2 lb (64.5 kg) to victory in the Alma Stakes at Caulfield, he set a weight-carrying record for a two-year-old, which was not broken until 1954. He finished off 1924—his first season—by winning the AJC Champagne Stakes carrying 9 st 6 lb (60 kg).

Heroic began his three-year-old season in Sydney in typical fashion by putting on a shocking display at the barrier and pulling throughout to run ninth, as favourite, in the Warwick Stakes.

As a Melbourne horse he was soundly booed and jeered that day by Sydney punters. A week later, however, many of those same racegoers happily cheered him, as the 'local horse', when he defeated the New Zealand champion Gloaming over 9 furlongs in the Chelmsford Stakes at Randwick.

Gloaming had been beating Australia's best for years and the parochial Aussie racegoers took Heroic to their hearts immediately when he broke the race record in defeating the New Zealand owned and trained champion.

Heroic's finest moment and one of his worst displays of bad manners occurred in the same race, the AJC Derby of 1924. The Derby was then run in the spring and Heroic started raging favourite at 10 to 9. The only two others considered to have any hope were the great stayer Spearfelt and the Rosehill Guineas winner with the delightfully politically incorrect name of Nigger Minstrel.

As Sydney racegoers know, the Derby starts in the straight at Randwick, where the leger enclosure, now long gone, was once filled with massive, noisy crowds. In 1924 the crowd was huge and it upset Heroic, who bucked and kicked as his long-suffering jockey, Hughie Cairns, attempted to get him into line behind the barrier wires.

When the barrier went up Heroic buckjumped and headed to the outside fence. Cairns attempted to straighten him and take him to the inside rail, but the strong-willed chestnut kept running out. The result was that the field raced away around the first turn as the Derby favourite zigzagged down the famous Randwick straight in a display more reminiscent of a Keystone Cops comedy sequence than a classic thoroughbred race.

In an oddly run race the field travelled at snail's pace behind a runaway leader, Sir Dighlock. Heroic, many lengths last at the mile, was able to sustain a huge run into second place at the half-mile, 20 lengths behind the tearaway leader.

The famous rise at the top of the Randwick straight took care of Sir Dighlock, who quickly compounded when Heroic raced past him. The two other fancied runners then attacked the champion chestnut, who gallantly held them off to win by a head from Nigger Minstrel, with Spearfelt another head away in third place.

Heroic was then rushed home to Melbourne for a crack at the VRC Derby and, only a week after his truly heroic victory in the AJC Derby, started favourite at 6 to 4 on a bog track in the Caulfield Guineas.

Once again the barrier rogue put on a display of bad manners, digging in his hooves and refusing to go into line until the clerk of the course cracked a stockwhip at his rump. He dwelt at the start when the barrier went up, but raced around the field to win the mile race by 3 lengths being eased up.

Heroic once again made the headlines when he was barred from running in the VRC Derby of 1924.

His owner, Jack Corteen, raced all his other horses in partnership with owner George Tye. The two owners had combined their resources and stables and had their horses all trained by Cecil Godby at his private training establishment at Alandale, out of Melbourne.

After the great betting plunge that enabled Corteen to buy Heroic at a record price, the old stayer Purser had revitalised his career to win the AJC Winter Stakes in 1923 and the All-Aged Stakes in 1924. He then returned to Melbourne and was entered for the Caulfield Cup, along with another very good horse owned by Corteen–Tye, named The Monk.

It was given out that The Monk would run in the Caulfield Cup and Purser, an eight-year-old who had been given 9 st 5 lb (59.5 kg) for the race, would not. Purser ran very poorly in the Coongy Handicap. Although Hughie Cairns claimed he had been hit in the face by a clod, the horse only plodded in to finish 11th, and he would have to set a weight-carrying record to win the Caulfield Cup.

Both horses were accepted for the Caulfield Cup, however, and it wasn't until after 2 p.m. on race day that The Monk was a late scratching and Purser, to be ridden by Gloaming's regular jockey George Young, was sensationally backed in from 50 to 1 to 15 to 1. The old horse, who carried St Simon blood close up on both sides of his pedigree, was up to the task and won easily, setting a new weight-carrying record for the famous mile and a half race.

A hostile demonstration after the race was followed by an enquiry the following week and the shock announcement that owners Tye and Corteen, trainer Godby and jockey Cairns, who had ridden

Purser in the Coongy but not in the Caulfield Cup, were all banned from racing for a year.

This meant that all horses owned by Tye and Corteen were also banned. Heroic, the VRC Derby favourite, was thus unable to start in the Derby or the Melbourne Cup and bookmakers pocketed many, many thousands of pounds.

More sensations were to follow. Appeals were heard and dismissed, Heroic was spelled, and then sold to Corteen's good friend Martin Wenke for 14,000 guineas. The VRC questioned both men and refused to accept that the sale was legitimate, and Heroic was then sold at a public auction and knocked down for the record price of 16,000 guineas.

Heroic was purchased by a colourful character in Charles Kellow, a well-known former champion cyclist who had made his fortune selling those new-fangled motor cars in the first two decades of the century and performing entrepreneurial stunts such as delivering newspapers to country towns by motor car during the rail strike of 1903, and setting a record in 1908 for driving from Melbourne to Sydney (25 hours and 40 minutes!).

No horse in Australian history made as many headlines as Heroic—at least headlines that didn't concern racing results—and every move in the saga was reported in the press and devoured eagerly by his adoring public.

Kellow sent Heroic to Jack Holt to be trained and the task must have aged the great trainer considerably. The horse won only three of his first 15 starts for Holt and his barrier manners became even worse than before. At the Randwick Autumn Carnival of 1925 he won the Autumn Stakes, and four days later was entered in two classic races on the same day, the All-Aged Stakes over a mile and the Cumberland Stakes over 14 furlongs. The record books show him as 'unplaced' in both races, but the truth is that he simply refused to start both times and took no part in either race!

Heroic won the Memsie Stakes and Caulfield Stakes in 1925 but was as erratic as ever, placing and finishing unplaced all through the spring. At wit's end with the erratic champion, Jack Holt proposed a daring plan to Kellow. He would train Heroic to sprint and attempt to win the 1926 Newmarket Handicap with the wayward champion.

Holt's friend, rival trainer James Scobie, had the good New Zealand stayer Pilliewinkle, and the two men wanted to try for the Newmarket–Australian Cup double with their two horses.

Kellow agreed—he needed to recoup many thousands lost on Heroic through the spring—and the plan was put into action. Holt's stable jockey, Billy Duncan, had had enough and was happy to step aside and allow Heroic's former jockey, Hughie Cairns, who had served out his one-year riding ban, to take charge of the horse again.

For once Heroic jumped away with the field and charged home to win the classic sprint, his only win in 11 starts between October 1925 and April 1926. Pilliewinkle fulfilled his part of the deal by winning the Australian Cup, and Kellow recouped huge amounts to restore his bank balance.

Back in Sydney, for the autumn of 1926, Heroic decided he would start in the Cumberland Stakes that year and duly won the race, but failed carrying 9 st 7 lb (60.5 kg) in the Sydney Cup, as he did the following year carrying even more, a hefty 10 st (63.5 kg).

Heroic showed his true class when he went on a winning spree at the Victorian Spring Carnival of 1926, taking out six races in a row: the Underwood and Memsie Stakes, Cox Plate and William Reid, CF Orr and St George Stakes.

Two weeks after his St George Stakes win he was unplaced attempting to win the Newmarket sprint for a second time, carrying a whopping 10 st 2 lb (64.5 kg).

Heroic's final victory saw him win at 2 miles for the first time in his career, in the Governor's Plate at Flemington in March 1927. After four unplaced runs at the Sydney Autumn Carnival he was retired, aged five, to start his career at stud in the spring of 1927.

More sensations were to follow as Heroic went on to be the nation's leading sire for four consecutive seasons. From nine crops he sired 184 winners of 964 races. Among his progeny were the mighty Ajax and Melbourne Cup winner Hall Mark.

Another sensation followed when the champion sire suddenly became impotent after nine seasons of great results at stud. Nothing could solve the problem and Heroic lived on for another six years until his wayward behaviour finally took its toll. A bolt of lightning in a sudden storm caused the old horse to gallop wildly across the paddock and slip over on the wet grass in December 1939. He broke a leg and was put down at the age of 18. His record of 21 wins, 11 seconds and four thirds is no real indication of the erratic champion's true ability.

# The 'Age of Champions': 1924–26

### JIM HAYNES

IN THE HISTORY OF Australian racing there has probably never been such a golden age as that which occurred in the mid–1920s.

Heroic, The Hawk and Gloaming were all racing and winning major races, and four other great champions in Spearfelt, Windbag, Manfred and Amounis joined them during this time.

## Spearfelt (foaled 1921)

Spearfelt was a small horse who was bred in the Goulburn Valley in Victoria but raised at Widden Stud in New South Wales after his mother died while being transported there with her foal at foot. He may well be the only bottle-raised horse to win the Melbourne Cup, and the little champ-to-be was purchased cheaply, for a mere 120 guineas, by Mr D.C. Grant, who was looking for a cheap colt with Carbine bloodlines to be trained by his friend, Melbourne trainer Vin O'Neill.

Spearfelt was a grandson of Spearmint, an Epsom Derby winner and son of Carbine. He won five races at two, then took the VRC Derby before starting favourite in the Melbourne Cup of 1924.

The little colt ran into interference and finished an unlucky third behind Backwood.

The following year he won the VRC St Leger and the King's Plate, but fell heavily in the Sydney Cup and then contracted pneumonia. He was still not fully recovered and was racing below his best when he ran mid-field in the Melbourne Cup that year behind Windbag.

He was fully recovered by the spring of 1926 and won the AJC Spring Stakes before finishing third behind Manfred in the Melbourne Stakes.

Trainer Vin O'Neill thought Spearfelt was poorly ridden in the Melbourne Stakes and replaced jockey George Young with Hughie Grant for the Melbourne Cup three days later. Manfred pulled up sore after his Melbourne Stakes victory and was scratched from the Cup which Spearfelt won, equalling Windbag's record time of the year before, 3 minutes 22.75 seconds.

The record crowd of 118,877 at the Cup that year remained an Australian record for a sporting event for 43 years, until broken by the Carlton–Essendon Grand Final crowd in 1968.

Spearfelt's career was blighted by sickness and injury and he won only nine races, but he was a brilliant champion. He was also a success at stud, counting many good horses amongst his progeny, including the 1943 Melbourne Cup winner Dark Felt.

## Windbag (foaled 1921)

Windbag was bred at the famous Kia Ora Stud in New South Wales by Percy Miller and was by the imported English stallion Magpie, who would go on to be Australian Champion Sire in 1928–29. His dam was the New Zealand mare Charleville, a grand-daughter of St Simon, which meant that St Simon was on both sides of Windbag's family, as Magpie was St Simon's great-grandson.

Windbag was a 'bad walker' and was famously knocked down at the Inglis Yearling Sales to agent Ian Duncan for 160 guineas. Duncan then decided he couldn't take the horse due to his poor gait and Clive Inglis graciously cancelled the sale and convinced the breeder's brother, Robert Miller, to race him.

From this embarrassing start Windbag became the Sydney champion horse of his day, winning 18 races in his career and a Melbourne Cup.

In fact, he had a very unusual Melbourne Cup preparation. He started racing in July 1925, winning over 6 furlongs at Randwick, and stayed in training right through the winter and spring, taking the Spring Stakes, Craven Plate and Randwick Plate at the Sydney Spring Carnival before heading to Melbourne, where he ran third behind Pilliewinkle in the Melbourne Stakes before winning the Melbourne Cup.

The 1925 Melbourne Cup was history-making as it was the first to be broadcast on radio, by the ABC. Manfred led for most of the race and the pace was hot, but Windbag outstayed his younger rival to win by half a length in record time with Pilliewinkle, the Australian Cup and Melbourne Stakes winner, a close third. Spearfelt also raced in the Cup that year, but was not well and finished well back.

Windbag didn't sire a Melbourne Cup winner, but he did sire many good horses including Chatham, the outstanding miler who won two WS Cox Plates in the 1930s.

## Manfred (foaled 1922)

Although Windbag, the older, tougher stayer, beat Manfred in the 1925 Cup, the younger horse was a strong-minded individual whose effort to win the AJC Derby in 1925 eclipsed Heroic's effort of the previous year.

Manfred shared a few things in common with Heroic. Both were sired by Valais, both were notorious barrier rogues, and both put up unbelievable efforts to win the AJC Derby.

In the AJC Derby of 1925 Manfred, who had won the Champagne Stakes at two, refused to start until the clerk of the course rode at him with his whip. He finally set off, seven seconds after the barrier had risen, and trailed the field by a good half furlong before settling for jockey Billy Duncan, who did not attempt to fight the horse but allowed him to settle at his own pace. He caught the field at the mile and raced level with Frank McGrath's champion Amounis before racing clear at the top of the straight to win easily.

Manfred also counted the Cox Plate, VRC Derby, Caulfield Cup, Caulfield Stakes, Melbourne Stakes and October Stakes in his tally of 11 career wins—an impressive resume.

Manfred had Bend Or on both sides of his bloodline, and his dam was a great-grand-daughter of St Simon via his brilliant son Persimmon. He was a great success at stud and sired many winning horses, including The Trump, who completed the Caulfield Cup–Melbourne Cup double in 1937.

## Amounis (foaled 1922)

Amounis was an unlucky horse in some ways; he ran into Manfred at his best and later Nightmarch and then the mighty Phar Lap. He had the distinction of beating Phar Lap in the VATC St George Stakes of 1930, when Phar Lap was three and Amounis was seven. He also stopped Phar Lap's great winning streak of 24 victories by defeating the 'Red Terror' by a head in the Warwick Stakes of 1930.

Like Windbag, Amounis was bred by Percy Miller at Kia Ora and was by Magpie. His dam, Loved One, was a great-grand-daughter of St Simon, giving Amounis the familiar champion's bloodlines of 'St Simon on both sides'.

In Sydney Amounis won two Epsoms, a Rosehill Guineas, Chipping Norton, All-Aged Stakes, Craven Plate and Warwick Stakes and, in Melbourne, three Linlithgow Stakes, two Essendon Stakes and two Cantala Stakes, as well as a WS Cox Plate, and Futurity and St George Stakes. He then won the Caulfield Stakes and the Caulfield Cup at eight. In fact Amounis has the distinction of having won at least one race that would today be a Group 1 event in every year of his career from age three to age eight.

With a record of 33 wins, 11 seconds and eight thirds from 79 starts, Amounis was the 'iron gelding' of his age.

In the century since Jorrocks was the darling of racegoers, many great horses had stirred the hearts of the Australian racing public. By 1930 radio, newsreel film and improved travel and communication made it easier to follow the exploits of the great inspirational champions of the turf, and the Australian appetite for racing and champion horses had grown even greater. The stage was set for the most loved champion of them all.

# Phar Lap: Australia's favourite horse

## JIM HAYNES

PHAR LAP'S SPECTACULAR CAREER has been continually documented and mythologised in books and films for 80 years, and his tragic end has been analysed and debated again and again.

In spite of his iconic status, it would be hard to imagine any champion whose career had less auspicious beginnings than the 'Red Terror'.

Both his sire and dam were failures on the track and, in breeding terms, both were outcasts, unwanted even by breeders of mediocre racehorses at the poorer end of the racing game.

In researching the breeding history of Phar Lap's sire, Night Raid, dam, Entreaty, and grand-dam, Prayer Wheel, the phrase I came across most frequently was 'got rid of'.

Night Raid was bred in England but was not a well-conformed horse when young and, although he was well bred, his breeder 'got rid of' him for a mere 100 guineas as a yearling. He was trained by a good trainer named Tom Hogg but only ever ran third in a poor-class 'selling' race, so Hogg 'got rid of' him to Australia, where he was trained in Sydney by Peter Keith and managed one win in a restricted race at Randwick, and even that was a dead heat.

Keith then 'got rid of' him to breeder Paddy Wade, who stood him at stud in Wagga Wagga, New South Wales, but the horse could not even attract mares from local owners, so Wade decided to 'get rid of' him to New Zealand breeder A.F. Roberts and sold him for half what he had paid for him.

Phar Lap's dam, Entreaty, had an even worse history. Her dam Prayer Wheel was a failure on the track and a failure at stud and was culled from the breeding stock of Trelawney Park aged 15 and sold for 20 guineas. It was not even known if she was in foal at the time, but she was, to the imported stallion Winkie.

Prayer Wheel was sold again before giving birth to a black filly. Named Entreaty, the filly was put into training but damaged a shoulder and raced once only, at five, and performed poorly. She was left in the paddock and forgotten by her owners until they heard that Roberts was looking for second-rate mares to be served by outcast stallion Night Raid, so they promptly 'got rid of' her to Roberts for 60 guineas. Phar Lap, born in 1926, was her first foal, from Night Raid's second crop.

More than anything, Phar Lap's success demonstrates the importance of being able to see potential in bloodlines and ignore racetrack results and preconceptions.

Harry Telford had the ability to do just that—and he didn't have the budget to do much else!

If we ignore results and look at breeding we see, as Telford did, that Night Raid was a grandson of both Bend Or and Spearmint and had Galopin blood on both sides and St Simon and Carbine (and thus Musket) blood. Prayer Wheel had Musket blood on her dam side and Entreaty had St Simon and Galopin blood via her sire. It was a potent mix.

Telford was a battler, a Sydney trainer who was born in Ballarat but grew up in New Zealand. He was obsessed by bloodlines and spotted the chestnut colt—lot 41 in the catalogue for the 1928 Trentham Sales—and implored his brother in New Zealand to buy the colt 'if he was sound'. His 'limit' was a paltry 200 guineas.

Telford's main problem was that he didn't even have the 200 guineas to back his judgement and had to convince one of the owners he worked for to pay for the horse.

The owner Telford decided to 'convince' was David Davis, who ran a successful import business in Sydney. Davis was born in Russia into a Jewish family who emigrated to the USA and was a US citizen, which partly explains the decision to race Phar Lap in the USA five years later.

Davis agreed to fund the purchase and Telford's brother Hugh was in the sale ring at Trentham when the last lot of the day, lot 41, was led in. Hugh was not quite alone; one other bidder was present, but he was acting as agent for a buyer who had gone home and was unsure about his limit, so the colt was knocked down to Hugh Telford for 160 guineas on a day when 2300 guineas had been paid for a previous lot and prices on average were between 1000 and 2000 guineas.

Not only were Phar Lap's immediate family poorly performed, the colt himself was gangly and ungainly, well over 16 hands as a yearling (big even by today's standards) and a slow developer.

On the journey across to Sydney on board the *Wanganella*, Phar Lap became seasick and did not eat; he also broke out in pimples, which covered his face. He arrived looking more like a cartoon horse than a racehorse.

David Davis was so unimpressed on seeing the horse he had been cajoled into buying that he refused to pay for his training. Once again Harry Telford backed his own judgement and arranged to lease the horse for three years, cover all costs and pay Davis one-third of all prize money. An Asian friend of Telford's evidently suggested the Thai word 'farlap' meaning lightning flash, perhaps a reference to the colt's glossy deep chestnut coat when he had recovered his health. The superstitious Telford, with November glory in his mind even then, wanted a seven-letter, two-word name as these had a good Melbourne Cup-winning record. So, the horse became Phar Lap.

Phar Lap was disinterested and lazy on the track and kept growing until he stood at 17 hands, so Telford had him gelded. Even so he ran poorly at eight of his first nine starts as a late two-year-old and early three-year-old. He did show a glimpse of what was to come by winning a Juvenile Maiden at Rosehill at his fifth start, after finishing last at his previous.

He then finished second in the Chelmsford Stakes and went on the first of his great winning jaunts, taking the Rosehill Guineas, AJC Derby, Craven Plate and VRC Derby before being sent out at even money favourite for the Melbourne Cup.

Phar Lap had run the same time for both Derbies and broke Manfred's record by a quarter of a second. In the Cup, with only 7 st 6 lb (47 kg), he had to be ridden by lightweight jockey Bobby Lewis.

It is often mistakenly stated that Lewis took the mount from Phar Lap's 'regular jockey' Jim Pike, who could not make the weight. The truth is that the colt had been ridden in his first 14 races by eight different jockeys, although Pike had ridden him in both Derbies and would become his regular jockey, riding him at every one of his 16 starts as a four-year-old—for 14 wins. Pike rode the great chestnut 30 times in total, for 27 wins and two seconds.

The 'Red Terror' could really be a terror to ride and he refused to settle for Lewis in the 1929 Cup. The jockey said later he just could not get the horse's head down or stop him reefing and pulling and so reluctantly he let him lead, only to be run down and finish third behind Nightmarch and Pacquito.

Nightmarch, the first good horse to be sired by Phar Lap's sire, was from the 'outcast' stallion's first crop and was a year older than Phar Lap.

The Phar Lap bubble had burst: the 'wonder horse' seemed to be just another 'good 'un', especially when he was beaten into third again, behind Amounis, on his return to racing in the St George Stakes in the autumn.

The spring of his three-year-old season would prove to be a mere aperitif to Phar Lap's career on the racetrack. In the 18-month period starting from March 1930, and ending with his eighth placing, carrying 10 st 10 lb (68 kg), in the Melbourne Cup of 1931, the 'wonder horse' started 32 times for 30 wins and two seconds, winning every major race in Sydney and Melbourne from a mile to 2 miles.

Those wins included the WS Cox Plate twice, two more Craven Plates to add to the one he won at three, the Melbourne Cup with ridiculous ease, carrying 9 st 12 lb (62.5 kg), and all the other classic races of the Spring and Autumn Carnivals in both cities.

The great horse won weight-for-age races by 20 lengths and broke the existing records for all distances between 1½ miles and 2 miles.

He started at prices like 14 to 1 on, and it is common knowledge that he remains the shortest-priced horse to win the Melbourne Cup, and the only ever odds-on winner. What some racegoers may not know is that he actually shut down the betting ring on no less than 12 occasions, when no bookmakers would take bets on the races he won. He also travelled to Adelaide and won two classic races there.

Jim Pike always said his greatest victory was when he took on the sprinters and beat them in the Futurity Stakes at Caulfield. On a bog track carrying 10 st 2 lb (64.5 kg), the big-hearted champion missed the start and then took off around the entire field to run down the good sprinter Mystic Peak.

Drama and sensation were part of Phar Lap's career. He was shot at before winning the 1930 Melbourne Stakes and then hidden away at St Albans near Geelong before winning the Cup three days later. He almost emulated the greats of former eras, like his ancestor Carbine, by winning four major races over eight days, three major races in a week and four major races in a month several times.

Phar Lap could probably have also won the Caulfield Cup of 1930, and the fact that he was left in the field and scratched quite late was controversial at the time. It was, indeed, part of a cunning plan.

Nothing outside the rules of racing took place, but some consider the actions of Telford and fellow Sydney trainer Frank

McGrath rather sneaky, while other racing men say it was a stroke of genius.

The plot revolved around three great horses: Phar Lap, Amounis and Nightmarch.

Nightmarch had defeated Phar Lap in the Melbourne Cup of 1929, but, the following spring, Nightmarch was defeated four times in a row by Phar Lap. Nightmarch's owner, Mr A. Louisson, had been heard to say that he would take the horse back to New Zealand for the New Zealand Cup if Phar Lap contested the Caulfield Cup.

In a conversation with Telford, Frank McGrath suggested that his great stayer Amounis, the only horse to defeat Phar Lap twice, would win the Caulfield Cup if Nightmarch and Phar Lap didn't start. He suggested that Telford leave Phar Lap in the Caulfield Cup field until Louisson took his horse home. In that time they could get very lucrative odds about their two horses winning the Caulfield–Melbourne Cups double.

The plan worked perfectly. Seeing that Phar Lap was set to contest the Caulfield Cup, Louisson took Nightmarch home and he duly won the New Zealand Cup. Then Telford scratched Phar Lap, stating that he didn't want to over-race the horse, and Amounis won the Caulfield Cup. Phar Lap, of course, famously and easily won the second leg and the two trainers sent a battalion of bookies near bankrupt.

Both Davis and Telford have been accused of over-racing their champion and Davis has been criticised for starting Phar Lap, against Telford's wishes, in the Melbourne Cup of 1931, with the cruel weight of 10 st 10 lb (68 kg), and for taking the horse to America.

Davis, however, seems in retrospect to have been a fair-minded man. He was grateful to Telford for finding the horse and allowed him to remain as part owner for a modest £4000 when the lease expired. It was also Davis who had Phar Lap's skin, heart and skeleton returned to Australasia after his tragic death.

It is also worth remembering that Telford had already won a Melbourne Cup with Phar Lap, while Davis had not.

Myths develop quickly in racing as in other fields of dreams and the truth is often forgotten when fiction and films are created from fact. Telford has been criticised for leaving young Tommy Woodcock in charge of the valuable champion in the USA, but the fact is that Telford's daughter had just died and he was organising her funeral. It is also true that a team of four, which included jockey Bill Elliott and vet Bill Nielsen, travelled to the USA with Woodcock and Phar Lap. David Davis was also in the USA managing the campaign. So the horse's assault on the US was meticulously planned.

It is a mark of Phar Lap's ability that the VRC changed the weight-for-age rules in 1931 to include allowances and penalties, in an attempt to bring the extraordinary horse 'back to the field'. They also gave him a massive 22 lb (10 kg) over weight for age in the 1931 Cup.

Further testament to Phar Lap's greatness are the sensation he caused in the USA and the ease of his win in the invitational Agua Caliente Handicap, in Tijuana Mexico, at his first start on dirt after a long sea journey and an 800-mile road trip. He was also recovering from a bad stone bruise to a heel and raced in bar plates for the first time—and broke the track record. That win, his only start outside the relatively minor racing arena of Australia, made him the third-greatest stakes-winning racehorse of all time, in the world.

Phar Lap's tragic death and the theories surrounding it have been well documented, as well as becoming entrenched in racing folklore. The nation mourned and the autopsy showed a severe gastric inflammation from duodenitis-proximal jejunitis, a condition exacerbated by stress.

Later studies, as recently as 2008, showed the presence of arsenic in large quantities, which has led to all sorts of theories, ranging from Percy Sykes's statement that all horses at that time had arsenic in their systems, to theories of deliberate poisoning. Phar Lap had evidently been fed foliage cut down after being sprayed with arsenic-based insecticide.

Two things seem certain: the well-documented symptoms the horse suffered are totally consistent with duodenitis-proximal jejunitis, and there was a lot of arsenic in his system. The rest is conjecture.

Phar Lap was such a towering figure that the history of thoroughbred racing in Australia is divided into 'before' and 'after' Phar Lap. All champions since him have only ever been 'the best since Phar Lap'. So it's entirely appropriate that this summary of our early champions and crowd favourites ends with him.

Comparing horses of different eras is silly, but people keep doing it. The exercise was described as 'folly' by the US *Blood-Horse Magazine*, which nevertheless, in 1999, ranked the top 100 horses ever to race in America. The panel placed Phar Lap, on the strength of one start in Mexico, 22nd.

When the findings were published, one of the panel recalled a conversation with Francis Dunne, who had been a placings judge at Agua Caliente and later a senior racing administrator in New York State. Dunne was asked, after Secretariat's Triple Crown win in 1973, whether Man O'War or Secretariat was the greatest horse of them all. He replied, 'Neither: I saw Phar Lap.'

# Why we came to love Schillaci

## LES CARLYON

I AM WAITING FOR the bus after the last race at Sha Tin when the urger glides up on a rumour and a prayer. In the sultry heat of late-afternoon Hong Kong, he thinks he is Peter Lorre. Dragging on a fag, he first looks around for hidden cameras, then leans forward and intones: 'I think I've got a really good horse back home.'

Yep, it is the big one. And me thinking it would merely be some tittle-tattle about Macau acquiring a nuclear arsenal.

He looks again and takes another drag. Before I can suggest we use the shoe phone, he goes on.

'They say he could be something special.'

Why do they always say these things?

Still, rituals must be followed. As with the other thousand times I have been told this fairytale, I effect deep interest and do a little Peter Lorre stuff myself. After all, the inference is that one loose word could see me being placed in quicklime by certain parties who do not wish me well.

This, remember, is racing. Idiots will tell you it's an 'industry'. Well, it may be, but before that it's a romantic comedy with a subtext of intrigue. Damon Runyon and Lewis Carroll write the scripts.

Most of these 'really good horses' are last seen at Manangatang wearing pacifiers and toupées, and attended by chiropractors and remedial farriers.

Anyway, this beast I hear about in Hong Kong has won but two races, a Kyneton maiden, worth $2925, and a mid-week at Sandown.

All this happened in 1991. The horse was Schillaci, the big grey who ended up a folk hero and now will never race again, which means we are all losers.

*They* were Lee Freedman, Schillaci's trainer, and his brothers Richard, Anthony, and Michael.

The 'urger' was Schillaci's co-owner, David Christensen, a company director and accountant, a committeeman at Flemington and Caulfield, and a very upright gent. Only as an owner does he take on his Peter Lorre persona, although this has paled now that he has given up smoking.

As it turned out, he had something better than a 'really good horse', and this had nothing to do with Schillaci winning eight group ones and two million bucks. Plenty of horses have won more races and more money.

Jeune is a really good horse. So is Danewin. But these and others merely inspire admiration. Schillaci belongs to another order, the guild that takes in Vo Rogue, Kingston Town, Manikato and Old Super. No, I'm not lining these five up on ability; what links them is more mysterious than that.

All could inspire affection. They came to be loved rather than admired. Because of the way they did things, they made people feel good and the sport seem grander than it is.

Schillaci was a great sprinting three-year-old, up there close behind Ajax, Vain and Manikato. He won fancy races and rewrote time records and humped big weights. This isn't why he came to be loved.

What endeared was the way he kept walking up, so honest, season after season. And the way, like Manikato, he stared down pain.

In the end, his grey coat had faded to near-white, his galloping action had lost its fluency, and his walk had become a shuffle. Yet he tried as hard, ran as fast, and won as many good races as in his carefree youth. When he was entitled to cheat, he didn't.

As a six-year-old, Schillaci had punters standing around mounting yards clapping until their hands ached. When he won his last race, the Futurity at Caulfield last Autumn, Lee Freedman briefly turned away from the media scrum and said aloud but entirely to himself: 'What a magnificent horse.'

Rebecca Newman, Schillaci's strapper, took the gelding to one corner of the yard and they clapped him there. She took him to the opposite corner and they clapped him there. This went on for ten minutes. And the glory of his win was grander than most of the crowd knew.

Some of us had seen Schillaci at trackwork the day before. Hurting everywhere, he was. As he shuffled out of the stripping shed for two easy laps on the sand, one word exploded in your mind. Lame.

Schillaci stumbled, lurched, slouched, and several times stood stock still, a ghostly statue, grand but worn. Lesser beasts, full of oats and bravado, pranced and danced; Schillaci just looked tired. When he came off the track, they lifted his forelegs into tubs of ice. As Rebecca Newman recalled: 'You could almost hear him say: Here I go again.' At the races next day, a famous trainer told Christensen: 'I saw your horse this morning and he's bloody near a cripple.'

Some cripple. Near the finishing post in the Futurity, Schillaci laid his long ears back, much like a heeler about to nip a bullock, and beat Jeune and Mahogany.

A few weeks ago, Schillaci was back at Flemington for another campaign. 'He was going really well,' Michael Freedman says. 'He looked great.'

In the dark, with Damien Oliver up and going only a little faster than even time, the grey hurdled a white bandage lying on the wood-fibre track near the 600-metre mark, landed awkwardly, and in less than a second, blew away a large part of his off tendon and all of his career.

'At first, I didn't notice much wrong with him,' says Oliver. 'But coming off the track, I knew he was lame. I felt sick.'

Rebecca Newman was waiting for them. 'Damien said, "I don't think Schillaci's very well." I looked down at his leg and thought, "Oh . . . oh, dear."'

John Van Veenendaal, the veterinarian who treated Schillaci, says the grey wrecked about 40 per cent of the tendon. The irony was that Schillaci had never had tendon problems. His trouble for two years was degenerative arthritis in the coffin bones of both front hoofs. Spurs had formed on the bones near the top of the hoof line. The gelding was also plagued by corns. Schillaci had grown into a massive horse, weighing 560 kilos, maybe more, and in the end his hoofs were just too small for his body.

Early morning at Brackley Park, the Freedman property at Avenel, north of Seymour. The sky is a cloudless blue dome and the new grass sags under the dew. You feel cold and old Schillaci is warm to touch. He crunches on lucerne hay and flicks his ears to the slightest sound, be it a tractor or swallows nesting in the stables. He nuzzles you, looking for a carrot, then lays his ears back in disdain when you come up empty handed.

Schillaci will live the rest of his life here because the Freedmans asked to keep him. Christensen was touched. 'I'm delighted that Lee and his family think so much of the horse they want to give him a happy home. Knowing that makes me even more proud of him.'

Dave Hitchin, the farm manager, leaves a filly to remove Schillaci's rug. The grey nuzzles Hitchin's pullover, smells the filly on it, and squeals like the stallion he isn't. Kylie Baines takes him out to have his photo taken. At first, he is tender on his bad leg. Then he sees the colts in the day yards and starts to swagger. He wants to plunge and rear and let them know he's better than they'll ever be. As on race days, all pain is forgotten. Schillaci is some character.

And, even, with that leg swaddled in bandages, some sight: tall, better than 16.2 hands, and long, incredibly long. He is power without coarseness, refinement without prettiness. A big eye: kind, intelligent and dark. A great sweep of shoulder and a length of rein to match. Bulging forearms and, behind, swelling bunches of muscles from hip to hock, the rear end of a quarter horse on the legs of a thoroughbred.

That powerful body is half the reason Alan Bell, a Rosehill veterinarian and trainer, bought him for $70,000 as a yearling; the other half is Schillaci's blood. He descends from mares bred by the legendary Stanley Wootton, who imported Star Kingdom and, with that one stallion, changed the pattern of Australian breeding. Bell figured he was buying generations of Wootton's genius. He offered Christensen a piece of the horse a few months later. Christensen recalls Bell said something like: 'I think this horse could be exceptional.'

Schillaci didn't race at two. He was gelded and given time to grow up. Early on, he was with Richard Freedman at Epsom. Richard, as is his way, tended to undersell the horse. But brother Anthony says, 'He'd declared him a champion before he'd even raced.' Schillaci had been sitting eight-wide in trials—and winning. Which may explain why he was odds-on for that first start at Kyneton.

At his fourth start, he won the Lightning Stakes. At his next two, he won the other legs of sprinting's triple crown: the Oakleigh Plate at Caulfield, in track record time, and the Newmarket at Flemington. Then, in perhaps the best win of his career, he took the Galaxy at Randwick, his fourth group one for the season. He was young; he could fly, and he didn't hurt anywhere.

After the grey's first win in the Lightning, Lee Freedman told the mounting-yard throng: 'This horse is another Manikato.' At trackwork last week, Freedman recalled the reaction. 'They all said to me, "Well, you've just gone straight off your head. You've gone stone mad."'

Some madness. After his three-year-old season, and despite aching hoofs, Schillaci won another four group ones, including two

Futuritys. When he won a sprint on Caulfield Cup Day last year, he received a longer and rowdier ovation than Paris Lane, the Cup winner.

Lee Freedman isn't given to mushy sentimentality. Asked how he saw Schillaci, he thought long before replying.

'You get lovely racehorses,' he said softly. 'You know, they win good races for you, but this one . . . ?' He sighs and his voice rises. 'Ah, he was something more: he was a lovely animal. There was no enigma with him: what you saw was what you got.'

After the accident, Freedman was drinking with friends at a Toorak hotel. The friends began toasting Schillaci and Freedman began to feel teary. He left and went shopping.

Rebecca Newman, tiny and vivacious, is sipping iced coffee and walking back to the Freedman stables at Flemington after track-work. It doesn't seem right: Schillaci, the carrot addict, doesn't live there anymore.

'I've lost my best friend,' she says. 'There'll never be another like him. Such a character: you'd just stand there feeding him carrots and he'd do anything.

'He was so kind. On the track, you'd have to hunt him up all through his work. But when you turned him to come home, he'd turn on like an electric light and want to canter all the way home.

'Oh, he'd do things wrong. Going out sometimes, he'd stand as still as a statue, refusing to move. Occasionally, he'd whip around and dump you. Then he'd stop and stare down, as if to say: What are you doing down there?

'To strap him at the races . . . well, that was just indescribable. The crowd would follow you everywhere. People would ask me for one of his shoes. When he was retired we got fan mail. A father wrote on behalf of his son. He wanted to thank us for the pleasure the horse gave his boy.'

Long before the grey ruined his tendon, Rebecca had become proprietorial. Schillaci would annoy her when he did his 'statue act'. What she resented much more, however, were well-meaning people getting behind the grey to hunt him forward. She could scold him, but not outsiders.

'I'm going to miss him terribly,' she says.

Aren't we all.

*6 October 1995*

# Sunline: A freak of nature

## JIM HAYNES

'THEY ALL LOVE SUNLINE.'

It was the bloke standing beside me in the TAB. The place was abuzz with comments, the usual ill-informed, well-informed and half-informed opinions that you get in any TAB when it is more than likely that a protest will be lodged. Men talking to anyone who will listen, or to no one in particular, or to no one at all.

But this was different.

It was not only the Cox Plate; the horses involved were the best three horses racing at the time!

It was 27 October 2001.

I'd backed Viscount, the Inghams' immaculately bred and trained three-year-old. I thought he was a classy conveyance and well suited at weight for age against the two champs, Sunline and Northerly. I still think the same. He should have won.

Sunline had led into the straight with Viscount behind her, waiting to start his winning run, and Northerly had been working home down the outside.

In his efforts to lift Northerly and reach the mighty mare, Damien Oliver had ridden the Western Australian champion out vigorously. Northerly had strained every sinew to the limit until the effort was too much. Then he ducked in under pressure, just as Sunline rolled out slightly for the same reason.

Viscount was the meat in the sandwich; he was crunched in between the two older horses, lost all momentum and was lucky to stay on his feet. Sunline's head went way up in the air as she, too, lost momentum, and Northerly, the main offender and the only horse of the trio to keep his momentum, pulled ahead to win by half a length.

The booing started as the horses returned to the birdcage.

That's when I commented through my pocket to the bloke beside me, 'No wonder they're booing,' I said, 'Viscount was robbed!'

He looked at me in that sad way older racing addicts have when confronted by ignorance. Then he said, 'They're not worried about the Inghams' horse, mate, they're booing 'cos Sunline didn't win— they all love Sunline.'

Maybe he was a Kiwi, but he was right anyway. They all *did* love Sunline.

Certainly all New Zealand loved her; when she died there was a news special on national television.

And why wouldn't they love her? Not only was she undefeated in her home country, she travelled to Australia and beat our best, and then went to Hong Kong and beat the mighty Fairy King Prawn over a mile in a world-class international event. She was the best middle-distance horse of her era and certainly the best mare to ever race over middle distances in Australasian turf history. Her record proves it.

When the protests came that day there were three of them: Sunline against Northerly, and Viscount against the other two, so second against first and third against first and second.

In a travesty of justice, all were dismissed.

I still maintain that Viscount should have won. And all fair-minded racing fans consider that Sunline's record against Northerly should show one victory and two losses, instead of three losses.

I still maintain it should have been Viscount first, Sunline second and Northerly third.

In any case, we all agree the mighty mare should have been put ahead of Northerly—a champion in his own right—just once in her career!

'But Northerly won by half a length,' I hear the voice of reason saying, 'and that was why the stewards gave him the race.'

'Yes,' I answer in my imagination, with more than a hint of frustration, 'and he won by that far because the interference was *so bad*!'

Punters have long and bitter memories of racing injustices.

While I was preparing this collection, it was announced that Sunline had lost her long battle with laminitis and had been put down.

That sad news made me think back to how I'd seen her in victory and defeat, in the flesh, not on the TAB television screens.

I have two vivid memories of Sunline. I saw her race maybe half a dozen times, but two memories are unforgettably clear. Because they were the most memorable two-horse-wars I ever saw.

Randwick is a track that really sorts out the champs from the pretenders down the straight. Sunline started there 12 times, usually carrying big weights, for six wins and four placings.

I saw her win her second Doncaster in 2002, defeating Shogun Lodge after they raced side by side for two entire furlongs. That was the best nose-to-nose tussle I ever saw at Randwick.

The crowd was in a frenzy; it was too close to call at the end. I thought she'd been beaten, but the photo showed her courage had paid off by a nose. The pundits thought she had too much weight that day to possibly win over the toughest mile course in the world.

I still can't believe you could get odds of 5 to 1 about Sunline in the ring when they jumped. And I still can't believe I didn't take it!

Strangely enough the mighty mare also featured in the best battle down the straight I ever saw in Melbourne, at Caulfield, in the Caulfield Stakes in 2002.

I have written about that great race elsewhere in this collection. It was a match race between Sunline, when she was approaching the end of her career, and Lonhro, who was nearing the peak of his career. There were some pretty handy horses in the supporting cast of the drama that day, but they were really only there for the crowd scenes, just making up the numbers.

Trevor McKee and his son, Stephen, owners of Sunline, and the Ingham brothers, who owned Lonhro, rate as true enthusiasts and lovers of racing. It is credit to the McKees that Sunline, who could have been quickly retired to stud, raced on as a mare to give us all so many wonderful memories. The McKee motto was always, 'We're here to race.'

Mind you, Sunline was an awesome force on any racetrack at any age, even at seven. She was strong and robust and towered over most of her male counterparts. She never looked frail, weak or delicate of disposition, attributes which many consider to be feminine. In fact, Greg Childs, who rode her for 32 of her 48 starts, described her as 'a freak of nature' and attributed her amazing ability to what he called her 'masculine qualities'.

She was feminine enough, however, to leave behind two sons and two daughters when she passed away prematurely at the age of just 13.

As usual the crowd at Caulfield that day mostly supported Sunline. Not many Victorian racegoers were fans of the New South Wales horse in the cerise colours, although they would come to admire him—and his progeny—in seasons to follow.

It was a mighty struggle between the young stallion and the seven-year-old mare, all the way down the straight, but neither horse shirked the task. Lonhro won by a head, with the rest of the field fighting out third place 6 lengths behind.

But Sunline will be remembered for the races she won, not those she barely lost.

Her two Cox Plate wins are enough to place her among the immortals. In the first she defeated Redoute's Choice, Commands, Testa Rossa, Tie The Knot and Sky Heights—an impressive line-up of legendary horses! And she won the second by a record 7 lengths, defeating Derby and Caulfield Cup winner Diatribe along with

Referral, Show A Heart and Shogun Lodge, as well as Testa Rossa, Tie The Knot and Sky Heights yet again.

Add to those two Cox Plate wins her other Group 1 victories, two Doncaster Handicaps, two All-Aged Stakes, two Waikato Sprints, two Coolmore Classics (carrying 60 kg each time), a Flight Stakes, a Manikato Stakes, her controversial second to Northerly in a third Cox Plate, and her international victory in Hong Kong, and you have a record unbeaten in Australasian racing history.

From her Group 3 victory in the Moonee Valley Oaks, as a three-year-old filly, until the end of her career at age seven, Sunline only ever competed in races at Group 1 or Group 2 level.

Her win rate was 68 per cent and her place rate 94 per cent, and she raced at least two seasons beyond what most consider to be the correct age for racing mares to retire. She was the top stakes-winning horse in Australasian history in her day, and the top stakes-winning mare in the world. She is the only horse ever voted Australian Horse of the Year three times.

How does her record compare to other great mares?

Well, given that comparisons from different eras are rather silly to begin with, the only racing mares who even come close to Sunline are Wakeful, Desert Gold, Tranquil Star, Flight, Emancipation and Makybe Diva.

Wakeful had a win rate of 58 per cent, well below Sunline's a century later. Her place rate, at 41 from 44 starts, is amazingly close (at 93.3 per cent) to Sunline's 45 from 48 (94 per cent). Each mare was unplaced only three times.

Wakeful was more versatile than Sunline, winning from 5 furlongs to 3 miles and carrying 10 st (63.5 kg) to run second in the Melbourne Cup, less than a length behind Lord Cardigan, carrying 22 kilos less at 6 st 8 lb. Wakeful comes very close to giving Sunline a run for her money, but where she won ten races that would now be considered Group 1 level, Sunline won 13.

Desert Gold was a New Zealander like Sunline. Her amazing run of 19 wins in a row easily eclipses Sunline's best run of eight consecutive wins. Desert Gold, however, did most of her racing in

New Zealand at a very different level to Sunline and, although she won a number of classic New Zealand races and had a great five-year-old season in Australia, winning quite a few weight-for-age events, her record at the very top level does not match Sunline's.

Desert Gold raced through the dark days of World War I for an overall record of 36 wins, 13 seconds and four thirds from 59 starts, very close to Sunline's record. Her place rate is a very respectable 90 per cent, 4 per cent less than Sunline's. Her win rate, at 61 per cent, again comes close to Sunline's 69 per cent, but not close enough.

Tranquil Star had an iron constitution. She started 111 times for 23 wins. That was her main claim to fame, her amazing stamina. She would have been a match for the great masculine mare, Sunline, as far as stamina went, and, like our heroine, she raced until she was past the age when most mares retired; in fact Tranquil Star raced a season more than Sunline, well into her eighth year. Unfortunately, she doesn't really measure up in other ways.

In her three-year-old season Tranquil Star became only the second female to win the St Leger. In her fourth year, however, Tranquil Star raced 21 times for only two wins and eight placings. Her Caulfield Cup win was commendable and, like Sunline, she won the Cox Plate twice in a row.

Also, despite breaking her jaw in a bad fall at Moonee Valley, Tranquil Star went on, with a wired jaw, to win the Memsie Stakes, William Reid Stakes and the Mackinnon Stakes for the third time!

Tranquil Star was, however, a beaten favourite on a record 18 occasions! The racegoers who had time to go on the punt during World War II must have been far more tolerant than they were in Sunline's day!

Within months of Tranquil Star's retirement, a new heroine emerged to excite the wartime and post-war crowds. Flight, famously bought for 60 guineas by Brian Crowley, would go on to race 65 times for 24 wins, 19 seconds and nine thirds.

While her statistics don't measure up to Sunline's, we are often told that Flight had to race against one of the greatest horses of all time in Bernborough, who she only managed to beat the day he broke down in the Mackinnon Stakes in 1946. She did, however, race into her sixth year and managed to emulate Sunline with two wins in the Cox Plate, in 1945 and 1946. She also won two Craven Plates, and the Mackinnon, CF Orr, Adrian Knox and Colin Stephen Stakes.

Like Sunline, Flight produced only four foals before passing away. The only filly foal was Flight's Daughter, who became the mother of champion Golden Slipper winners, Skyline and Sky High. Sky High stood at stud in the USA and sired Autobiography, best handicapper in the USA in 1972.

Flight won only six Group 1 races, less than half of Sunline's total. Her claim to fame is based as much on her impact as a broodmare as it is on her two Cox Plate wins. So any real comparison to Sunline may take years to assess.

Emancipation had many characteristics in common with Sunline. She was a great middle-distance mare and won many of the same races Sunline won: the Doncaster, All-Aged Stakes and George Main Stakes among them. In her three-year-old season she won ten from 13 starts and her record overall was nine from 15; and as a four-year-old, her Group 1 tally was seven.

Emancipation failed when she travelled away from Sydney and she also failed to run out 2000 metres. She was unplaced behind Strawberry Road in the Cox Plate.

As a broodmare Emancipation, like Flight and Wakeful, made her mark. Her son Royal Pardon was placed in the AJC Derby and won good races; her daughters, Suffragette and Virage, produced champions in Railings and Virage De Fortune.

We may have to wait a generation or two before we see if Sunline's blood will resurface into champions, as did the blood of Flight, Wakeful and Emancipation. With only four living foals before her untimely death, it may be hard for Sunline to match the broodmare record of her predecessors. However, with the miraculous Sunline, who knows?

It is a strange fact that the brilliance of great race mares appears to skip a generation and reappear in the foals of their daughters, and sons to a lesser extent.

There is ample proof, as we have seen, of the daughters of great race mares being poor performers but great producers. There are also examples of sons and grandsons being great sires. Wakeful's son Baverstock only managed to win one race, but became a hugely successful sire, as did Flight's grandson Sky High.

We will have to wait to see what influence Sunline has on future generations. And that is also true of one other great mare to whom she is often compared.

Nine days before Sunline scored her last race win in the Group 2 Mudgeway Stakes at Hasting in New Zealand, a mare having her second race start and bred to northern hemisphere seasons won her maiden at Wangaratta. The mighty staying mare Makybe Diva had arrived.

There is an account of her career and place in racing history later in this collection, so I will make her comparison to Sunline quite brief.

We are possibly comparing the greatest middle-distance mare that ever lived to the greatest staying mare Australia has ever seen.

However, we can go through the process of comparing records, just for the sake of it.

As a stayer, Makybe Diva obviously ran in more 'lead-up' races towards her major goals, so her record of 15 wins, four seconds and three thirds from 36 starts looks quite poor against Sunline's 33 wins, nine seconds and three thirds from 48.

The figures give Makybe Diva a win rate of 42 per cent and a place rate of 61 per cent, well below Sunline's remarkable 69 per cent and 94 per cent. But we are doing no more with such statistics than comparing oranges to apples.

Group 1 wins? Well, it's no contest. Sunline won almost twice as many times at Group 1, with 13 victories at the elite level to Makybe Diva's seven. And when we look at overall wins at group level, it's ten to Makybe Diva and 27 to Sunline.

It's tempting to do what many have done, including the Melbourne *Herald-Sun* in an article comparing contemporary champions in December 2009, and say 'Sunline was simply a one-off freak'.

That's hardly good enough though—you can't dismiss a champion because he or she was 'freakishly talented'. After all, that's what being a champion often amounts to!

When she died her regular jockey Greg Childs, who had taken his family to visit her after her retirement, described her as 'a freak of nature' who took all New Zealand on a great journey.

'She was a big influence on my life,' Childs said. 'She lifted my profile and my bank balance . . . she helped pay for the house we are living in.

'It's not only the jockey, it is the family as well, my wife and my kids,' said Childs, 'they all love Sunline.'

# Firecracker

## JIM BENDRODT

I TURNED AND LOOKED back. Now, that is something many folk contend should not be done. But I did.

I'd sat all day at the edge of the sale ring while the thoroughbreds paraded and men paid tens of thousands for them. I'd looked with covetous eyes at horses I'd have given my very soul to own, but this was a place where hard cash talked, and I had no cash, hard or otherwise.

And so at last I had walked away because the prices were beyond me, and when I'd travelled some 50 yards towards the exit, I heard the auctioneer's derisive roar upbraiding those whose highest bid was 50 guineas.

I said I turned and looked back, and in the distance I saw a tall black horse, and once again I heard the auctioneer roar, 'What, 50 guineas? Surely, gentlemen, you haven't looked at this one!'

I started walking back, and I heard someone call 52 and a half and then, after a bit, 55, and the auctioneer shouted, 'I've got 57 and a half just over here.'

I said, 'You've got 60, mister.' And then his hammer smashed onto the rostrum.

That's how I bought Firecracker, by Cistercian out of Persian Nan. And the folk who knew Persian Nan said the mare was mad.

Well, maybe so, I didn't know his mother, so I couldn't tell you, but I do know that her son was equine dynamite. I've had so many horses but, among them all, I've never owned a horse like him.

I paid my 60 guineas at the auctioneer's desk, and I remember that the balance in my wallet wasn't much. Then I found the number of his stall, and went to see him. I found the man who cared for him and seven other yearlings. I gave him a little money, and then I said, 'Well, let's have a look at him.'

'So *you* bought the blighter, did you?' the man asked, and added, 'Well, you've got a handful.' He pulled the top and bottom bolts of the heavy door and opened it. 'You be careful,' he said, 'this coot is mad. I come from the station he was bred on, and it took five of us three days to catch him in the paddock where he's been running wild for months.'

He sidled cautiously towards the colt's near side. He had tied the horse's head to a strong ringbolt with a heavy length of rope, a thing no horseman worthy of his salt would do. 'Get over, you!' he roared, and smashed the horse in the soft underbelly with his clenched fist, and the colt struck at him with the speed of light . . . and so did I.

My right hand took his shoulder and whirled him round so that he looked at me in blank astonishment. 'Take it easy, lad,' I said, and looked at him for a little time. 'Now get out,' I ordered, 'and stay out.' He left the stall without another word, and did not come back.

We got the black colt home eventually to the humble stable that I rented for him, and began to break him in. I say 'began' because that about describes it. We couldn't break him in, and we never did, to the degree that is desirable. He was a queer horse, lean and hard and streamlined, with a lovely fine-drawn head and a remorseless wicked eye.

They are usually so gentle, so easily handled, these baby horses from the famous studs. A little touchy maybe, a trifle nervous, perhaps more difficult than a pleasant-natured dog, but not much trouble as a general rule. But Firecracker! Well, why go into it in detail? By an imported English stallion from the black mare Persian Nan, and knowing folk said Persian Nan was mad!

Well, her son was surely crazy in his first four months with us, and then he settled down and, up to a point, but not beyond it, would do as he was told, but it was always the horse that drew the line as I remember it, though we tried to.

It was in the midst of the Depression years when I bought Firecracker, and 60 guineas was a lot of money then. You may know the Palais Royal, or you may have heard of it, no doubt. The giant dance hall I owned was staggering through the lean hard times with every sail set to catch its hard-won silver pieces. We didn't get 6000 people back then, as we did in better times.

We got Firecracker ready and entered him at Menangle in a race of 5½ furlongs, just enough for Firecracker. He won at 6 furlongs eventually, but 'only just', as the horsemen put it; but that was later. At three years old he moved over 5½ furlongs like a swift machine, and then he'd stop. He wouldn't go another yard, except at a canter.

On Monday night when the show was all over, I called my Palais Royal staff together.

'Boys,' I said, and then I bowed a trifle towards the grinning girls, 'and ladies, I think the time has come to have a little talk. Now let's see, there are about 125 of you and I've been having quite a time taking care of you in this damn Depression. I think I'm right when I say most of you have been with me for years. I know you all have a faith and trust in me.'

A somewhat raucous bellow from the background interrupted me at this point. I paused and then continued, 'Well, we're going to have a gamble. Your wages for your work this week are in the bank for payment on Friday, about £600, I think. I've got the change the cashiers use, and I've hocked everything I own, which isn't much, and tomorrow I'm going to put the proceeds on a horse.

'If he wins, he'll save the Palais Royal. If he gets licked, well—that's the end of us, and I'm afraid you'll have to go to work at last.

Now how about it? Two to one is the price you'll get, no matter what the price is that he starts at, and the rest is to go to keep this old show open.'

I could see Bill Swift. I could see him grin as I talked to them. Bill was the lad they'd follow in a case like this, so I talked to him, and he grinned back at me derisively, and once he interrupted with his deep rich Irish voice, 'Sure, boss, and it's a generous little soul you always were, so help me, and it's round your little finger that you'll be twisting us poor stupid goats as usual.'

'Bill,' I said, 'how well you know that, night and day, only one thought moves me, and that's your blasted welfare, else how could it be that you are my staff manager at your luscious salary, when half the world is starving?'

'Sure and it's three-quarters of my luscious salary that you've been borrowing from me to feed your crackpot horse, who would otherwise be starving like the rest of them, and now it's the lot you'll take to bet on the feckless loon tomorrow, and that'll be the end of it, so it will, or me mother's name was Rachel.'

The delighted treble of the girls' laughter fought with the rumble of the male voices when he answered me. He was a natural salesman, this Bill Swift.

He was so many other things to me. Years before I'd advertised for a fighting man. I ran a show in those days, a fine big rink in a hard tough section near the waterfront, and I needed help because respectability was its slogan, and its patrons needed guidance in the civilised amenities as ordained by me. And so I had to have a 'man of his hands' to help me in my inroads on my precious patrons' natural inclinations.

So many likely fellows came in answer to the advertisement, and when one stood before me I would say, 'And now, my lad, do you think you could whip me in a dust-up?' and, because of policy or some other reason, they all said 'No', until Bill came.

A great tall lad about my own age, from a wind-jammer in the harbour, thick in the middle even then, with a caveman's torso and lethal hands. With bright blue eyes under thick red brows, and a torrid head of hair. And when I said, 'Well, Bill, do you think you could whip me?' he said without an instant's hesitation, 'My flaming oath!'

So I took him to the rink's high roof where my small gym was, and we pulled the gloves on. He was a rough-and-tumble fighter, whose equal I knew but once before, but he was a child in the tricks of Mr Queensberry. I doubt if he'd ever seen a pair of boxing gloves. It was the rapier against the blundering broadsword, but I knew this was my man right from the start and ever since he'd been with me through tumultuous years of triumphs and disasters.

I think the things I liked best about Bill were his Irish sense of humour and his loyalty. With him, loyalty went to far extremes, and this little yarn will tell you just how far it did go.

Some years before we had rocketed out of Melbourne in my Marmon Speedster, Bill Swift, Steve and Bill Romaine, and I. We climbed the Gippsland mountains over the yellow slippery highway, and a summer cyclone kept us company. The narrow road was greasy, un-tarred, unpaved, and, at a point where the mountain was a wall on one side, my back tyres slipped, and the Marmon skidded sideways.

When she stopped, the car's rear wheels rested a bare 3 inches from the outer edge of a gentle slope that skirted the road itself, and beyond the edge of that slope where the wheels rested there was nothing. Two thousand feet below, the treetops growing in the valley looked like children's toys. The bonnet of the car thrust upwards at an angle to the road itself.

You know those old cars. You held the foot-brake on with sheer strength. The handbrake was nearly always useless. You didn't have hydraulic power in braking systems back then.

I knew I'd hold the foot-brake down for quite a long time, and I knew that when I got tired, as I must eventually, my leg would lose the power that kept the pedal level with the floor. I knew then that we'd go tumbling down to where the treetops waved so far below. I told Steve and Bill Romaine to get out quickly, but I said to do it quietly and with care. I didn't want to shake the car. Along the running-board and over the bonnet, and then onto the road. That was the way they reached safety.

And then I said to Bill Swift, 'Now, Bill, get going. I can't keep this pressure on forever.'

Bill looked at me and growled, 'No, boss.'

'But Bill, why two of us?' I asked. 'There's nothing you can do, that's obvious. You get out.' I looked at him and his heavy face was hard as granite, so I tried again in a different way: 'Please, Bill.'

'No,' he said, and nothing else.

I watched him reach for his tobacco pouch and papers. He rolled a cigarette and leaned over and put it in my mouth, then rolled another one. Above and about us the cyclone howled. He held a hooded match to my cigarette, and I said curiously, 'Why, Bill?'

He answered, 'Aw, hell, there's times a man likes company. Let's forget it.'

Then for a time there was nothing except the crazy roaring of the wind, and then Bill looked at me and his voice was gentle when he asked, 'Getting tired, boss?'

'Yes, a bit, Bill.'

Then I saw his eyes lift above my head and he said urgently, 'Take it easy, boss. Keep that foot down hard, then take a look.'

I turned my head and there, coming round the shoulder of the mountain, a hundred yards away, was a bright red Buick Phaeton.

The driver had a steel tow rope, and he said he came from Denmark, which was a queer thing because my father came from Denmark, and you wouldn't have found another Dane in all that thousand miles of mountain wilderness, especially one with a power-laden Buick Phaeton and a steel tow rope, on that tempest-ridden day.

You have to hand it to a man like that Dane. He knew as we knew, because we warned him, that when he took the strain my car might slip that bare 3 inches and, if it did, then he'd go tumbling down with us to where those treetops twisted in the gale so far below.

We thanked him a little later when the Marmon stood four-square on the road, and we drank his fiery advocaat and went on our way.

So that was Bill and that was loyalty. A handy thing. And rare. So now I beckoned Bill to bend down while my crowd of dance-hall people waited.

'Bill,' I whispered, 'it's worth the chance. They'll get their £600 in wages on Friday, then we'll have to close, and they'd get nothing else except the dole. Now, if Firecracker can make it, we'll have lots of money to carry on for weeks, and this Depression cannot last forever. How about it?'

He looked at me with his bright blue eyes alight with laughter. 'Sure, and I always said you'd talk the leg off an iron pot, but you're crazy, boss. Gold-digger will beat that long-legged loon of yours by half a mile.'

So I tried again and this time I was cunning because I didn't argue. I simply said, a little sadly, 'Quitting is a queer thing for the Irish, Bill.'

He shook his head like an angry bison, and then stood up and his great voice filled that echoing dance hall.

'Now, blast the lot of you,' he roared, 'what's all this talk about anyhow? This bonny horse the boss has got is just a certainty. Sure, and it's a fine idea and good enough for the little bit of money he wants from us. Now, get about your work. We'll get our wages Friday, and for a lot of Fridays after that. It's a grand notion, so it is.' Then *sotto voce* to me, 'May the good Lord forgive me for being Australia's greatest liar, because it'll be that chestnut rascal Gold-digger that'll be paying off tomorrow afternoon.'

By the price of him, the bookmakers agreed with Bill, because when we reached Menangle Gold-digger was at a nervous 6 to 4. We had come up in the Marmon Speedster over the dusty country roads on a lazy summer day, and there were eight of us all told in a motor built for four. They were the smartest of my big boys from the Palais Royal.

You didn't run a dance hall like that one without some head-aches. Five and six thousand people in a night are a lot to care for in one big public place within four walls. They came and chattered, dance and flirted in that gaudy mausoleum, and as the night wore on the giant building shook and quivered with the thrust of stamping feet, or whispered like the wind brushing sand along a beach when the musicians played a waltz.

The smoke from cigarettes would curl up in lazy blue-grey layers to the caverns in the roof where brilliant lanterns hung in clustered thousands, and after a bit these would grow dim blood-red in colour, or hazy emerald-green, or faint old-rose. The jungle beat in the music thrust and throbbed relentlessly on the eardrums of the dancing multitude until they postured and grimaced and genuflected like a herd of mesmerised buffoons.

But you didn't succeed in a place like that because of coloured lights and mass hypnosis. You knew that among these multitudes there would be people who came to prey on lads and lasses out for fun. They didn't come to listen to the music. You had to keep the liquor out of crowds like these; I would as soon have nitro-glycerine in a place like that as sparkling wine. So you had your private army to guard your patrons from marauders, to rule your dance hall with an iron hand, and you knew you'd often have to use them in the hectic midnight hours when your famous dancing rendezvous exploded in your face.

I'd brought the best of them with me. I'd given them each one-eighth of all my money and their wages, and the funds I had borrowed on my car, my race glasses and on any other mortal thing I could get my hands on. Then, half an hour before the race, I gave each of my lads a square of bookmakers to work on. They were to commence to bet at a given signal. These bookmakers are hard to trap, especially at Menangle, but there were things that favoured me. I heard two of them talking before the race started.

'Tom, what's this Firecracker?'

'Firecracker?' Tom echoed. 'Oh, 'im. Some goat that fellow Ben-drodt trains.'

'What! Trains 'im, does 'e? Well, wouldn't that rock you! What next will 'e do? 'E couldn't train a rabbit to run up a burrow.'

'Naw,' said Tom. ''E's got Cook riding 'im.'

'What!' the other fellow said in pained surprise. 'Cook! Why, 'ow did 'e get 'im to ride it, I wonder?'

'Friend of 'is, I guess,' said Tom. 'Anyway, we needn't worry about Firecracker, 'e's never had a run. Gold-digger is a certainty.'

When betting opened, Firecracker was at 10 to 1 and, when the money flowed for Gold-digger, I took my hat off and ran my fingers through my hair and, in a flash, eight good men commenced to bet as one.

In 90 seconds Firecracker was at 5 to 1 and, in 90 more, you had to fight to get the bookies to lay you 6 to 4. And no wonder. My lads were old in this game, and they had bet a lot of money—for Menangle. The vouchers they carried in their pockets would keep the Palais Royal going for a decent time to come if Firecracker won. But could he?

I legged Bill Cook up and said to him, 'Now, Bill, this is serious. So pay attention to what I tell you. This fellow's got to win, because, if he doesn't, five minutes afterwards I'll just be passing Suva going strong. No foolin', Bill, you've got to win it.'

And Bill, who rarely paid attention to anything I said, or for that matter to anything that anybody said, looked down at me and asked in consternation, 'But, boss, what's he done? He's never had a race. I can't come home without the horse, you know, it isn't done.'

'Quit fooling, Bill,' I said. 'Firecracker is a little peculiar.' Then, as alarm spread over his face and I saw him take a tighter grip on the reins, I hastened to add, 'But he's fast, Bill, very fast. He's only peculiar because his mother was Persian Nan, and she was a wee bit mad, so they tell me. You talk to him going to the post and get his confidence. Don't hit him for heaven's sake, or you'll need a parachute to bring you down. And be careful at the barrier, Bill, because that's where he really gets peculiar. He'll only go for 5½ furlongs and then he'll stop as if he's hit a wall. So hug the rails as if you loved them, and don't make him go an unnecessary yard. Out and home, Bill, that's the ticket.'

'Aw, for God's sake,' Bill replied morosely. He clucked at Firecracker and Firecracker obediently erupted through the gate onto the course and disappeared into the distance, with Bill Cook doing stunts that would have turned a Cossack green with envy.

They didn't have announcers back in the days I write about, and I couldn't see the start without my glasses. But the track was dry and sandy, so I knew when a bunch of horses travelled in a cloud of dust to a turn a quarter of a mile or more away. But I couldn't see the colours, and I didn't hear the crowd. I knew a sort of dull, sick feeling, and it seemed that every second was a year.

Then in the distance I could hear their hooves thudding on the hard dry ground as the field swung towards the furlong pole, and I could see a tall black horse skimming along the rails with a golden chestnut close behind him, and the rest 10 lengths away. And then I became a cold stone statue, and the world a place where nothing seemed to focus.

Then a smashing blow hit me between the shoulder blades, and an Irish voice roared joyously, 'By the holy saints, it's Firecracker! It's the feckless loon himself, so help me Bob!'

# Lonhro never liked Moonee Valley

## JIM HAYNES

'AND LONHRO STANDS MOTIONLESS, gazing off into the distance as he so often does before a race . . . he'll be the last to be loaded.'

It was April 19, 2004.

As the course commentator's voice echoed across from the stands, Lonhro gazed towards the traffic crawling endlessly along Alison Road, then turned his head for a last long look across the wide expanses of Royal Randwick towards the NSW University buildings to the south.

On nine of the 11 occasions Lonhro had raced here at Randwick he'd been victorious. Today was to be different, but somehow it hardly mattered.

It was Queen Elizabeth Stakes Day, last day of the Autumn Carnival, and the feature race was to be Lonhro's swan song, the final curtain call in a magnificent and well-orchestrated racing career. It was a race in which he had nothing left to prove, but it was an opportunity for the AJC to bring much-needed media attention to racing. It was also a chance for those who had watched and loved the horse for four glorious racing seasons to say farewell.

It was, in fact, uncannily similar to his father's farewell day at Randwick seven years earlier. There was to be a real sense of déjà vu.

Both he and his famous sire, Octagonal, finished their racing careers in the Queen Elizabeth Stakes. On both occasions the AJC made the day into a carnival and promoted it as a chance to farewell a champion. On both occasions the party was spoiled and the fairytale ending denied when the retiring champion was defeated, finishing second in the feature event.

Yet, in both cases, it hardly mattered—the race itself was simply a coda to a great career.

Octagonal had nothing left to prove when the AJC put on a party for his farewell in 1997. Having passed his target of winning an Australasian record of more than $6 million in prize money several weeks before, the 'Big O' could have simply headed off to stud. There was really no reason to risk running the champion again in the Queen Elizabeth Stakes when he had nothing left to prove and was worth many, many millions as a stallion.

Indeed, a reporter asked Jack Ingham that very question after Octagonal won the Tancred Cup at Rosehill: 'Why risk the horse now, when he has achieved his goal and everything you ever expected of him?'

With typical Inghamesque logic, Jack simply looked the reporter in the eye and asked, 'Don't *you* want to see him race again?'

As an AJC committee member Jack was also no doubt aware that he was giving the club a chance to attract much-needed support and media attention—he was a gracious man, Jack Ingham.

Octagonal was defeated in his farewell race by a useful stayer called Intergaze, who would go on to win an Australian Cup.

And then here we were, seven years later, watching his illustrious son stand at the 2000-metre start, gazing off into the distance before taking his position in the barrier, only to be defeated by Grand Armee, a very good horse trained by Gai Waterhouse, which had also defeated Lonhro in a Doncaster Handicap.

Grand Armee's cause was helped to an extent by an atypical poorly judged ride by Darren Beadman, who allowed the winner to get away with a slow pace and an easy lead, giving Lonhro no real chance of running him down in the straight.

Unlike his father Octagonal, who crept up on the racing world through his two-year-old season, Lonhro had lived his entire life in the spotlight. Being the first foal of Octagonal's first crop he entered the world in a blaze of publicity. His mother, Shadea, had won the Group 3 Sweet Embrace Stakes and had been placed in both the AJC Sires Produce and Champagne Stakes.

As soon as he was born at the Inghams' Woodlands Stud, his anxious owners asked for a firsthand report and were told that the foal was 'small but perfectly formed'.

This report gave Suzanne Philcox, who had the task of naming all the Woodlands' foals, a good pointer towards an appropriate cryptic name for the foal. His name is a deliberate misspelling of the stock exchange code for the London Rhodesian Mining and Land Company, LONRHO. The CEO of this company was the controversial Roland 'Tiny' Rowlands, who was always sarcastically referred to as 'small but perfectly formed' by the satirical magazine *Private Eye*, which exposed some of his perfidious activities in the 1980s and 1990s. The misspelling was to avoid possible legal difficulties and enable the thoroughbred registrar to accept the name.

Lonhro finished second at his first start in November 2000 and was then spelled before winning easily over 1100 metres at Rosehill. A trip to Melbourne followed, resulting in an impressive win in the Blue Diamond Prelude and a close fourth, behind True Jewels, in the Blue Diamond itself.

The Inghams and trainer John Hawkes saw Lonhro as a potential weight-for-age horse and took their time with him. He was spelled until July and then contested the Missile Stakes as a two-year-old, finishing third. This was the last time in his entire racing career that Lonhro would lose two consecutive races.

Woodlands' other champion two-year-old of that year, Viscount, won the AJC Sires Produce and Champagne Stakes while Lonhro was in the spelling paddock.

When he returned to racing, the first son of Octagonal had developed into an impressive big, almost black horse who was to be unbeaten at three. He took out the weight-for-age Warwick Stakes, the Ming Dynasty Quality, the Heritage Stakes and the Stan Fox Stakes one after the other, all at Group or Listed Race level. He was then sent to Melbourne to race against a class field, including stablemate Viscount, in the Caulfield Guineas. He won running away by one and a half lengths.

A minor injury saw Lonhro spelled again, leaving stablemate Viscount to wear the famous all-cerise colours in the 2001 Cox Plate.

Sandwiched between Northerly laying in and Sunline shifting out, Viscount was robbed of a Cox Plate victory in a controversial decision that saw the 'past the post' placings upheld after multiple protests.

Lonhro and another Woodlands horse, Freemason, would later avenge to a degree the 'unfair' defeat of their courageous stablemate at weight for age. Lonhro famously defeated Sunline in the Caulfield Stakes of 2002, and the dour old stayer Freemason handed Northerly an unexpected defeat at weight for age in the Tancred Cup at Rosehill on Golden Slipper Day in 2003.

Lonhro returned to racing in February 2002 to win the Royal Sovereign Stakes and the Hobartville Stakes, both at Group 2, before a virus saw him put away again until the spring. Amazingly the Royal Sovereign Stakes was the first of 25 consecutive races in his career which saw him start favourite.

Lonhro returned to racing in the spring, once again in the Missile Stakes over 1100 metres. Ridden for the first time by Darren Beadman. He won effortlessly by 4 lengths. Previously he had mostly been ridden in Sydney by Rod Quinn, though Digger McLellan and Jim Cassidy had also won on him. In Melbourne it had been Darren Gauci and Brett Prebble. But from the start of his four-year-old season until he retired, Lonhro was ridden by Darren Beadman and no one else.

The imposing sleek dark horse they were now starting to call 'the Black Flash', although he was never 'officially' black, was sent out red-hot favourite at his next start in the Warwick Stakes, over 1400 metres.

Perhaps he was a little flat second-up after a long spell, or perhaps the step up from 1100 to 1400 was too much, for he failed by half a head to run down Guy Walter's good horse Defier.

Lonhro was to finish behind Defier four times in his career, twice in the Cox Plate, although the gelding was easily defeated three times by Lonhro at Group 1 level in Lonhro's five-year-old season.

Defier was a gallant and unlucky horse who finished second in the Cox Plate twice, in 2002 and 2003. Lonhro finished sixth in 2002, his worst-ever result in a race, and third in 2003.

After the 2003 race Defier's trainer Guy Walter cheekily quipped, 'Finished behind us again,' to John Hawkes in the birdcage at Moonee Valley.

Hawkes famously replied, 'Yes, but ours still has his undercarriage.'

Lonhro was never at home at Moonee Valley and his two Cox Plate runs were probably the most disappointing in his stellar career. The man who knew the horse best, trainer John Hawkes, thought Lonhro never liked Moonee Valley for some reason—perhaps the StrathAyr surface didn't feel right to the big stallion.

Perhaps he disliked the closed-in cauldron-like atmosphere. He didn't stand and stare for long before entering the barriers in his two runs at Moonee Valley.

Although he was never to run to his best in the Cox Plate, he went on as a four- and five-year-old to win 17 of his 23 starts, all at group level, at distances ranging from 1100 to 2000 metres.

There are those who claim Lonhro was a false champion who had many 'easy kills' in group races, never won a Derby or a Cox Plate, and failed to prove himself as a handicapper in the Doncaster of 2003.

There is no doubt that John Hawkes had the luxury of being able to pick the champion's races. Woodlands had other great horses, notably Viscount, racing at the time and could plan complementary campaigns for their horses.

It is also true that Lonhro was never at home at Moonee Valley. It was the only track he ever started on at which he never won a race. His two starts there were perhaps among the worst three or four performances of his career—although a sixth and third in the Cox Plate are not bad for 'worst ever' performances.

He carried 57.5 kg top weight to finish fourth in the Doncaster behind Grand Armee, carrying 6 kilos less, on a wet track and, as a sprinter/middle-distance horse, he was never going to run in Derbies or Melbourne Cups.

Those who question the horse's bravery and stamina, who doubt that he inherited his father's bulldog determination, should have been at Caulfield Stakes Day 2002.

I travelled out to Caulfield that day to see Lonhro run against Sunline. The Caulfield Stakes that day was basically a match race between Sunline and Lonhro, with a few other very good horses like Republic Lass, Prized Gem, Distinctly Secret and Tully Thunder making up the numbers.

It was a rematch in a sense. Two weeks earlier in Sydney Lonhro had finished fourth, one place behind the mighty mare, in the George Main Stakes won by Defier. It was one of those races in which a small field produces an odd tempo and tactics. Defier, Excellerator and Shogun Lodge managed to keep Lonhro pocketed until it was too late to get out and chase effectively.

Sunline was a freak; at seven she was as strong and robust a horse as I ever saw. She towered over most of her male counterparts and was fit and at her peak for the spring carnivals.

Not many of the crowd seemed to be supporting Lonhro, just the Ingham family and a few others who had strayed south of the border for the spring racing.

Lonhro proved that day that he had inherited his sire's incredible will to win.

Beadman moved Lonhro up onto the outside of Sunline as they rounded the big home bend at Caulfield and he was a half-length behind her when they straightened.

The famously religious jockey appeared to have faith in his colt's ability to run a metre faster per furlong than the mare at weight for age. He rode Lonhro out steadily and made ground on Sunline centimetre by centimetre. It was a two-horse war with the rest of the field forgotten, a true test of stamina, strength and courage between two champions, with neither horse giving in at any point and each stretched to the extreme. At the post it was a clear victory to the big black horse carrying the famous cerise colours.

Perhaps Lonhro's greatest victory was to come 18 months later at what was his Melbourne farewell, the Australian Cup at Flemington.

The sporting Melbourne crowd cheered him again and again that day as he came back to the winner's stall having won a miraculous and memorable victory over the three horses Melbourne racegoers loved best at that time—Mummify, Elvstroem and Makybe Diva.

After having his momentum stopped dead twice in the straight and being turned almost completely sideways, the 'Black Flash' pushed out, started up his big engine again, and made up impossible lengths in a hundred metres to run down a good three-year-old in Delzao at weight for age. In doing so he also defeated that season's VRC Derby winner, Elvstroem, the Caulfield Cup winner Mummify and the Melbourne Cup winner Makybe Diva.

Those who wish to find fault with his record of 26 wins from 35 starts might like to consider that his Group 1 winning strike rate of 64 per cent is the best ever recorded since the system began. His overall winning strike rate of 74 per cent is far better than that of Tulloch, Kingston Town and Phar Lap. Indeed it is second only to Carbine, arguably the greatest racehorse that ever breathed, and a horse who raced a century before Lonhro was born.

It is true that Lonhro's campaigns were well planned and orchestrated to get the best results. However, it is also true that he raced in an era of great racehorses, and he didn't exactly avoid them!

Lonhro raced against and defeated Sunline, Viking Ruler, Dash For Cash, Viscount, Shogun Lodge, Tie the Knot, Universal Prince, Magic Albert, Republic Lass, Freemason, Platinum Scissors, Grand

Armee, Private Steer, Clangalang, Belle Du Jour, Elvstroem, Mummify and the great Makybe Diva.

His progeny have already sold individually for more than $1 million and Denman, from his second crop, was the most exciting colt to be seen in Australia for years, before being sent to race in Dubai and Europe.

Denman is named after the town in the Hunter Valley near Woodlands Stud, where Lonhro now stands as a stallion. In between his stud duties, the beautiful near-black horse often stands motionless, gazing off into the distance.

Apparently Lonhro enjoys looking out across the upper reaches of the Hunter Valley. It's a long way from Moonee Valley ... and Lonhro never liked Moonee Valley.

# Father Riley's Horse

## A.B. ('Banjo') Paterson

'Twas the horse thief, Andy Regan, that was hunted like a dog
By the troopers of the Upper Murray side,
They had searched in every gully—they had looked in every log,
But never sight or track of him they spied,
Till the priest at Kiley's Crossing heard a knocking very late
And a whisper, 'Father Riley—come across!'
So his Reverence, in pyjamas, trotted softly to the gate
And admitted Andy Regan—and a horse!

'Now, it's listen, Father Riley, to the words I've got to say,
For it's close upon my death I am tonight;
With the troopers hard behind me I've been hiding all the day
In the gullies, keeping close and out of sight.
But they're watching all the ranges till there's not a bird could fly,
And I'm fairly worn to pieces with the strife;
So I'm taking no more trouble, but I'm going home to die,
'Tis the only way I see to save my life!

'Yes, I'm making home to mother's, and I'll die a Tuesday next
And be buried on the Thursday—and, of course,
I'm prepared to meet my penance, but with one thing I'm perplexed
And it's—Father, it's this jewel of a horse!
He was never bought nor paid for, and there's not a man can swear
To his owner or his breeder, but I know,
That his sire was by Pedantic from the Old Pretender mare
And his dam was close related to The Roe.

'And there's nothing in the district that can race him for a step;
He could canter while they're going at their top:
He's the king of all the leppers that was ever seen to lep,
A five-foot fence—he'd clear it in a hop!

So I'll leave him with you, Father, till the dead shall rise again;
'Tis yourself that knows a good 'un; and, of course,
You can say he's got by Moonlight out of Paddy Murphy's plain
If you're ever asked the breeding of the horse!

'But it's getting on to daylight and it's time to say goodbye,
For the stars above the east are growing pale.
And I'm making home to mother; and it's hard for me to die!
But it's harder still, is keeping out of gaol!
You can ride the old horse over to my grave across the dip
Where the wattle bloom is waving overhead.
Sure he'll jump them fences easy; you must never raise the whip
Or he'll rush 'em! now, goodbye!' and he had fled.

So they buried Andy Regan, and they buried him to rights,
In the graveyard at the back of Kiley's Hill;
There were five-and-twenty mourners who had five-and-twenty
    fights
Till the very boldest fighters had their fill.
There were fifty horses racing from the graveyard to the pub,
And their riders flogged each other all the while.
And the lashin's of the liquor! And the lavin's of the grub!
Oh! poor Andy went to rest in proper style.

Then the races came to Kiley's—with a steeplechase and all,
For the folk were mostly Irish round about,
And it takes an Irish rider to be fearless of a fall;
They were training morning in and morning out.
But they never worked their horses till the sun was on the course
For a superstitious story kept 'em back,
That the ghost of Andy Regan, on a slashing chestnut horse,
Had been training by the starlight on the track.

And they read the nominations for the races with surprise
And amusement at the Father's little joke,
For a novice had been entered for the steeplechasing prize,
And they found that it was Father Riley's moke!
He was neat enough to gallop, he was strong enough to stay!
But his owner's views of training were immense,
For the Reverend Father Riley used to ride him every day,
And he never saw a hurdle nor a fence.

And the priest would join the laughter, 'Oh,' said he, 'I put him in,
For there's five-and-twenty sovereigns to be won.
And the poor would find it useful, if the chestnut chanced to win,
And he'll maybe win when all is said and done!'
He had called him Faugh-a-ballagh, which is French for 'Clear the
    course',
And his colours were a vivid shade of green:
All the Dooleys and O'Donnells were on Father Riley's horse,
While the Orangemen were backing Mandarin!

It was Hogan, the dog poisoner—old man and very wise,
Who was camping in the racecourse with his swag,
And who ventured the opinion, to the township's great surprise,
That the race would go to Father Riley's nag.
'You can talk about your riders—and the horse has not been schooled,
And the fences is terrific, and the rest!
When the field is fairly going, then ye'll see ye've all been fooled,
And the chestnut horse will battle with the best.

'For there's some has got condition, and they think the race is sure,
And the chestnut horse will fall beneath the weight,
But the hopes of all the helpless, and the prayers of all the poor,
Will be running by his side to keep him straight.

And what's the need of schoolin' or of workin' on the track,
When the saints are there to guide him round the course!
I've prayed him over every fence—I've prayed him out and back!
And I'll bet my cash on Father Riley's horse!'

*

Oh, the steeple was a caution! They went tearin' round and round,
And the fences rang and rattled where they struck.
There was some that cleared the water, there was more fell in and
    drowned,
Some blamed the men and others blamed the luck!
But the whips were flying freely when the field came into view,
For the finish down the long green stretch of course,
And in front of all the flyers—jumping like a kangaroo,
Came the rank outsider—Father Riley's horse!

Oh, the shouting and the cheering as he rattled past the post!
For he left the others standing in the straight;
And the rider—well they reckoned it was Andy Regan's ghost,
And it beat 'em how a ghost would draw the weight!
But he weighed in, nine stone seven, then he laughed and disappeared,
Like a banshee (which is Spanish for an elf),
And old Hogan muttered sagely, 'If it wasn't for the beard
They'd be thinking it was Andy Regan's self!'

And the poor of Kiley's Crossing gave their thanks at Christmas-tide
To the chestnut and his jockey dressed in green.
There was never such a rider, not since Andy Regan died,
And they wondered who on earth it could have been.
But they settled it among 'em, for the story got about,
'Mongst the bushmen and the people on the course,
That the Devil had been ordered to let Andy Regan out
For the steeplechase on Father Riley's horse!

# The Bernborough story

## DAVID HICKIE

BERNBOROUGH WAS FOALED IN 1939 at Harry Winten's Rosalie Plains Stud, in the Dalby district on Queensland's Darling Downs, near Toowoomba.

His dam was the 18-year-old mare Bern Maid and his sire was supposed to be by the imported sire Emborough, a horse that had won the Manchester Cup in the UK, but there is some doubt about this and his sire may have been Monish Vella.

Bernborough, racing under the nomination of a Mr Albert E. Hadwen of Brisbane, was unplaced at his first Toowoomba start on 26 January 1942 and then ran in a maiden event for two-year-olds. Bernborough finished second to a scrubber called Dunfor, but a protest was successful. Bernborough then won four more two-year-old races at Toowoomba.

As a three-year-old he raced three times for three wins and as a four-year-old he had two starts, once coming third and once unplaced. He had eight runs, all at Toowoomba, as a five-year-old for three wins, one second and was four times unplaced.

His Toowoomba record therefore stood at 11 wins from 19 starts—impressive, but not sensational, and certainly not the sort of credentials upon which many turf experts would later base their judgement that Bernborough, of all Australian thoroughbreds, was the greatest.

In later years many people closely associated with the Bernborough camp, which won a lot of money knowing when to back the 'one day on—one day off' champ, revealed details which give reason to believe Bernborough could have won all those Toowoomba races in a canter.

## Part 1   The Daylate–Brulad 'ring-in' scandal

The background to Bernborough's restricted early racing went back to Queensland's infamous Daylate–Brulad 'ring-in' scandal, when the Queensland Turf Club's investigation led to the life disqualification of Oakey farmer Fred Bach.

In December 1938 a horse named Brulad, owned by Bach and trained by Con Doyle, flashed home at double-figure odds to run third behind Tollbar in the QTC Champagne Stakes at Eagle Farm. A week later the bay gelding, by Brutus out of Lady Chillington, was heavily backed at 3 to 1 and won the 5-furlong Oxley Handicap at Eagle Farm, despite badly missing the start. The time, 61.5 seconds, was the fastest registered by a two-year-old for the season.

Brulad was sent for a spell, returning in February 1939 for three disappointing unplaced runs. Then the horse began to show form. He ran third at Eagle Farm, before being well supported and defeating the odds-on favourite, top colt Brisbane River, in the 6-furlong Juvenile Handicap at Eagle Farm in April. After that win, Fred Bach was offered £1000 for Brulad but refused to sell.

Brulad was beaten in his last three starts of that season and then, as a three-year-old, failed to show any form and was beaten in six successive starts. The horse was now in the stable of Clive Morgan, who sent the horse back to Bach in February 1940, suggesting he needed a long spell. Morgan never saw the horse again and Fred Bach told the trainer that Brulad had died. The same year a four-year-old brown gelding, Daylate, by Listowel out of Fernie-hurst, was registered in the ownership of a certain J. Jackson.

Daylate's first start resulted in a second place in a Hack Handi-cap at Warwick, in October 1940. A month later he won easily at Bundamba. Fred Bach was at the course and backed the horse for a small fortune. 'If I had one win a year like I had at Bundamba,' Bach later boasted, 'I would be thoroughly satisfied.' Daylate then ran third at Bundamba and fourth in a Trial Handicap at Eagle Farm.

On 4 January 1941, Daylate ran in another Trial Handicap at Eagle Farm. Leading jockey Russell Maddock was engaged and the horse was heavily backed in the betting ring. A mysterious 'Lady in Black' was reputed to have collected more than £1000 in win-nings from bookmakers in the on-course betting ring alone. In 1941 that was enough to buy a couple of modest suburban homes in Brisbane.

The horse raced with the leaders until the 2-furlong mark and then dashed clear to win easily, beating a horse called Bullmar who was ridden by a youthful George Moore. Years later Maddock revealed, 'I was asked only the night before the race to ride Daylate by the owner.'

No hint emerged that day of any behind-the-scenes drama, but the following Saturday QTC chief steward J.J. Lynch, accompa-nied by two racecourse detectives, arrived unannounced at the Doomben stables of Daylate's trainer J.H. McIlwrick. The news spread like wildfire that authorities had made a thorough examina-tion of Daylate.

A reporter tracked down Lynch and asked him why he had inspected Daylate. 'I cannot discuss that with you,' came the stern reply. It was also reported that two unnamed trainers, later identi-fied as Con Doyle and Clive Morgan, who had previously trained Brulad, had also been asked to examine Daylate.

Neither trainer would make any comment but the rumour spread that Daylate bore a remarkable resemblance to Brulad, which Fred Bach had officially certified to the QTC office as being dead. Then Daylate suddenly disappeared from McIlwrick's stables.

What had happened was that a country steward named Steve Bowen, enjoying an off-duty day at Eagle Farm, had raised initial doubts about Daylate's identity and declared the winner was in fact Brulad. Similarly trainer Morgan told racecourse detective Charles Prentice that Daylate was Brulad. Prentice was at first dubious, but Bowen maintained he was certain because Brulad had a particularly unusual mane, which hung in three sections across his neck whenever the horse tossed his head—Daylate's mane fell in the same distinct pattern.

So Prentice and stewards Lynch and Williams set off in search of the mysterious owner of Daylate, 'J. Jackson', who had a postal address at a cattle station near Bowenville. When Prentice asked to speak to Jackson, the station mistress told him that all correspondence for J. Jackson was in fact handed to a Mrs F. Bacon, who was Fred Bach's daughter.

Meanwhile a policeman turned up at Bach's property near Oakey one night but was mysteriously shot at and wounded. Fred's son Jack was later tried for the crime, but acquitted—he had an alibi to prove he wasn't at the farm that evening.

When Prentice and his companions went to Bach's farm, Fred Bach wasn't there, but his son Jack told them Brulad's body had been burned after the horse had died. Prentice later officially reported, 'It was learned that the horse called Brulad had returned from Brisbane in a sick condition and subsequently died on Mister Frank Bach's property at Blaxland. Mister Jack Bach said he saw Brulad when the horse was dead and assisted his brother to burn the carcass.'

When Prentice went to see Frank Bach, however, Frank said he knew nothing about Brulad and had not helped Jack burn the carcass of any horse. It was when Prentice returned to Brisbane that Daylate suddenly disappeared from McIlwrick's stable.

Prentice, one jump ahead, had decided to 'stake out' the stables and caught Fred Bach absconding with Daylate. At about 10 p.m. he saw Fred Bach enter the yard. At 10:15 p.m. he heard 'knocking and hammering' and a few minutes later Bach led Daylate from the property. When he'd gone about 50 yards Prentice intercepted him and said, 'Good night'.

When Prentice asked his name Bach replied 'Jackson', but Prentice retorted, 'You are Fred Bach.'

Bach then said, 'You are Mister Prentice, how are you?' and shook hands.

When Prentice asked, 'Why are you mixing yourself up in this sort of thing?' Bach appeared 'flurried' and said Jackson was down the road. Prentice saw two cars further down the street and in one were two men who refused to give their names.

Eventually Bach confessed, 'Now you've got me. There's nobody else in this. There is only me. I am Jackson. I suppose I'll get life. I'll take full responsibility for everything.'

At a subsequent QTC enquiry Fred Bach denied he had admitted being Jackson and refused to answer most questions. A CIB handwriting expert testified that the same person who had signed nomination forms for Daylate in the name of Jackson had also signed nomination forms for Brulad in the name of Bach.

On 20 January 1941, QTC stewards disqualified Fred Bach for life. The ban also applied to his son, Jack.

## Part 2   Bernborough's mysterious ownership history

Fred Bach had two sons, John (known as Jack) and Frank. In 1940, some months before the Daylate–Brulad controversy, Jack had purchased the old mare Bern Maid, with a foal at foot, at the Rosalie Plains Stud dispersal, for 150 guineas.

Bach subsequently claimed to have sold the foal to A.E. Hadwen but, when the horse was entered for a two-year-old event in Brisbane in 1942, QTC stewards rejected the nomination. An official reason was never given but it was generally accepted that it was because of the colt's connection with the Bach family. Officials believed that the real owner was still Jack Bach.

The horse was then sent to Sydney, ostensibly by Hadwen, and trialled at Rosehill, but the AJC affirmed the Brisbane ban and refused any nomination for the colt. So Bernborough was banned from racing on any of the major tracks across Australia.

Only the Queensland country course at Toowoomba accepted the bona fide of Bernborough's sale. This they did after an enquiry, allegedly conducted by Darling Downs steward George Kirk, into the authenticity of a receipt signed by J.R. Bach for the sale of Bernborough to Hadwen for 140 guineas.

Hadwen said he bought the horse on 22 June 1940, after asking Bach to find him a good horse. Bernborough was then purportedly leased to trainer J. Roberts and raced solely in Toowoomba for four seasons, winning 11 races under often enormous weights.

Finally, in October 1945, the champion was sent to Sydney as a six-year-old, to be sold at public auction. Flamboyant restaurant and nightclub owner Azzalin Romano duly purchased him for Harry Plant to train at Randwick.

Romano had been told to purchase the horse by Plant and paid 2600 guineas for him. After the sale to Romano the QTC lifted its ban on Bernborough. Hence the champ raced on city tracks only in his sixth and seventh years—winning 15 of his 18 races in Sydney, Melbourne and Brisbane, at distances from 6 furlongs to one and a half miles.

Bernborough was a six-year-old bay stallion, then, when jockey Athol George Mulley first rode him. Mulley later recalled, 'Bailey Payten, to whom I was apprenticed, told me there was a very good horse from Queensland to come up for auction. He said he would like to buy him. He was prepared to pay up to £10,000 or, being conservative, at least £5000.'

Payten told Mulley, 'I could afford to buy him, but it wouldn't matter how much money I've got he can't be bought, so I won't worry.'

Years later Mulley explained this cryptic comment by hinting that Romano was not the sole owner of Bernborough and told of an argument he overheard between the two men concerned late one night when trainer Harry Plant was not present.

'My old boss, Bailey Payten, always maintained that there was no chance of anyone else ever buying Bernborough when he was put up for auction in Sydney,' Mulley said. 'He said that too many influential men of the day were involved and suggested that a certain bill of sale would have made interesting reading.'

Author Frank Hardy later wrote that Mulley told him, 'There was a mystery about the sale. Over the years, at parties, listening to various conversations, I gathered that certain important people in Sydney had arranged the sale and that apparently the original Queensland owner still retained a half-interest in the horse.'

Whatever the secret manoeuvrings away from public view, Bernborough was sold at public auction in October 1945 for 2600 guineas and duly arrived at the Randwick stables of trainer Harry Plant, a former Queensland buckjump champion and one-time professional horse breaker. Bernborough had previously raced on only one track—Clifford Park, Toowoomba.

## Part 3   A true champion

At his first Sydney start, in a Flying at Canterbury on 8 December 1945, Bernborough met severe interference and finished on the heels of the placegetters. Plant, who'd trialled the horse in secret and knew he had a champion, had told Romano to plunge heavily. Romano backed the horse to win a proverbial fortune, lost the lot, and insisted Plant replace jockey Noel McGrowdie.

Then followed Bernborough's legendary sequence of 15 straight wins under huge weights, ridden by Athol George Mulley. The sequence began with a Sydney treble in the Villiers Stakes with 9 st 2 lb (58 kg) by 5 lengths; the Carrington Stakes, with 9 st 6 lb (60 kg); and the Australia Day Handicap, with 9 st 5 lb (59.5 kg).

Mulley was 21 when he first rode Bernborough to victory in the Villiers at Randwick on 22 December 1945. He had begun riding less than four years before, at age 17.

'I was approached to ride Bernborough just for the one race and I took the ride only for one simple reason—I didn't have a riding engagement for the Villiers,' Mulley later recalled. 'I didn't know I was taking the ride on a champion. I rode him in trackwork at the old Victoria Park course before the Villiers and he was a big strong horse. He had beautiful shoulders. He measured 17 hands and 1 inch, the same height as Phar Lap, but he was better balanced than Phar Lap. Bernborough's conformation was perfect.

'I found out afterwards that he measured 67 inches from his ears to the top of his withers, and exactly the same from the top of his withers to his tail; that is a perfectly balanced measurement.' Later Bernborough's full galloping stride was measured at 27 feet (8.2 metres), 2 feet longer than Phar Lap's stride.

'That first day at the track I noticed how well balanced he was and that as a walker he was terrific,' Mulley said, 'and he had a marvellous temperament for a stallion. But if I told you I knew how good he was, I'd be telling a lie. Nobody knew then.

'I obtained my first feeling that Bernborough was a champion when I won on him in the Villiers. There were no starting stalls in those days, it was a stand-up start. He was second last on settling down and about eighth at the turn and, when I called on him, that's when I first noticed how he dropped his off-front shoulder. I pulled the whip, but I didn't use it, just waved it at him, and a furlong out he leapt straight to the lead and won by 5 lengths. And I knew I had ridden a champion racehorse.'

Mulley was given the mount again for the Carrington Stakes, over 6 furlongs, which Bernborough won carrying 9 st 6 lb (60 kg) in 1 minute 10.25 seconds.

And so it went on, 15 consecutive times, until Bernborough and Mulley were household names throughout Australia.

After his three Sydney wins Bernborough headed for Melbourne and the big autumn races. He won the Futurity Stakes by 5 lengths carrying 10 st 2 lb (64.5 kg) and the Newmarket Handicap with 9 st 13 lb (63 kg). Mulley later told how he was offered £5000, a fortune in those days, to 'pull' Bernborough in the Newmarket.

After the Futurity triumph Romano rushed up to the 21-year-old Mulley and declared, 'Georgie, my boy, I am proud of you. Name anything you like and I'll get it for you. I will even let you marry my daughter!'

Twenty-five years later Mulley told Frank Hardy, 'Bernborough's greatest performance, in my opinion, was his Newmarket win at Flemington. He had had a very hard race in the Futurity a week or so before and he carried 9 st 13 lb (63 kg) in the Newmarket and beat a field of class sprinters, including Versailles ridden by Scobie Breasley. Coming back from the 7 furlongs of the Futurity to the 6 furlongs of the Newmarket was Bernborough's greatest feat. Ordinary horses can increase their distance from 6 to 7 furlongs, 7 to a mile and so on, but only great horses can come back in their distances in top-class company.'

Mulley had ridden Bernborough in three races in Sydney, but the Futurity at Caulfield in February 1946 was the jockey's first ride ever in Melbourne.

'In the Villiers at Randwick,' Mulley recalled, 'I had to make up some ground on the turn into the straight and, coming into the turn he dipped his off-front shoulder. I'd say, without exaggerating, it was at about a 45-degree angle. I'll never forget it: in all my experience I never rode a horse with that peculiarity before or since. He dropped his shoulder and he got tremendous speed once he did that and could continue his run right to the post. He had a run of 2 to 2¼ furlongs. You had to judge it and he liked to begin it in the middle of his turn or near the end of his turn.'

There was no turn, of course, in the Newmarket, which is run down the 'straight six' at Flemington.

'There was more than one horse in that race whose jockey's job was to down Bernborough,' recalled Mulley. 'I know that because to pull Bernborough in the Newmarket I was offered £5000. I refused, of course, and a man pushed his way into my hotel room and threatened me, and he told me Bernborough wouldn't win anyway, because there were jockeys scouting for him.'

The record shows that Bernborough was cannoned into by two horses as soon as the barrier went up; and after travelling 2 furlongs he received another bad check.

'I pulled Bernborough to the centre of the track about 2¼ furlongs from home,' explained Mulley. 'He dropped his shoulder and unwound his famous cyclonic run . . . and then the "accident" happened. A horse veered out and came at us but luckily Bernborough was such a great horse and so strong that he just hit him on the shoulder and knocked him away and he never even lost his stride.'

Bernborough continued his mighty finish and got up in the last stride to collar the good sprinter Four Freedoms, ridden by Bill Cook and carrying 2 stone less in weight, right on the line.

'It turned out that Bernborough had run the last furlong in ten seconds,' Mulley later recalled, 'and won by half a head. It was his greatest win.'

To that point Bernborough had strung together five sensational wins on the trot in major races and Romano revealed that he'd already been inundated with hundreds of letters from all over Australia. He responded by sending out 300 photographs of the horse to the fans.

Back in Sydney in April 1946, Bernborough won the Rawson Stakes, Chipping Norton Stakes (beating Flight and Russia) and the All-Aged Stakes.

Bernborough then headed north to the Brisbane Winter Carnival where, on successive June Saturdays, he added to his record with wins in the Doomben Ten Thousand, carrying 10 st 5 lb (65.5 kg), and the Doomben Cup with an incredible 10 st 11 lb (68.5 kg). Romano and stable followers collected £40,000 from winning wagers on the two races and through the feature doubles.

Although Mulley named Newmarket as Bernborough's greatest race, many turf aficionados rated his Doomben Cup win superior. Bernborough began slowly, as usual, and was 14 lengths from the lead at the mile post. He eventually caught the leaders right on the finishing line, having humped 10 st 11 lb (68.5 kg) to victory in a top feature race and carrying 28 lb (12 kg) in dead weight.

'That was Bernborough's secret,' Mulley explained years later. 'I always felt he could race as fast with 10 stone as he could with 7 stone—weight made no difference to him. That's what made him a champion, his ability to carry big weights.'

Veteran Brisbane race-caller Keith Noud claimed: 'Bernborough's Doomben double in 1946, a feat yet to be duplicated, were the two great performances above all others used to underline the argument that he was the greatest horse, up to 2000 metres, yet to race in this country. The full force of that opinion is based on the massive weights he carried in those races.'

After the sensational Brisbane triumphs Romano, who had a photo of Bernborough that he always carried with him and described as his 'lucky mascot', presented Bernborough's silks to Mulley at a special function.

Now a seven-year-old, Bernborough won his next five starts, all at weight for age. They were the Warwick Stakes, Chelmsford Stakes and Hill Stakes in Sydney, and the Melbourne Stakes and Caulfield Stakes in Melbourne. As a result he was allotted an incredible 10 st 10 lb (68 kg) for the 1946 Caulfield Cup and 10 st 9 lb (67.5 kg) in the Melbourne Cup.

What made those huge handicaps all the more remarkable was that eight months before the weights for the Cup were issued, very few racegoers in Australia had even heard of Bernborough. Moreover the horse was now at an age when most thoroughbreds are considered past their prime. At that time the weight-carrying record for the Caulfield Cup stood to the credit of Amounis, who had won with 9 st 8 lb (61 kg) in 1930.

'His weight-for-age wins were never as impressive as his handicap wins,' Mulley later said. 'But Bernborough should have been reserved for weight-for-age races in the spring of 1946. He'd had a lot of hard racing and his legs were bound to give out under handicap weights in big fields. He should never have run in the Caulfield Cup. But they wanted him to run in everything. They would have run him in the Stawell Gift, only it had been cancelled during World War II.'

A sport-loving, hero-worshipping nation just out of war needed an idol. And the massive, heart-stopping Bernborough filled the role precisely. He was indifferent to distance, and no weight the handicapper gave him seemed to dull his strength. Most importantly, he always won with a blistering finish that brought crowds roaring to their feet. No matter how far back he was at the furlong, everyone knew Bernborough would mow down his rivals.

'There was something special about the horse,' Frank Hardy wrote, 'the balance, the giant strides, the will to win. And about the way Mulley rode him, allowing him time to settle down and timing his paralysing finishing run to the split second.'

Bernborough became the greatest drawcard racing had ever known. That's why 107,167 patrons streamed to Caulfield racecourse for the 1946 Caulfield Cup. The press made great play of the fact that one woman, a mysterious 'woman in black' who turned out to be an Estonian woman, Miss Joanna Taks, had bet her winnings 'all-up' 15 times in a row on the champion and intended to do so once again.

The day after the race the *Melbourne Truth* newspaper reported:

Taks, who took Melbourne by storm with her huge bets on Bernborough in the Melbourne Stakes and Caulfield Stakes, risked her money once too often yesterday and lost £6000. Miss Taks said last night that she would not back Bernborough again. 'I'm going straight back to Sydney and will retire as a punter,' she said. 'I backed Bernie because he looked so lovely, but he lost, and now I have the big headache.' Had Bernborough won, Miss Taks would have collected £13,250 from four bookmakers.

Romano himself was reported to have amassed about £110,000 in winning bets from Bernborough's phenomenal run, as well as the considerable stake money. On the eve of the Caulfield Cup he told the press, 'If only he can win, I shall be the happiest man in the world.'

Bernborough started 2 to 1 favourite after a wild betting spree and bookies gambled heavily against him. The race has since been repeatedly tagged 'the most controversial race ever run in this country'.

His winning streak finally came to an end when he finished fifth behind Royal Charm. Bernborough missed the start slightly and, after severe interference, flashed home from an impossible position in the straight. Carey shifted sharply from close to the rails as Bernborough came flashing down the run home, and the flying favourite cannoned into his rump.

Bernborough was stopped in his tracks, lost his momentum and staggered. Mulley balanced him quickly but the others were too far ahead and the post too close. Across the line it was Royal Charm, Columnist, Two Grand, Carey, and Bernborough fifth, still coming strong at the finish.

The race report noted that 'Bernborough was gathering the opposition in swiftly as they passed the post'.

Romano and Plant were so upset at Bernborough being such a long way back during the run that they replaced Mulley with 'Bustling' Billy Briscoe for the horse's next start in the LKS Mackinnon Stakes. Plant and Mulley never spoke to each other again.

After the Caulfield Cup defeat Romano received 200 letters imploring him to scratch Bernborough from the Melbourne Cup. This was not only because of the champion's huge weight, but also because Romano had stated, as far back as the previous March after his sensational Newmarket victory, that Bernborough would have 'only a few more handicap races' and then be reserved for weight-for-age events.

'He belongs to the public now,' Romano had declared then. 'I've got back what I paid for him and we are not going to ruin him by racing him under fantastic weights in handicaps.'

The Mulley–Romano–Plant rift after the Caulfield Cup became one of the most notorious aftermaths to any major race in Australian turf history.

Almost 40 years later Mulley told Bert Lillye of the *Sydney Morning Herald*:

> I am the only one still alive to tell. Owner Romano, trainer Plant and stable foreman Ned Cullen have all gone . . . I will tell you something that I have not revealed before. There was always a

meeting between Romano, Plant and myself to plan Bernborough's race programme. Mister Romano and I were both against starting Bernborough in the Caulfield Cup but we were overruled by Plant. I argued that no horse could win with that weight and that Bernborough should be restricted to weight-for-age races. Romano agreed with me.

But then the hint that Romano was not the sole owner of Bernborough came into play. And there the mystery remains.

Mulley married a few weeks after the Caulfield Cup. Despite the success of their association through Bernborough's magic succession of wins, Romano sent no wedding present, nor was he invited to the ceremony.

For many years Mulley had to suffer the rumours and allegations that he 'pulled up' Bernborough in the Caulfield Cup.

After examining the evidence years later, Pat Farrell wrote in the *Sydney Daily Mirror*, 'To say that Mulley pulled Bernborough up is the most profoundly ridiculous assertion ever known in a sport where ridiculous assertions abound.'

In any event Bernborough, with replacement hoop Briscoe aboard, tackled the fateful Mackinnon Stakes four days before the Melbourne Cup of 1946 and broke down with an injured sesamoid bone. Romano and Plant raced from the stands to their stricken champion, hobbling in pain at the top of the straight, and the distressed Romano could not speak for an hour after the race, which was won by the great mare Flight.

Bernborough was saved by veterinary surgeons and in December 1946, he was sold to Louis B. Mayer, head of Metro-Goldwyn-Mayer pictures, to stand at stud in the USA. The price was reported to be £93,000 at the time, but was later claimed to be less. (Mayer's annual salary of an equivalent to £312,675 was top of the published income lists in the USA at the time.)

Mayer subsequently sold Bernborough to a syndicate of Kentucky breeders.

Many Australians, who regarded Bernborough as their own, were horrified by the whole affair and an uproar followed the sale. Romano remained unpopular with the general public for a long time.

However, after one visit to the USA, Romano reported that his former champion was 'living like a prince'. He even had a thermometer in his palatial stall to ensure a comfortable temperature.

In the USA Bernborough sired the winners of more than $4 million in prize money. His progeny included many stakes winners, most notably Bernwood, who ran a mile in 1 minute 33.8 seconds to set a new national record.

# Zaimis

## JIM BENDRODT

*Zaimis was foaled in 1934. Although moderately performed in England he had a strong pedigree with St Simon appearing three times. Named after a famous Greek prime minister, he was shipped off to stand at stud in Western Australia and produced nine stakes winners of 15 races.*

THIS IS THE TALE of a dark bay horse who, bred in the lap of luxury, left his fine safe home to wander down the latitudes in a steel-grey ship. Of how, after many weeks and many thousands of miles of danger-ridden travel, the Storm Gods laid a trap for him when he was almost safe again. Of how he, in his last extremity while death swept up on him, lifted his classic head to the frantic skies and sent out a desperate call to a little lad who loved him. And of how the lad, deep in the arms of Morpheus, just slept on.

Should you who read this story not know a thoroughbred, then this tale will be hard enough to credit; but those who know and understand them will say the thing I write about is just fantastic. That is why I tell you now that what I sit down here is plain, unvarnished truth—no more. Now, here's the story . . .

He came trundling down the lanes and byways of wartime

England, clad in his fine, rare woollen rugs, guarded by men who knew his blood was precious. Always through life such men had surrounded him, careful to fend the slightest danger off. Never, except in little paddocks, had he known freedom, unless it was when his mighty muscles bunched and swept him triumphantly along some English green sward, and even then a lad crouched along his neck to guide and care for him. Always a friendly hand, a cunning eye, to guard him. That's what made his last ordeal so doubly hard.

Down the streets of Liverpool he came, eventually to the side of the steel-grey ship that would carry him safely to this land in which I live—if she missed the submarines! And even then, they cared for him just like a baby. They led him quietly into a narrow stall which was strapped to the rails and stanchions on the welldeck aft—a box that was stout and strong as hands could make it with hardwood timber and strong steel bolts—but a box, my friends that the Storm Gods laughed at, as I shall tell you if you will bear with me a while.

Then they left him, with a pat on the neck, and a friendly word, and the sailors took him over. Now a sailor is a merry lad to whom his ship is as familiar as your bedroom is to you, but it is a rare thing if he knows anything about a horse. There is something incongruous about a sailor and a horse. They just don't go together. Yet the seamen did the best they could do for him in those early days. They could not know the things that bothered him and, even if they had known, there was not much that they could do about it.

The *Leaside Park* crept out of Liverpool in the dead of night, while far over her mast heads in the blackness the bombers roared away for Germany. She sailed into her place in a great convoy, and slid quietly seaward, with the destroyers whipping the grey ships into line, like shepherd dogs. It was not the bombers that worried the horse. Long ago, he had learned to watch them with quiet-eyed wonder.

Blackness was a thing that he was used to; but the low growl of ships' sirens, the hooting of foghorns, and the silver voice of bells, were things that worried him, though he took them quietly enough, shut away in the inky blackness of his narrow stall. But when they got to sea, that heaving deck on which his box stood was something new and terrifying, and the unaccustomed motion made him sick. For days he pawed restlessly in his stuffy quarters, and would not eat, but there was no complaint from him. The sailors did what little things they could to make him comfortable, and, as is the way of sailors, trusted him to bring them luck.

When the top door of his stall was open he could gaze seaward over the after-gun mountings. By being very careful in his narrow space, he could just lie down, if he had wanted to, and go to sleep, but he didn't want to—he just stood up, night and day, week after week, month after month, with that incredible patience horses have.

Now, an outward-bound sea-tramp takes time to settle down, particularly in wartime. All through those first few days men worked and wondered. In the back of their minds, both night and day, an alarm bell poised. Out in those dreary wastes of water deadly warheads waited, snuggled in the bows of a silent craft that shot to kill. Those were no times for song and shanty. Those were times to quietly watch and wait, and pray, if that was the kind of thing you cared to do. But the *Leaside Park* escaped them all. One day in the mid-Atlantic, some pennants fluttered at the destroyer's stumpy mast, and she turned south and wandered off alone.

I have sailed the seas in frowzy tramp steamers and penthouse liners, and I've travelled in diverse ways and circumstances. I've journeyed in tired old rusty 'tea-kettles', clad in a pair of cut-down pants and a dingy shirt. I've slept on an iron deck from which the clang of shovels, beating on steel bulkheads in some hellhole far below, awakened me to savage toil. And then, again, I've sailed in seagoing hotels, in a private suite with a man to adjust my cuff-links and clean my shoes, but I've found one thing that is common to them all. Once the grey northern latitudes drop below a far horizon, then is the time that sea folk start to play.

The *Leaside Park* laid her course for Panama, and in a day or so she was sailing beneath brilliant skies on jewelled waters. The great horse shook his head and ate his food. They took his heavy rugs off, and in his lair, among the crated tanks and aeroplanes, he settled down. The sickness left him.

There was a little square of steel deck, perhaps 14 by 14 feet, a tiny pocket-handkerchief of rusty iron, facing the big bay's stall. On three sides of it the boxed engines of war crowded every available inch of space. On the fourth side, with the low ship's rail intervening, was the ocean. It was on that seagoing stage that the bay made his last great fight for life, but long before that happened it was the space on which the sailors met to pay him homage.

'Brought us luck, 'e did!' they said of him, and in their hours off watch, or as they went about their daily business, they'd stop and talk to him, and pat his neck and rub his ears. And so, because the business of the ship goes on night and day, there was nearly always someone with him. He played no favourites in those early days. When the Captain came in his braided cap, he would incline on his head with simple dignity and accept the great man's gift of sugar; but when the midnight black gang came off watch in the early hours of the morning, he'd be waiting there to welcome them. These grimy men, with naked torsos, with black-rimmed eyes like circus clowns, and dead-white faces from which the stokehole's heat had drained all colour, were his friends, and he'd put his muzzle down and lick their blackened hands for salt. In the velvet nights the men would gather on the little square of deck and sing their quaint sea songs, and make their music, while from his open doorway he would watch them carefully and nibble hay.

I said he played no favourites. Well, that was true at first, and then he changed.

Sailors, I believe, are never horsemen, but there is an exception to any rule you care to make, and Red was one. I never knew his full name, but he was a pantry-boy with a carrot top and a freckled face, and inevitably they called him Red, and he loved horses.

I suppose he cared for ships and oceans too, or he would not have sailed on the wartime tramp, but in his snug sea-bag there were many books on horses and on jockeys—the great Tod Sloan, the imperturbable Donohoe, the brilliant Eddie Accaro—these were the folk the little lad adored, and here, on his ship, was a horse such as they had ridden to fame. A thoroughbred horse, with satin coat and long slim legs, mentioned more than once in the books he read at night-time.

When the agents ship a horse to foreign parts, they, in collaboration with the Captain, appoint a member of the crew to care for him, among that seaman's other duties. Usually the carpenter or bo'sun is the person. And so it was in this case, but eventually it was Red who got the job. From that time he was the horse's favourite.

'Look at 'im,' a sailor said, as the horse turned from the carrot he had offered him to welcome Red. 'Fair in love with 'im 'e is.' Then, as the big bay nibbled delicately at the lad's ear, 'Rather eat *'im* 'e would,' the sailor said, disgustedly, and threw the carrot overboard and walked away.

The master of a ship carrying precious bloodstock has an added worry on his mind. He is almost always a man who prides himself on the condition of the animals he carries, when at last he delivers them at some far destination, but as a rule he knows little about them except that he must follow close directions given by the agents.

And so the Captain watched the big horse carefully. On one soft, warm night, he walked aft on comfortably slippered and noiseless feet, and paused some 10 feet away from the horse's stall. In the shadows he saw a little figure astride the bay, with his knees drawn close to the horse's wither, and his freckled hands playing along the outstretched neck. He could hear a soft murmur as the lad whispered words he could not catch, and he heard the bay horse nicker deep in his throat, a soft, fluttering sound of infinite contentment, warm and exciting in the quiet night. Without a word, and very quietly, the Captain turned away and went back to his bridge. In the morning he called the mate.

'Mister,' he said, 'tell the steward we'll have that redhead lad of yours look after that blasted horse in his spare time. Tell Chips to do something else. Perhaps you'd better check over the stowage of those tanks. This weather won't last forever.'

The *Leaside Park* crept south and west, week after week. Almost it seemed she dreamed her lazy way down through the latitudes. Sun-drenched day followed sun-drenched day, and at night an indigo sky blazed with stars. These ships are slow. She seemed to slide through the amethyst sea carefully, piling on either side of her curling waves that broke into little capfuls of cream and blue, and these ran whispering and hissing along her steel sides. No sign of life. No other ship. No sight of land. Sometimes a whale broached on the far horizon, as if this strange intruder had awakened him from age-old dreams to come forth and welcome it with a derisive jet of arching water. Sometimes a flying fish would flop on deck, and beat in frenzy with iridescent wings.

In the long, hot days the ship's bells told the time in dull monotony, but in the midnight hours they sounded cool and clear in sharp, sweet music. And so she crept on ever southward, a squat, grey stranger, in a fabled world of whispering tropic winds and placid waters.

Through the drowsy summer days the horse grew sleek and satisfied. His quarters filled out, and his coat became more and more like satin, and he grew to look for Red. The boy himself lived in a sort of seventh heaven of delight, thrilled with the boon of a fine companionship.

But nothing that is perfect ever lasts. Almost imperceptibly at first, the weather altered. Just little changes here and there. But the Captain knew. He called them 'the mate'.

'Mister,' he said, 'the glass is falling like a lift. I've never seen anything like it before. Something pretty tough is coming up. Call all hands, and get to work on that deck cargo. Double everything holding it, and bend a couple of extra cables round that horse's box. Tie it down hard, and tell the kid to stay with him, and try to keep him quiet. Get going. We haven't much time.'

Over to the southwest, a patch of inky cloud marred the marvellous beauty of the day. It grew, even as Red watched it, and spread across the whole horizon, and crept upward and outward over the azure sky. The sea changed from amethyst to a sort of sullen malign yellow, and the sun became a livid glowing ball. The ocean seemed a lake on which the grey ship travelled. A lake growing smaller and smaller as the horizons closed in on her. Then this lake began to twist and writhe as if some gigantic hand tormented it.

The grey ship plunged and rolled restlessly. There was not a sound except the sounds the hurrying sailors made. Then in a flash the sun was gone. The black horizons to the southwest flamed, and in this devil's light they saw a torrent of white water racing down on them. An instant more, and the Storm Gods struck—sprang the trap they had fashioned in far Antarctica—roaring and bellowing down on the little ship, with insensate, stupid rage, to maim and kill and drown. The world dissolved in chaos, became a raucous, flame-drenched universe through which the *Leaside Park* groaned and shuddered.

I couldn't tell you what went on in that horse's mind when the cyclone hit them. If he was terrified, he gave no sign, because Red told me so. The floor of his box was good hardwood. His front feet were shod with little steel slippers, and on the wood these gave him grip. His back feet were bare, as is the custom. Red shut his top door, ran a supporting rail from end to end off the stall, making it half the width, so that the horse couldn't roll too much if he kept his feet.

Red stayed with him all through the day, and long into that awful night, and no one but those two knew just how they made it. It was two in the morning when the boy was done. He told me afterwards that he left the horse to get some food. That bare ten minutes was all he thought he'd be away. He never intended to leave his great horse struggling there in that narrow stall amid that fearful pandemonium, alone.

But that little lad, I said, was done. He had to go. The horse's stall was just aft of the officers' mess. The little square of steel deck I spoke of ran along its portside wall. The boy told himself that he could hear the horse even in the raging storm. I said he was half asleep, but he was more than half asleep. He was nearly sound asleep as he fought his way to the little galley in search of food. Then suddenly, he didn't want food. He turned and stumbled to the mess room. Behind a table in a corner, a settee ran along the wall. Like an automaton he edged his way behind the table and sat down.

Then, as a marionette's head might do, if jerked by knowing fingers, Red's head fell forward on his outstretched arms. Then, before his face touched that table, he was sound asleep. That was when the Storm Gods struck again.

The horse had called once when the boy had left him, a sort of soft bubbling flutter deep in his throat. Then he set himself anew to fight this battle on that crazy, plunging ship, and he would have won it too, I'm convinced of that, all by himself. The wooden floor helped him. His steel slippers gripped it well. The wall of his box was padded, and the extra rail buttressed him, and so in the dead of night he struggled on. A thoroughbred! Oh, sure, I told you that.

Two hours passed. The plunging ship crept on. From high on the bridge, eight bells sounded, clear and shrill, in a night gone mad. And then? Well, then, perhaps half a mile to port, the great waves gathered, merging themselves for that tremendous blow. Mountains of tumbling water marshalling into one great weapon, as the Storm Gods made their mighty play.

The wave struck the *Leaside Park* just abaft the bridge, on the ship's port side. Down through the engine-room skylights the water tumbled. Over the deck cargo it smashed and roared, raced to the welldeck aft, and splintered the stallion's box to pieces.

How he got out no man will ever know. I saw what was left of that box myself, and marvelled, when the ship got to port. I cannot tell you how he got out; but he did get out. He snapped the thin manila rope that tied him to his manger, and in the maelstrom of raging water he fought his way to that little square of steel deck I have talked about. A slip—one mere step away from that iron square—and the horse was done. But, by some amazing equine miracle, that good horse knew it, and battled on.

No one saw him fighting there like some four-footed equilibrist for his balance, bleeding from many wounds, on that deadly night—with no friendly hand to help him. But that he did this thing is unarguable, as you shall see.

Then, after the groaning ship had lifted herself from that monstrous wave's cold embrace, she sank back again into the bosom of the sea, as if weary of it all. The twisted port rail, 4 feet from the horse, sank under, and the black waters reached him with icy fingers. To his knees—his shoulders—the water came. Then he felt a steel-shod foot slip on a steel-shod deck that gave no grip as wood had done. At last his courage faltered. Terror enveloped him. He lifted his classic head to those frantic skies, and sent his shrill wild call for help to a boy who slept and could not hear him.

Red dreamed on. Wedged in his corner sound asleep. Tonight, as on so many other nights, he dreamed of horses. Of riding horses in silks and satins, among cheering multitudes. The land he came from uses bugles to call the horses to their posts. Deep in his dreams he heard the bugles call, shrill and clear. He stirred uneasily. Deep in his subconscious mind he sensed that something was amiss. His dream of horses faded out. Tormenting nightmare gripped him. A weird fantasy of strife and tumult. He stirred again—his head lifted—then he awoke, and sat bolt upright, his mind still gripped with the fear of his crazy dream.

Then, high and thin and clear over the bedlam of the night, he heard the great horse call. So *that* was the bugle he had dreamed about. The bugle that, even in his dream, had seemed so sharp and shrill. He was gone from that room like a freckled wraith, defying the laws of gravity, desperate with fear.

He'd slept only a few yards away—yet to him it seemed hours before he reached the horse. Then with one strong young hand he held tight to the broken halter, and talked to his friend, and reached up and patted him and soothed him—just as he had done so many times, when all that the nights had held were stars and peace.

And so, through the remainder of the hours of blackness, the boy and the horse fought it out together, each helping the other, each drawing courage and confidence from their strange companionship. No physical strength possessed by one small boy could have tipped the scale, but his cheerful voice, his gentle hand, together with the mere fact that he was near at all, was all the bay horse needed.

When the black turmoil of night at last gave way to a yellow, murky dawn, the sailors found them there and, except for cuts and bruises, both were safe and sound.

The Captain, coming aft, paused and surveyed the scene in blank astonishment. He watched his men, with cunning hands, weave hempen safeguards. He examined the shattered horse stall in amazement. He had watched over the grey ship through the anxious night, and half the time his bridge had been deep in water. He looked again at the two on their little square of steel deck, with unbelieving eyes, and shook his weary head.

All night long on his bridge high above the chaos raging below him, the Captain had fought for his footing. Time after time, the plunging steel monster he rode and guided through the blackness had hurt and bruised him. But there, high over this sea-swept wreckage, he'd had a hand hold, a little shelter to guard him from the Storm Gods' fury. But these two! This salt-encrusted stallion, with the blood dripping from his broken forehead—this little lad with his windswept flaming hair and smiling eyes. What hell had they had?

He looked again at the gap where his port-side rail had been, then lifted his eyes to the dreary skies for just a moment. 'This thing makes no sense in any language,' he muttered. 'How could any horse . . .' He paused and perhaps for a full minute more he surveyed the scene before him. Then he shook his tired head again in utter disbelief and, without another word, he turned and lurched away.

On a Western Australian stud farm, a great bay horse watches the sun etch the crest of the mountain ranges with purple and lemon and faint old rose. In the pastures that stretch towards him from their base, soft-eyed matrons with foals at foot browse quietly. The stallion lifts his head and calls to them masterfully, compellingly, as a king might call. His name is Zaimis.

# T.J.'s top two: Tulloch and Kingston Town

## JIM HAYNES

TOMMY SMITH HAD AN eye for a horse.

He came to Sydney with his first horse, Bragger, in 1941. He had bought the reject out of the paddock in Wagga Wagga in spite of the owner telling him the colt was mad and would never make a racehorse.

Tommy and Bragger lived side by side in two boxes at Kensington racetrack until Tommy and the horse had proved his previous owner wrong. It was touch and go for a while, though; Bragger bolted at his first barrier trial at the old Victoria Park track, threw the jockey, hurdled a fence and ended up on the beach at Botany Bay before Tommy managed to catch him.

Bragger went on to win 13 races, including the Rosehill Cup, and set Tommy on the path to success as a trainer.

Tommy's eye rarely let him down. He famously bought Playboy for Sydney owner E.R. Williams, who later raced good horses like Pride of Egypt and dual Cox Plate winner Hydrogen, and was annoyed when Williams said he didn't like the horse.

Williams later decided to take Playboy, but Tommy's nose was well out of joint and he refused to sell him, raced him in his own colours, and won the AJC Derby with him in 1949, along with the AJC St Leger, Craven Plate and CB Fisher Plate.

Tommy Smith was well established when Tulloch came along, but it is perhaps true to say that Tulloch stamped him as a great trainer and Kingston Town capped off his career.

The two champions had much in common, as well as some obvious differences. Tulloch and Kingston Town were both brilliant middle-distance horses that could stay, but they inherited that ability in different ways.

Tulloch was bred at the famous Trelawney Stud in New Zealand. He was by King George VI's galloper Khorassan, who was bred by the Aga Khan and had bloodlines back to Nearco (and thus Carbine), from the handy staying mare Florida. Tulloch was bred to be dour, but was also born with brilliance aplenty.

Kingston Town, on the other hand, was bred to be brilliant and go over distance when required. His sire was Bletchingly, a son of Biscay and a grandson of Star Kingdom, and his dam, Ada Hunter, was a grand-daughter of Italian legend Ribot, who had multiple St Simon blood and was unbeatable over a mile and a half, literally. In fact he was never beaten at any distance, winning all 16 of his race starts, from 1000 to 3000 metres and including the Prix de l'Arc de Triomphe twice.

There was one thing Tulloch and Kingston Town had in common—they were both rejects.

Tulloch 'took Tommy's eye' at the New Zealand sales and he bought him, in spite of his 'sway-back', thinking he would easily find an owner for him. T.J. Smith was by then a top trainer and owners lined up to buy horses he chose.

However, no one wanted Tulloch and Tommy was resigned to racing the colt himself when a chance meeting with Mr Evelyn Angus (Lyn) Haley changed everything. It seems Tommy had completely forgotten a conversation in which Haley had asked him to look for a yearling in New Zealand. Lyn Haley bought the horse and named him after his mother's hometown in Scotland.

Kingston Town was bred by wealthy owner David Hains at his

property on the Mornington Peninsula. Like Tulloch, he was an unimpressive yearling, being spindly and awkward where Tulloch was small and sway-backed. Hains decided to sell the colt but the best offer was $5000, well below the $8000 reserve price. Hains was annoyed but unwilling to accept the paltry offer. He reluctantly decided to keep the horse and sent him up to Sydney to see if the great T.J. Smith could make anything of him.

Tulloch and Kingston Town were both bad-tempered and hard to handle.

Tulloch, whose stable name was the prosaic 'Bobby', was a biter and kicker who would lash out when annoyed and nip anyone he could. His strapper, Neville Johnson, was usually wearing a bandage somewhere when 'Bobby' was in the stable.

Kingston Town, known as 'Sam' in the stable, was also a biter and was so badly behaved as a two-year-old that he was gelded. At his first start at Canterbury he refused to race when the gates opened, then tried to throw Malcolm Johnson and finally tailed the field to the post, finishing last.

At two years of age Kingston Town won at his only two other starts after being gelded, whereas Tulloch started 13 times aged two for six wins and seven seconds. He won the Sire's Produce Stakes in Victoria, New South Wales and Queensland and defeated the champion two-year-old Todman easily when winning the AJC version of the race.

As three-year-olds the two horses both became true champions. Tulloch started 16 times for 14 wins and two placings, while Kingston Town's record was 15 starts for 12 wins, a second, a third and a fourth.

In Tulloch's case T.J. Smith himself admitted the two placings, in the St George Stakes and Queen Elizabeth Stakes in the autumn of 1958, were a result of him not having the horse fit enough when he resumed after a three-month spell. It was a different matter with Kingston Town; his second in the VRC Derby was due to him tearing a lump off his hoof when he lost a plate. His third in the Caulfield Guineas and fourth in the Caulfield Cup were a result of the horse getting on his wrong foot around the Caulfield track.

Kingston Town always preferred to race clockwise. His record in Melbourne was four wins from 14 starts. In Sydney he won 22 from 25 starts, and in Brisbane it was two from two.

Both horses won the AJC and QTC Derbies among their many classic wins at three. Tulloch added the VRC Derby; Kingston Town won the Sydney Cup.

Each horse had 'one that got away' in their stellar three-year-old seasons, races they never started in but would probably have won easily. For Tulloch it was the Melbourne Cup, and for Kingston Town the Cox Plate.

The fuss over Tulloch running or not running in the Cup has been well documented. It is true he was given a record weight for a three-year-old, but it is hard to see how he could have lost the Cup at the height of his powers, even with 52.5 kg, after his spectacular and effortless victory in the Caulfield Cup. Nevertheless Haley decided to scratch him and 'Haley's Comet' was not given the chance to blaze a path to glory in the Cup.

In the case of Kingston Town it is a little more complex. He did not seem to handle the Melbourne way of going and T.J., on the strength of the colt's inability to handle Caulfield, decided the Derby on Flemington's roomier track would suit him better than the Cox Plate on the tight Moonee Valley track.

In hindsight this seems a tragic assumption. Kingstown Town started three times at Moonee Valley for three wins, in three WS Cox Plates. As it was, at three he raced at Flemington instead, damaged a hoof, changed legs all down the straight and missed winning the Derby by half a head. We can only imagine what would have happened had he won his first Cox Plate at three, instead of four.

Tulloch missed almost two years with a life-threatening scouring illness and returned triumphantly to win five races from five starts at age five; he then took the Cox Plate, Craven Plate, Mackinnon Stakes, CB Fisher Plate, AJC Queen Elizabeth Stakes and Autumn Stakes at six and just missed winning the Sydney Cup with 63 kg after being boxed in until the last furlong. He lumped 64 kg in the only unplaced run of his career in the 1960 Melbourne Cup and went out in a blaze of glory by winning the Brisbane Cup over 3200 metres, carrying 62.5 kg.

Kingston Town won four from six at four, including the Cox Plate; seven from nine at five, including the Cox Plate; and five from eight at six, including the Cox Plate. He was narrowly defeated in the Melbourne Cup of 1982, carrying 59 kg, but his effort to win his third Cox Plate, after legendary race-caller Bill Collins had famously broadcast 'Kingston Town can't win', will live forever in the memory of everyone who heard the call or saw the race.

Tulloch failed dismally at stud and Kingston Town retired to David Hains's property at Mornington, where he was bred.

Kingston Town was euthanised, aged 14, after a kick from another horse damaged a knee, which failed to heal. Tulloch died relatively young also, at 15. An autopsy revealed that Tulloch's heart weighed more than 6 kg, almost the equal of Phar Lap's, which weighed 6.3 kg. The average racehorse has a heart weighing about 3 kg.

'Bobby' and 'Sam' are long gone, but they are 'immortals' in the rich history of Australian racing, as is Tommy Smith, who sure had an eye for a horse.

# How to look at a horse

## LES CARLYON

FROM THE FIRST TWO yearling sales, the message has come down: this year buyers want 'athletes'. After the Magic Millions sale, a spokesman for the auctioneers said buyers, and bless every lovely one of them, wanted 'athletic, racy types'. After the Sydney summer sale, the man from the selling agents said: 'People are now trying to buy an athlete rather than merely buying on pedigree.'

I am not sure any of this is as original as it sounds. Harry Telford once bought a chestnut colt sight unseen from a catalogue, and Phar Lap turned out sort of athletic. But, mostly, trainers have always tended to put type ahead of pedigree, good legs ahead of good families.

And rightly. The absentee owner can stoke up a warm inner glow as he sits up in bed and drools over this catalogue page he has bought. The trainer has to live every day with the flesh and blood. He figures that if it can't talk and sulks most of the time it probably won't run.

All right, so let's wander into the occult. How do you spot one of these athletes at the sales? We all need one badly. Well, for a start, it's much harder than spotting a fancy pedigree.

The truth is any fool can spot a hot pedigree. You leaf through the Bunker Hunt dispersal catalogue and, lo, here's a filly by Northern Dancer from Dahlia. Northern Dancer is the most commercial stallion in the 300-year history of the breed. Dahlia, apart from being nicely bred, was a racecourse champion for three seasons. It takes no divine insight to conclude that this filly, so long as she is vaguely 'athletic', will make big bucks. She did—nearly $2 million.

Leafing through the catalogue for the upcoming New Zealand sale, you come on a bay colt by Sir Tristram from Taiona. This means he is a brother to Sovereign Red, Gurner's Lane and Trichelle. The blood is so hot that only one and a quarter generations are needed to fill the catalogue page. Again, it takes few brain cells to conclude that the boys from the footy club won't be buying this fellow with the proceeds of the pie night.

You can learn much about genes without leaving your living room. The literature of the turf abounds with tomes on famous stallions, nicks, crosses, in-breeding, line breeding, dosages and the laws of Mendel, the pea-growing monk. But there are few volumes on athleticism in the future racehorse.

Genetics, of course, is a science. I'll rephrase that in haste. When it comes to racehorses, genetics is sort of a science. Matters of conformation, on the other hand, are subjective art. I'll re-word that one, too. Matters of conformation are occult art. You can learn a little only by leaving your living room and looking at flesh and blood. Any horse. Anywhere.

A trainer looks at a yearling with a witch's brew swirling in his head and in his heart. The brew contains instinct and intuition. It contains the logic of an engineer—and rabid prejudice. It contains his idea of what constitutes a toff. It contains all his experience with this or that breed, or with horses with this or that fault, all the advice from the old man—handy things such as: washy chestnuts are always bad luck, son. Mind you, much was written about what was desirable in the horse in the days before derbies and TABs. Henry VIII ran to a little flesh and fancied himself as a sire. He liked size on a horse. He decreed that no stallion under 15 hands be allowed to reproduce. Shakespeare was often driven to lyricism about horses. He said they should have 'broad buttock' and 'fetlock shag and long'. Bill would have been a whiz with the brewery horses. Richard III, blundering around Bosworth Field after his house of York had blown out the gate, wasn't the least fussy. He said he'd take anything; the auctioneer missed his bid.

None of this really helps. Damon Runyon at least defined the 'non-athletic' racer with his portrait of Itchy Ironhat's bay mare Emaleen: 'She has four bad ankles and in fact the only thing that is not the matter with her is tuberculosis and maybe anaemia . . . she cannot keep up with the lead pony even when the pony is just walking.'

Well, that was a big help too, Damon. But it really is very hard with racehorses. The youngster is led out of the box; you inspect the chassis and, if you are feeling brave, pronounce it sound. But you cannot see the motor. You cannot see things like courage or the killer instinct, the things that make champions.

The trouble is this whole 'athletes' business comes down to compromise. To probabilities rather than certainties. To a loose set of rules, if you like. But with exceptions, always the exceptions. For instance . . .

You don't want a really small horse, do you? But then Northern Dancer couldn't attract a buyer as a yearling because he was a pony. As an elderly stallion he stands only about 15.1. But he knew how to get his neck out. Hill Rise towers over him in the black-and-white clip of the 1964 Kentucky Derby, but the Dancer had the V8 motor. Hyperion was so small as a youngster they considered putting him down. As a small three-year-old he bolted away with the Epsom Derby. In recent times at home, Drawn was small but it didn't stop him winning the Caulfield Guineas. So was Mr McGinty: he won six group ones. The adage holds: it's not the dog in the fight but the fight in the dog.

You certainly wouldn't want an unsound horse, would you? But maybe it's worth mentioning that Placid Ark, the best sprinter since Vain, may have flunked a conventional soundness test as he walked away, so gingerly, after shattering the record in the Linlithgow. Princequillo, who appears twice in the pedigree of Sir Tristram, was such a day-to-day proposition he caused his trainer to have a nervous breakdown. Princequillo was a top racehorse and a great sire.

Of course, you want a yearling with a nice topline, a short, strong back, just room for the saddle. A sway-back wouldn't look too 'athletic'. Tulloch had a sway-back. And a roach back wouldn't look too 'athletic', either. Century, the champion sire, has a roach back.

A smart head is a necessity. Matrice, winner of 27 races and the stallion who led the resurgence of 'colonial' sires, had a boofhead. Taj Rossi and Pago Pago, two of his champion sons, were plain about the head. Toparoa and Red Handed had heads only mothers could love. Both won Melbourne cups. You certainly wouldn't want something as unsightly as a parrot mouth. Dulcify had a parrot mouth.

And your youngsters need a good eye, big and generous. Bletchingly, the champion sire, had an eye that sometimes looks piggy, although he's a sweet horse to be around. And, of course, you wouldn't want a wind-sucker. Kingstown Town, Bletchingly's famous son, wore a cribbing strap for a spell.

You must have a horse who, as they say, fills the eye. Manikato, the chestnut warrior, had good limbs, but he always bespoke coarseness. Man o' War, who is in the American pantheon with FDR and apple pie, was coarse.

All right, well, you want a horse with balance, with some symmetry between height and length, one who gives the impression that it all hangs together, a horse like Beau Zam. Todman, who was greater than Beau Zam, always seemed too long for his height; he also had a shambling walk. Emancipation, the crack mare, sometimes looked as though she had been assembled from the pieces of three horses, with a mule donating the ears. Oh dear. All right, well, what about the legs? Legs are everything. At the gallop each leg has to take the full weight of the horse and jockey for an instant. You want to be able to drop a plumb line that passes through the centre of the knee, cannon bone and joint. You don't want these legs turned in or out.

It is undesirable for a yearling to be turned in. Biscay was turned in; so was Galilee. Forget that, then. To be turned out is much worse: the 'winging' legs tend to strike each other. Seattle Slew was slewed out in one leg: he won the US Triple Crown.

All right, well, what about being back at the knee? That's inexcusable, isn't it? Yes . . . except that some Grey Sovereign-line horses are a little back. And there was this yearling in America who made only $1100 because, apart from his unfashionable blood, he was back at the knee. On the track he won $6 million. They called him John Henry.

Compromises, compromises. There are a few matters we can surely be dogmatic about. All good horses, regardless of size or shape, seem to possess a big sloping shoulder (the greater the slope the greater the reach), a deep girth, and a good length of rein. A true champion must also have the quality you cannot see at the sales—courage.

And, despite the irritating exceptions above, it *is* better to stick with the probabilities. You do want good legs and balance—because for every John Henry there are countless cripples, because horses with bad legs break down before horses with good legs. But you still have to make little compromises: it is, after all, the world of the occult.

Personally, I got around this 'athletes' business long ago. I wait until some beast pokes his nose out to take the Tancred or the Cox Plate. At this instant, and with a flair for the obvious which is contemptible, I turn to whoever is dim enough to be standing next to me and pronounce: 'Now, *there's* an athlete!' Oh, it's cowardly, I know—but I usually get it right.

*18 January 1988*

# PART 2

# The Humour of the Track

# A lesson in laconic

## JIM HAYNES

THE RACETRACK SEEMS TO inspire humour, especially in Australia. Racing is such a part of everyday life in the 'Land Down Under' that racing stories, anecdotes and jokes abound in our oral tradition.

In the stories and verses which make up this section, the humour ranges from amusing reflections on childhood by footballer Crackers Keenan to the tall-tale-telling of famous poet Barcroft Boake, who was able to write far-fetched humorous tales like 'How Babs Malone Cut Down The Field' in spite of the chronic depression which caused him to hang himself with his stockwhip at 26 years of age.

Also included are a few of the 'delightful and insightful' tongue-in-cheek pieces written about racing by C.J. Dennis for the *Herald-Sun*, and a series of wry anecdotes by Banjo Paterson.

Banjo's memories of racetrack skulduggery in the 'old days' are wonderful glimpses into a time gone by, and yet they also remind us that little has changed as far as racetrack characters go. His anecdote about Breaker Morant is a favourite of mine.

I have also included a verse and a story about Banjo's fictional, but very realistic, pub full of sporting men that he called simply

'Mulligan's'. In the first poem Mulligan and his crew outwit the forces of authority with a clever 'con-trick' and, in the story, justice is perhaps done as they become victims of a cleverer con-artist on a trip to Randwick. These yarns have long been favourites of mine and demonstrate just how well Banjo knew bushmen of all types!

Certain kinds of racing characters have almost become clichés or caricatures in Australian humorous literature. The cunning old trainer (often a battler from the bush), the hardened old punter, the insensitive bookie, the unlucky jockey and 'mugs' of all shapes and sizes.

One of the most common types of racetrack joke is that where fate conspires to spoil what seems to be a sure-fire tip based on inside information, or perhaps some divine or supernatural prescience.

One such example is the story of the man who bumps into a neighbour on the tram going home.

'Hello, Bill,' says the friend, 'where have you been?'

'I've been to the races,' Bill replies.

'You don't usually go to the midweek meetings, do you?' says the neighbour.

'No,' says Bill, 'I only went today because I had a very vivid dream early this morning. I saw sunshine through fluffy clouds and a voice kept repeating "number seven . . . number seven . . . ". So I looked in the paper and there was a horse carrying saddlecloth seven, coming out of barrier seven, in the seventh race at Sandown, at seven to one. So I went to the track and put $777 dollars on it.'

'What happened?' asks the neighbour.

'It ran seventh,' replies Bill.

Stoicism is a common element in racetrack humour. Another of my favourite stories concerns the old battling punter who heads off to the races with $20 in his pocket.

The old battler, let's call him Jim, backs the first winner at 10 to 1 and then goes all up on the next three favourites, who duly salute the judge, giving him a bank of $500 when the fifth race comes around.

Now, Jim has done the form carefully on this race and has a 'special' which opens at 6 to 1 and drifts out to 8 to 1. Unperturbed, Jim steps in, backs his 'special' and watches it win with his hands in his pockets and no emotion on his face.

Two more all-up bets on successful favourites take Jim's bank to almost $20,000 before the final race on the card.

This race features Jim's second 'good thing' for the day, a track specialist named Wire Knot, third up from a spell over his pet distance.

Jim extracts a $50 note from his wad, tucks it into his back pocket and puts the rest on Wire Knot, on the nose at 3 to 1.

Wire Knot misses the kick, flies down the outside late and it's a photo finish. The judge calls for a second print before awarding the race to the rank outsider, Mitre Guest. Wire Knot misses by a nose.

On his way to the bus stop Jim meets a mate who says, 'Hello Jim, how'd you go today?'

'Not bad,' says Jim, deadpan, 'I won $30.'

This stoic acceptance of the cruel hand of fate is a common feature of many racing anecdotes. Another common situation is that in which one character underestimates another's knowledge, or overestimates their own.

The Western Districts of Victoria are a great area for racing. This story was told to me by a great old yarn-spinner at Port Fairy, near Warrnambool.

It seems that an old cocky once turned up at a jumps meeting with a tough old steeplechaser, but with no jockey to ride it.

As the lad he had engaged for the ride didn't show up, the old trainer approached one of the professional city jockeys and asked if he would take the ride.

The jockey looked the old bloke up and down with a bored expression on his face and said, 'All right Pop, I'll take him around for you I suppose, the moke I was booked for has been scratched and it will warm me up for the important races later in the day.'

As the old bloke legged the jockey aboard, he whispered urgently,

'Now listen carefully, this horse will win easily if you remember one thing.'

'I'll do a good job on him, Pop,' the jockey said impatiently. 'Don't worry, I do know how to ride, you know.'

The old trainer persisted, 'This is important, listen. As you approach each jump you must say, "One, two, three—jump". If you do that, he'll win.'

The jockey was already moving the horse away from the old trainer as this advice was given. 'Sure, Pop, it'll be all right, don't you worry,' he called back over his shoulder.

Of course the smug city jockey took no notice of the old trainer's advice. Away went the field and the tough old chaser was up with the leaders as they approached the first fence. When the horse made no preparation at all to jump, the jockey desperately attempted to lift him. The horse belatedly rose to the jump, struck heavily and almost dislodged the startled 'professional'.

This incident caused them to fall right back through the field, the horse being lucky to stay on his feet and the jockey using all his skill to stay in the saddle. The jockey's mind was now racing to remember the old man's advice and, at the next jump, he succeeded in calling, 'One, two, three—jump!' and the horse easily accounted for the fence.

The jockey repeated the process at each jump and the horse jumped brilliantly, making up many lengths, but just failing to catch the winner at the post.

On his return to the enclosure, the jockey was confronted by the old trainer who said, 'You didn't listen to me, did you? You didn't say, "One, two, three—jump" at the first fence.'

'Yes, I did, Pop,' lied the jockey, 'but perhaps I didn't say it loudly enough. He didn't hear me, he must be deaf.'

'He's not deaf, you bloody fool,' replied the old trainer laconically. 'He's blind.'

The kind of humour displayed in the stories that follow ranges from the mild and gentle wit of realistic anecdotes to the outrageously unrealistic humour of tall stories.

orrocks the 'Iron Gelding', our first popular champion racehorse. (Courtesy of Dianna Corcoran/AJC)

Grand Flaneur depicted on a cigarette card. He was the only undefeated Melbourne Cup winner.

Carbine at age four with trainer Walter Hickenbotham and VRC Chairman R.G. Casey.
(Courtesy of ARM)

Carbine wins the 1889 Sydney Cup. This painting hangs in the AJC office at Randwick.
(Courtesy of AJC)

The mighty mare Wakeful posing for the camera for an early newspaper poster. (Courtesy of ARM)

A postcard showing Western Australian champion Eurythmic with F. Dempsey in the saddle. (Courtesy of ARM)

Amounis wins the 1930 Caulfield Cup and sets up the biggest Cups double betting coup of all time. (Courtesy of ARM)

Phar Lap runs away with the 1930 Melbourne Cup, becoming the shortest priced winner in history. (Courtesy of ARM)

Phar Lap wins his last race at Agua Caliente and races into immortality on 20 March 1932. (Courtesy of AJC)

Jim Bendrodt chats to his good mate, champion jockey Billy Cook. (Courtesy of ARM)

Bernborough leads out the field at Flemington before carrying 63 kg to victory in the Newmarket Handicap on 2 March 1946. (Courtesy of Ern McQuillan/AJC)

Bernborough ridden at trackwork by Athol George Mulley. (Courtesy of AJC)

Tulloch in action in an exhibition gallop, carrying the colours of A.E. Healey—the only colours he ever carried. (Courtesy of AJC)

A very young Gai Waterhouse sits on Tulloch's back as her father, Tommy Smith, holds the great champion. (Courtesy of Brett Costello/Newspix)

Malcolm Johnson brings Kingston Town back to scale after winning the George Main Stakes at Randwick on 26 September 1981. (Courtesy of Bob Seary/ Newspix)

Schillaci with Damien Oliver aboard wins the George Ryder Stakes at Rosehill in 1993. (Courtesy of Steve Hart Photographics)

Greg Childs brings the great mare Sunline back to scale after winning the Coolmore Classic at Rosehill on 9 March 2002. (Courtesy of Rohan Kelly/Newspix)

Lonhro with Darren Beadman wins the Caulfield Stakes from the great Sunline with Greg Childs on 12 October 2002. (Courtesy of Steve Hart Photographics)

Some of the humour of times gone by seems insensitive and politically incorrect by today's standards, while other stories from the past are based on characters and incidents that we would not be surprised to encounter on a modern-day racetrack.

Many larger-than-life characters have been part of the history of Australian racing, and a source of humour and tall tales. These characters range from great conmen like Robert Standish Sievier to small-time battlers like the mysterious Jimmy Ah Poon.

Sievier, also known as Robert Sutton, was the man who invented the role of the bookmaker as we know it today, being the first bookie to ever carry a bag and spruik his odds on a platform, at Flemington in the 1880s. He was, among other things, a soldier of fortune in the Zulu Wars, stage actor, racehorse owner, flamboyant bookmaker, criminal cardsharp and three times bankrupt.

Jimmy Ah Poon's appearance on Sydney's racetracks coincided with the career of the mighty Poseidon.

No one knows for sure but it seems Jimmy was a Chinese market gardener from Bankstown who had an uncanny knack of only backing one horse, Poseidon, and only when he won.

Poseidon won 18 times from 26 starts as a three- and four-year-old. His wins included two Derbies, two Caulfield Cups, the Melbourne Cup and the AJC and VRC St Legers, and it seems that Jimmy backed him on every occasion that he won but never when he ran second or worse.

Jimmy was known as 'Louis the Possum' by bookmakers because he could not pronounce the name of the horse which won him an untold fortune. Every time Poseidon was due to win Jimmy would turn up at the track and ask the bookmakers, 'What price Possumum?'

Jimmy disappears from Australian racetrack history after Poseidon's four-year-old season. Legend has it that he returned to China and lived like a Mandarin for the rest of his days on the estimated £35,000 fortune he acquired due to his uncanny prescience about the future successes of 'Possumum'.

One of my favourite politically incorrect racetrack stories concerns an old stablehand, the iconic desperate old battler, who was a victim of *alalia syllabaris*—that is, he stuttered.

This character appears in front of a bookmaker who is frantically writing out tickets and taking money hand-over-fist just before a big race.

'Waddya want, mate?' asks the bookie.

'I b-b-b-b-b-backed ...' stammers the stablehand.

'Come on, mate,' says the bookie, 'you backed what?'

'I b-b-b-b-b-backed ... a f-f-f-f-f-f-f-five t-t-t-t-t-t ...,' the flustered stablehand manages to get out, his face growing red in the process.

'Struth, mate,' says the impatient and insensitive bookie, 'you backed what!?'

'I b-b-b-b-b-backed ... a f-f-f-f-f-f-f-five t-t-t-t-t-t-to ...' comes the slow stuttering reply.

'Look, mate,' says the bookmaker, 'I haven't got time to hear your story now. You backed a five-to-one winner and lost your ticket or something ... Here's $50, I hope that's near enough, now get out of the way will you?'

The old stablehand is walking back to the horse stalls when he meets the trainer he works for. The trainer sees the $50 in his hand and asks, 'Bloody hell, where did you get $50?'

'W-w-w-w-w-w-well,' replies the stablehand, 'I w-w-w-w-went t-t-t-t-to t-t-t-t-tell that b-b-b-b-b-bookie, old M-M-M-Mr S-S-S-S-Smith I b-b-b-b-b-backed ... your f-f-f-f-f-f-f-five t-t-t-t-t-ton h-h-horse float over his M-M-M-Mercedes ... and he gave me f-f-f-f-f-f-fifty b-b-b-b-bucks!'

Or how about the trainer who is spotted by a steward slipping a pre-prepared 'speed ball' to his horse before a race.

'What did you give that horse?' demands the steward.

The trainer, who has several more of the pills in his pocket, replies, 'Oh, they're just homemade boiled lollies,' and he pops one into his mouth and goes on, 'the horse loves them,' he says, 'I'm having one myself, here, do you wanna try one?'

'Okay,' says the steward as he takes the pill, looks at it and puts it in his mouth, 'but I've got my eye on you.'

Minutes later, as the trainer legs him aboard, the stable jockey asks, 'Are we all set, Boss, everything as planned?'

'Yes,' the trainer replies, 'money's on and he'll win. And, if anything passes you, don't worry, it'll just be the chief steward or me.'

# Corn Medicine

## Harry ('Breaker') Morant

'A well-bred horse! but he won't get fat,
Though I've done the best I can;
He keeps as poor as a blessed rat!'
Said the sorrowful stable-man.

'I've bled and I've blistered him, and to-day
I bought him a monster ball;
But, blow the horse! Let me do what I may,
He won't get fat at all.

'I've given him medicines galore,
And linseed oil and bran,
And yet the brute looks awfully poor,'
Said the woebegone stable-man.

One glance the intelligent stranger threw
At the ribs of the hollow weed,
Then asked, with an innocent air, 'Did you
Remember to give him a feed?'

# Racetrack reminiscences

## A.B. ('BANJO') PATERSON

## A memory of Breaker Morant

AMATEUR RACING, for some reason or other, has always had some sort of encouragement from the Rosehill proprietary, and that club is the only metropolitan institution that caters for the 'lily-whites'. Their annual race at Rosehill is a sort of 'Custer's last stand'.

They used to also run an amateur steeplechase, and one of these was to some extent memorable, for among the riders was Harry Morant, whose tempestuous career was ended by a firing squad in the South African war.

Plucky to the point of recklessness, he suffered from a theatrical complex which made him pretend to be badly hurt when there was, really, not much up with him.

Morant was breaking in horses and mustering wild cattle somewhere up in the west, and he had been accustomed to ride after hounds in England.

Arriving in Sydney at the time of the amateur steeplechase, he set out to look for a mount.

Mr Pottie, of the veterinary family, had a mare that could both gallop and jump, but she was such an unmanageable brute that none of the local amateurs (and I was one of them) cared to take the mount.

Morant jumped at the chance, but as soon as they started the mare cleared out with him and fell into a drain, rolling her rider out as flat as a flounder.

He was carried in, supposed to be unconscious, and I was taken up to hear his last wishes.

The doctors could get nothing out of him, but after listening to his wanderings for a while I said, very loudly and clearly, 'What'll you have Morant?' and he said, equally clearly, 'Brandy and soda.'

## Weight was right

Once, years ago, a son of the then Governor of New South Wales secured a ride in a picnic race. Intensely enthusiastic and a very lightweight, this young gentleman turned up, full of hope, to ride his first race.

He got on the scales with his saddle, and it turned out that he was two stone short of making the weight!

Not one of the amateurs had a lead bag to lend him, but no one would dream of leaving the Governor's son out. He was the main attraction of the meeting.

The officials had never been confronted with anything like this, but the caretaker was a man of resource. He shovelled a lot of sand into a sack and strapped it firmly on the pommel of a big saddle; weight was right, and away the field went.

It was an amateur hurdle race and, every time that the horse jumped, a puff of sand flew up, like the miniature spouts blown into the air by killer whales.

Simultaneously jumping and spouting, the vice-regal contender saw the race out, unsuccessfully, it is true; but he got more applause than the winner.

## A-maizing escape

The most vivid memory that abides with me of South Coast racing is of a meeting held many years ago in the Shoalhaven district.

The attendance consisted mostly of the local agriculturalists, horny-handed sons of the soil quite formidable in appearance and character. The foreign element was provided by a group of welshers, side-show artists, prize-fighters and acrobats who followed the southern meetings as hawks follow a plague of mice.

The centre of the course consisted of a field of maize fully ten feet high and when one bookmaker decided to 'take a sherry with the dook and guy-a-whack' (a slang expression meaning to abscond without paying), he melted into the maize and took cover like a wounded black duck.

The hefty agriculturalists went in after him like South African natives after a lion in the jungle. For a time nothing could be seen but the waving of the maize and nothing could be heard but the shouts of the 'beaters' when they thought they caught sound or scent of their prey.

After a time all and sundry took a hand in the hunt; so the 'wanted man' simply slipped off his coat and joined in the search for himself, shouting and waving his arms just as vigorously as anybody else.

When the searchers got tired of the business and started to straggle out of the maize he straggled out too, on the far side, and kept putting one foot in front of the other till he struck the coach road to Sydney.

## Flash Jack's last race

It was at the hamlet of Jugiong that an event occurred, which is perhaps unique in turf history.

It was a publican's meeting, which means that the promoter was less concerned with gate money than with the sale of strong liquor.

The unfenced course was laid out alongside the Murrumbidgee

River and one of the Osborne family, graziers in the district, had entered a mare which was fed and looked after on the other side of the river.

Off they went, and the mare made straight for home, jumping into the river and nearly drowning the jockey who was rescued by a young Aboriginal boy.

Meanwhile Mr Osborne, under a pardonable mistake, was cheering on another runner in the belief that it was his mare.

Then there came a splashing sound at the back of the waggonette and Mr Osborne, looking around, was astonished to see his jockey.

'Well, I'll be damned,' he said. 'What are you doing here? Where's the mare?'

'She's home by now,' said the boy, a bush youngster known locally as 'Flash Jack from Gundagai'.

'And I'm going home too,' he added, 'I've had enough of it. In the last race my moke fell in front of the field and there was me lying on the track with nothing but horses' heels going over my head for half an hour and this time I was nearly drowned. I'd sunk four times when that black boy came in after me.

'I'd like a job, Mr Osborne, picking up fleeces in the shed if you ain't full up; but Flash Jack has rode his last race.'

## Ask the horse

Another old-time trainer was William Kelso, father of the present trainer. The original Bill Kelso was like his son, a very direct-spoken man and if you didn't like what he said you could leave it.

I was doing some amateur riding and falling about over steeplechase fences and, like a lot of other young fellows, I began to fancy myself as a judge of racing. So, one day I asked old Kelso, 'Mr Kelso, what will win this race?'

'Well,' he said, 'I'll tell you something. Do you know what I was before I went in for training?'

I said, 'No.'

He said, 'I was working for a pound a week and I'd be working for a pound a week still, only for young fools like you that will go betting. You leave it alone or get somebody to sew your pockets up before you come to the races.'

Well, it wasn't very polite but it was good advice.

The committee had him in once to explain the running of the race, before the days of stipendiary stewards. It took them a lot of trouble to get the committee together and they sat down, prepared for a good long explanation.

'Mr Kelso,' said the chairman, 'can you tell us why your horse ran so badly today?'

'No, I'm afraid I can't,' he said, 'you'll have to ask the horse. He's the only one that knows.'

## Rough justice

Before the rules about registration of meetings and registrations of horses became so strict some weird things were done, or attempted, in connection with the definition of a hack.

At an unregistered amateur meeting at Rouse Hill, no admission charged, there was a race for hacks, the definition being 'any horse habitually used and ridden as a hack'.

One competitor bobbed up with a well-known racehorse which had won a lot of welter races at Randwick and elsewhere. The horse had developed some sort of temporary leg trouble and, for the time being, was ridden every day by its trainer as a hack.

It came within the letter but not the spirit of the definition.

No one liked to take the responsibility of barring the animal; but the starter, the late Edward Terry, one-time member of parliament for Ryde, was equal to the occasion.

'Let him start,' he said, 'I'll fix him.'

Waiting till this dangerous competitor was walking the wrong way, he addressed the other riders.

'Go on, boys,' he said. 'Off!'

Away they went, and though the Randwick horse nearly got up

after being left a hundred yards at the start, he was just beaten on the post.

Thus justice was done, albeit in a somewhat crude way.

## Hard luck

One hears some curious hard luck stories at the end of a race meeting.

One lady, who had sprinkled her investments over the tote as though half-sovereign notes were pellets from a shotgun, was heard to say last Saturday that she had backed the first six winners and would have backed the seventh if she had had any money left.

Another punter said that he had pushed at the end of a long queue to get his money on at the very last moment.

'Unfortunately for me,' he said, 'when at last I got to the window ... it remained open and I got my money on!'

# My racing problems: The punter's art

### C.J. DENNIS

NOW THAT THE RACING season gathers to its exciting climax, a unique racing problem that has interested me for a number of years again presents itself for solution.

You are quite wrong if you imagine that my problem has anything to do with my own puny efforts to 'spot stone morals' with a view to pecuniary gain. It is far more impersonal than that. Punting to me presents no problem at all! It is a perfectly simple process.

When I wish to have a little flutter I merely bid a last farewell to a ten-shilling note and give it to a bookmaker. (At the precise moment of its passing one gently intones over the ten shillings the name of some favoured horse.) For this sum the bookmaker sells me a little piece of pasteboard bearing his name and certain indecipherable characters that look like Coptic Roots, or something.

This piece of pasteboard I cling to religiously—even fanatically—until the race is over. Then I tear it into little pieces, throw these to all or any of the four winds that happen to be blowing at the time, and the transaction is completed.

I have heard it rumoured that, should the animal I fancy win the race (which is absurd), the bookmaker will then buy back my piece of pasteboard at a price more or less in advance of what it cost me. Some day I should like to have an opportunity of testing this contention.

But, even without this happy consummation, the mere purchase of the pasteboard provides me with a mild thrill. For, if the horse I have chosen manages to beat at least one other horse in the race, a distinct glow of satisfaction flatters my prescience and unexpectedly shrewd judgement.

I should like to know how to capitalise this; for I feel that I have a unique flair for selecting certain horses that are frequently well able to run faster than certain other horses, or at least one other horse.

But my real problem is far more baffling than anything presented by the simple mechanical rights of punting. It is this—

Why is it that a large proportion of regular racecourse frequenters have extremely fat necks?

I know immediately what you would answer: that thin necks are also much in evidence; but I hope to be able to explain that also at a later date.

I wish it understood that I exclude from this enquiry all owners and trainers.

The men I refer to are very evidently gamblers who 'follow the game' with a queer devotion worthy of an even nobler aim; and their fat necks are abnormally fat. Look about you next time you are on a racecourse.

I had taken my problem to various learned men without getting much satisfaction; and then I remembered Percy Podgrass. Percy is a friend of mine and a scientist of sorts—of very many sorts, in fact; he attends guild lectures.

I have propounded my perplexing problem to Percy (alliteratively, like that) and he has promised to chew it over and bring back to me a working hypothesis. At least, I think it is a hypothesis and certainly not a hypothenuse; though Percy himself laughingly referred to it, with his quaint, diffident humour, as his hippopotamus.

I shall be glad, later, to afford readers the benefit of the Podgrassian research.

# Five bob on Sir Blink

## CRACKERS KEENAN

I REMEMBER THE FIRST time I ever had the urge to put a bet on a horse. I wanted to have five bob on Sir Blink in the 1958 Caulfield Cup.

Mum said it was disgusting that somebody of such tender years should want to back a horse. She didn't want to put the money on but her conscience must have bothered her after it won because she gave me £2. What really upset her was that I wanted to 'all up' it onto Sir Blink again in the Victoria Derby.

A horse who had been a champion two-year-old called Master Rane was the public elect. I think it won six or seven in a row as a two-year-old but Sir Blink was too strong for him.

Sir Blink was trained by Jack Godby and was owned by a Mrs Kellett. She called him 'Blinky', but that wasn't what I felt like calling my mum when I found out she didn't put my money on in the Derby. Sir Blink was a bit of an early favourite of mine; he was by Blue Coral out of Inky and had a big baldy face.

I eventually forgave my mother for not backing Sir Blink in the Derby for me. Someone tried to explain to me it was the Scottish blood in her that found the thought of playing up my earlier winnings far too extravagant.

Then she did it to me again a couple of years later. It was in the early 1960s and I picked out a daily double. I'll never forget it. The two horses were Rio David and Chokra.

Mum wouldn't put a bet on and they both won, paying a small fortune. Or at least it would have been. I haven't cried too many times in my life but that was one of them. It's very vivid in my memory, sort of like total recall.

By this stage we had moved off the farm into the big smoke—Yarrawonga. The town had 2500 people in so many double-storey buildings we didn't know what to do. I used to bet just about every Saturday. I'd go down to the TAB and ask people to put money on for me. I talked to all the desperates outside the TAB and got known—as a ten-year-old—as a good tipster, a kid that did his form. Blokes would actually come up and ask me what I fancied.

I used to get the *Truth* if I could because it was the best form guide to have, but my mum didn't fancy me buying the scandal rag, as it was in those days. Little did I know at the time that I'd eventually be writing for it.

I used to get every bit of information I could, and then my big day finally arrived when the old man took me to the races. We used to go to Wangaratta or Chiltern or Corowa, sometimes Berrigan. I couldn't wait to get there and race in and buy a racebook.

Mum and Dad would line all of us ten kids up and take us to the races. We knew all the trainers. Jack Freyer used to train for the old man at Corowa. Hal Hoysted trained for him as well. Jackie 'No Teeth' Murrell, who was Bill Murrell's cousin, also trained for my dad. So we'd go to the races and he'd drink and drive us home. It was terrible—we'd keep waiting to hit the white posts at the side of the road.

But they were great days. Most of the horses were no bloody good but we thought they were champions. A few of them went on to win in town, horses like Sullivan and others. We were sort of taken into the bosom of the racing fraternity.

They were the early memories. I remember Bill Murrell coming to pick up his horses after they'd spelled on our farm. Some of these horses were left untouched in the paddock for six months or so. Just running wild around the paddock. When it was time to get them on the float, they'd try to kick the sides out of the float and Bill Murrell would be there cursing and getting them going. They had names like Mad Mac and so on.

Bill Murrell would lob in about midday, have lunch, drink all afternoon and then, about five o'clock, he'd say, 'Let's get these mongrels on the float,' and then off they'd go to Melbourne. I don't know how they did it. They'd get them loaded up and away they'd go, drunk as skunks and headed to town. They certainly would not be doing it these days.

I was going to Yarrawonga Primary and I remember reading the *Turf Monthly* under my desk while pretending to be doing school-work. One of the first copies of *Turf Monthly* I ever bought was when Tulloch had gone to stud at Kia Ora in New Zealand and there were all these photos of his mares in foal. Rather poor taste I thought at the time, but it was rather interesting.

I decided about then that all I wanted to do was own racehorses. I ate, drank and slept dreaming about the horses I would own. I was showing a bit of promise as a footballer, but football never took over my life. Everything I ever wanted to do in life was centred around racehorses. It stays with you.

By the time I got to the Marist Brothers' Assumption College in Kilmore my gambling tentacles had spread far and wide. Being a good Catholic boy I knew that idleness was an instrument of the devil. So, as well as being firmly hooked on the punt, I decided to wile away my spare time by taking over as the school SP bookmaker.

I'd bet on race, pace and chase. I spent six years of intensive study at Assumption but it wasn't all on school matters. Pretty soon, anybody who wanted to have a bet, they'd come and see me. I'd get the form guide every day.

One of my assigned jobs was to go down to the gate and get the papers for the Brothers. Mostly it was the afternoon *Herald*. It wasn't the best form guide but I had to make do, so on the way back to drop off the paper, the form guide would disappear. I wanted to keep temptation away from those Marist Brothers. I didn't want them to get caught up in the punt. I was so dedicated to making sure they didn't have a bet I'd just hook out the racing pages. I always had the form guide and no one ever knew. Every Saturday, anybody that wanted to bet had to come to me.

Probably the best result I ever had as a bookie was when Tobin Bronze won the Caulfield Cup in 1967. But, champion though Tobin Bronze undoubtedly was, everybody and his dog wanted to back Red Handed, trained by Bart Cummings. The odd few who didn't want Red Handed still didn't go for Tobin Bronze.

I was about the only one who was keen on Tobin Bronze; he had won the Toorak Handicap the previous Saturday, but he had failed in the Caulfield Cup the year before. My confidence was a bit dented and I even rang Bill Murrell to ask his opinion. He was a Tobin Bronze man.

I said, 'What about Red Handed?'

Bill replied, 'Tobin Bronze is a bloody champion!'

I had great faith in Bill Murrell's judgement and my enthusiasm for the big copper chestnut was restored.

A bloke called Peter Twomey from Numurkah came up to me on the day before the race—and this bloke was pretty well heeled. You wouldn't want to know, he wanted to back Tobin Bronze. The horse was 4 to 1 favourite and I looked him straight in the eye and said, 'You can have 8 to 1.' He looked at me sort of funny and I said, 'Give us ya money, I love taking money from mugs any day of the bloody week. Give us ya money.'

I tried to grab his money but he whipped it away and put it straight back in his kick. 'You know something,' he said suspiciously. He put that money straight back in his pocket and walked away.

Tobin Bronze gave Jimmy Johnson an armchair ride and beat Red Handed by a neck, giving the second horse the equivalent of 7 kg. Then, of course, Red Handed came out 16 days later and won the Melbourne Cup.

Hardly anyone had backed Tobin Bronze and, to cap it all off,

I backed him down at the TAB. I found some desperate to put my money on for me.

I've never eaten so many bloody ice-creams in my life. I bought all my mates ice-creams, we were fair dinkum as fat as black rats at the finish. That was my best bluff of all time.

I just went on from there. Sort of progressed to being even more mad about horses. I would study anything to do with them. I'd get stoked up with yearling catalogues and *Turf Monthly*s and various other racing magazines.

Any time I got down to Melbourne I'd be straight into MacGill's, the famous Melbourne newsagent and bookshop, and buy anything about horses.

I was playing football regularly at Assumption by the time I was 14 but I was still more interested in horses than football. I was just an absolute student; I did six years of study in horses and reading form guides.

Despite all this, I finished matriculation and got a Commonwealth scholarship and all the rest and did reasonably well. There was always a lull after the Melbourne Cup, so I used to do a bit of schoolwork. It gave me about six weeks to get myself through. You had to get your priorities right.

Assumption was a boys'-only school then—it's co-ed now. Maybe my punting activities might have been curtailed a bit if there had been girls there in the 1960s, but somehow I doubt it. At least they didn't have Sunday racing then—the term 'day of rest' truly applied in my case.

I used to joke that I had to bet to get money, because my old man wasn't too forthcoming with pocket money.

If you were doing the form for a living you had to have the best and eventually I graduated to the *Truth*. It was the best form guide you could get, but it was very hard to come by at Assumption. The only forms you could get on a regular basis were the ones in the dailies and they weren't a patch on the *Truth*. If you got caught with the *Truth* at Assumption, you were treated to a sneak preview of what hell would be like.

All the perverts used to say they just bought it for the form guide; in my case it was true. I used to ask anybody who I thought could get me one to buy it for me. I'd say, 'Get me the *Truth*. You can have the tits—I just want the form guide.' We'd carve it up between us—the pervs would take the main section and I'd have the centre lift-out.

One day I got caught with the *Truth*, the whole *Truth* and nothing but the *Truth*. I'd removed the form guide for some later study but, before I could get rid of the rest, I got nabbed. The funny thing was that the Brothers were searching the lockers for cigarettes and I usually had some. That would have been preferable to them finding the *Truth*.

Monday morning at assembly one of the Brothers held up the paper in front of everyone and said, looking straight at me, 'This is the devil's work.'

One thing I remember, though, was that the paper was in pristine condition when they found it in my locker and when it was displayed at assembly it was dog-eared all over the place. You could tell they'd been going through it. I said to the bloke next to me, 'They've had a thumb through it, you know.'

I think they heard me, too. It didn't make any difference—I got the cane and a lecture and all the trimmings. But it didn't stop me trying to get the old 'Truform'. It got to be a ritual. I'd be sitting up in bed on Friday night doing the form and you'd hear the Brother coming and you'd have to find a quick hiding place for the rag.

Another time I got caught with it and the Brother said, 'How'd you get that?'

'I nicked it,' I said.

He was a punter, this Brother, because he said, 'Best form guide you can get, Keenan.'

'Better then *Best Bets*, anyway,' I said nervously.

Later on, he used to put my bets on for me. When I had a good thing—I'd only go to him if it was a 'good thing'—I'd say, 'Brother, this'll win.'

'Ah, yes,' he'd say, 'see me later up in the infirmary.'

I'd go up there and he'd say, 'What do you want on it, Keenan?'
I'd get my money out and he'd say, 'How good is it?'
'Straight from the trainer,' I'd say.
'One of Bill Murrell's?' he'd ask.
Usually the answer would be in the affirmative.

Despite all my boasting and lying, I didn't really know many trainers at that time. But this Brother would never let me down. If it got beat he'd always produce a ticket and if it won the money would always be there. I'd watch him go down the street on Saturday mornings with my money.

Some of us would go down to the Kilmore TAB on Friday nights and wait until somebody we knew, or thought we could trust, would wander up. 'Hey, mister,' we'd whisper. 'Will you have a bet for me, please?'

You'd usually find someone eventually. 'Hey, mister, can you put ten bucks on such and such for me, please?' Occasionally they'd disappear with your money, but there was nothing you could do about it.

I have mostly fond memories of my years at Assumption, mostly of punting and taking bets and poring over the *Truth* form guide.

A few years down the track I bought my first horse, a mare named Miss Burette. She was bloody terrible, placed just once and at Jerilderie. My second horse was Misneach. Richard Freyer, son of Jack, trained those two.

Then I sent Misneach to Denis Murdoch. Denis had the licence but he and I sort of helped one another out training her. We took her to Tatura one day thinking we could win with her. There were only three people on earth who really thought she could win: Denis, myself and Midge Cooper, who was riding her. She opened up at 12 to 1 and I stepped in to back her and the next minute she was at threes. The price was gone and we couldn't get set with any bookie. It came third and we found out later it had been backed strongly each way.

Then next week we replaced Midge, but he bobbed up in the

same race on the odds-on favourite. Well, Misneach had gone out at 8 to 1 and we had Donny Brown riding her, his last ride ever.

The little postman from Yarrawonga was a part owner of Misneach with me and this time nobody got the mail. The postman was there with his missus and we all grabbed the 8 to 1. I told them the more they put on, the more they'd get back.

Misneach won by a length and a half going away from the favourite. Donny Brown brought her back and we were all jumping around, talking about going to Melbourne to win races and Donny looked at us and said, 'Jesus, this is a hack!'

You wouldn't want to know—we gave it two more starts and it got a little bubble on its tendon and the tendon bowed, so I sold her at some sales. It did race again, but never won.

I knew Misneach had a good 'ticker', and that was borne out many years later.

In 1993 a girl walked up to me at Werribee races and asked me did I ever own a horse named Misneach. I replied, 'Yes, I did.'

'Well,' she said, 'she's 20 years of age and she's been my pony club horse for the past six years.'

I thought it would have gone to the lion's den at the zoo or into a pie somewhere years earlier. It made me feel good, actually, because when you've finished with a horse, you like to feel they end up all right, certainly not as pet food.

# The Oil From Old Bill Shane

## C.J. Dennis

I got the oil: too right. A cove called Shane.
Yes; ole Bill Shane. You've 'eard of 'im, of course.
Big racin' 'ead. There's no need to explain
The things he don't know about a 'orse.
Good ole Bill Shane. They say he's made a pile
At puttin'. Shrewd! I wis I 'ad 'is brain.
An' does 'e know the game? Well, I should smile.
They can't put nothin' over ole Bill Shane.

Yes; Shane, Bill Shane . . . Aw, listen, lad. Wake up!
Why everybody's 'eard of ole Bill Shane.
They say he made ten thousan' on the Cup
Last year, an' now he's got the oil again.
Wot? Owner? Trainer? Nah! Who 'eeds their guff?
Bill's a big racin' man—a punter. See?
Top dog. I alwiz sez wot's good enough
For ole Bill Shane is good enough for me.

Yes; he gave me the oil. I got it straight—
Well, nearly straight. Of course, I've never spoke
To Bill 'imself direck. I got a mate
Wot knows a bloke wot knows another bloke
Wot's frien's with Shane, an' so—you un'erstand.
Wot? me give you the tip? Aw, take a walk!
Yeh think I'd do a thing so under'and?
Bill Shane would kill me if I was to talk.

Well, listen . . . Now, for gosh sake, keep it dark.
An' don't let no one know it came from Shane.
Keep it strick secret. I would be a nark
To let you chuck yer money down the drain . . .

Wazzat you said? He's scratched? 'Ere! Lemme look!
Scratched! Ain't that noos to knock a man clean out?
I alwiz said this puntin' game was crook ...
Who? Shane? Aw, I dunno. Some racin' tout.

# Mulligan's Mare

## A.B. ('Banjo') Paterson

Oh, Mulligan's bar was the deuce of a place
To drink and to fight, and to gamble and race;
The height of choice spirits from near and from far
Were all concentrated on Mulligan's bar.

There was 'Jerry the Swell', and the jockey-boy Ned,
'Dog-bite-me', so called from the shape of his head—
And a man whom the boys, in their musical slang,
Designed as the 'Gaffer of Mulligan's Gang'.

Now Mulligan's Gang had a racer to show,
A bad 'un to look at, a good 'un to go;
Whenever they backed her you safely might swear
She'd walk in a winner, would Mulligan's mare.

But Mulligan, having some radical views,
Neglected his business and got on the booze;
He took up with runners*—a treacherous troop—
Who gave him away and he 'fell in the soup'.

And so it turned out on a fine summer day,
A bailiff turned up with a writ of 'fi. fa.';
He walked to the bar with a manner serene,
'I levy,' said he, 'in the name of the Queen.'

Then Mulligan wanted, in spite of the law,
To pay out the bailiff with '*one* on the jaw';
He drew out to hit him, but, ere you could wink,
He changed his intentions and stood him a drink.

---

*The 'runners' referred to here are professional footracers—like those who compete
for the Stawell Gift. The sport was very popular in the 19th century in the bush.

A great consultation there straightway befell
'Twixt jockey-boy Neddy and Jerry the Swell,
And the man with the head, who remarked 'Why, you bet!
Dog-bite-me!' said he, 'but we'll diddle 'em yet.

'We'll slip out the mare from her stall in a crack,
And put in her place the old broken-down hack;
The hack is so like her, I'm ready to swear
The bailiff will think he has Mulligan's mare.

'So out with the racer and in with the screw,
We'll show him what Mulligan's talent can do;
And if he gets nasty and dares to say much,
I'll knock him as stiff as my grandmother's crutch.'

Then off to the town went the mare and the lad;
The bailiff came out, never dreamt he was 'had';
But marched to the stall with a confident air—
'I levy,' said he, 'upon Mulligan's mare.'

He never would let her go out of his sight,
He watched her by day and he watched her by night,
For races were coming away in the West
And Mulligan's mare had a chance with the best.

And, thinking to quietly serve his own ends,
He sent off a wire to some bookmaking friends:
'Get all you can borrow, beg, snavel or snare
And lay the whole lot against Mulligan's mare.'

The races came round, and a crowd on the course
Were laying the mare till they made themselves hoarse,
And Mulligan's party, with ardour intense,
They backed her for pounds and for shillings and pence.

And think of the grief of the bookmaking host
At the sound of the summons to go to the post—
For down to the start with her thoroughbred air
As fit as a fiddle pranced Mulligan's mare!

They started, and off went the boy to the front,
He cleared out at once, and he made it a hunt;
He steadied as rounding the corner they wheeled,
Then gave her her head and she smothered the field.

The race put her owner right clear of his debts,
He landed a fortune in stakes and in bets,
He paid the old bailiff the whole of his pelf,
And gave him a hiding to keep for himself.

So all you bold sportsmen take warning, I pray,
Keep clear of the running, you'll find it don't pay;
For the very best rule that you'll hear in a week—
Is never to bet on a thing that can speak.

And whether you're lucky or whether you lose,
Keep clear of the cards and keep clear of the booze,
And fortune in season will answer your prayer
And send you a flyer like Mulligan's mare.

# The downfall of Mulligan's

### A.B. ('BANJO') PATERSON

THE SPORTING MEN OF Mulligan's pub and sporting club were an exceedingly knowing lot; in fact, they had obtained the name amongst their neighbours of being a little bit too knowing. They had 'taken down' the adjoining town in a variety of ways. They were always winning maiden plates with horses which were shrewdly suspected to be old and well-tried performers in disguise.

When the sports of Paddy's Flat unearthed a phenomenal runner in the shape of a blackfellow called Frying-pan Joe, the Mulligan contingent immediately took the trouble to discover a blackfellow of their own, and they made a match and won all the Paddy's Flat money with ridiculous ease; then their blackfellow turned out to be a well-known Sydney performer. They had a man who could fight, a man who could be backed to jump 5 feet 10, a man who could kill eight pigeons out of nine at 30 yards, a man who could make a break of 50 or so at billiards if he tried; they could all drink, and they all had that indefinite look of infinite wisdom and conscious superiority which belongs only to those who know something about horseflesh.

They knew a great many things never learnt at Sunday school. They were experts at cards and dice. They would go to immense trouble to work off any small swindle in the sporting line. In short the general consensus of opinion was that they were a very 'fly' crowd at Mulligan's, and if you went there you wanted to 'keep your eyes skinned' or they'd 'have' you over a threepenny-bit.

There were races at Sydney one Christmas, and a select band of the Mulligan sportsmen were going down to them. They were in high feather, having just won a lot of money from a young Englishman at pigeon shooting, by the simple method of slipping blank cartridges into his gun when he wasn't looking and then backing the bird.

They intended to make a fortune out of the Sydney people, and admirers who came to see them off only asked them as a favour to leave money enough in Sydney to make it worth while for another detachment to go down later on. Just as the train was departing a priest came running on to the platform, and was bundled into the carriage where our Mulligan friends were; the door was slammed to, and away they went. His Reverence was hot and perspiring, and for a few minutes mopped himself with a handkerchief, while the silence was unbroken except by the rattle of the train.

After a while one of the Mulligan fraternity got out a pack of cards and proposed a game to while away the time. There was a young squatter in the carriage who looked as if he might be induced to lose a few pounds, and the sportsmen thought they would be neglecting their opportunities if they did not try to 'get a bit to go on with' from him. He agreed to play, and, just as a matter of courtesy, they asked the priest whether he would take a hand.

'What game d'ye play?' he asked, in a melodious brogue.

They explained that any game was equally acceptable to them, but they thought it right to add that they generally played for money.

'Sure an' it don't matter for wanst in a way,' said he. 'Oi'll take a hand bedad—Oi'm only going about 50 miles, so Oi can't lose a fortune.'

They lifted a light portmanteau on to their knees to make a table, and five of them—three of the Mulligan crowd and the two strangers—started to have a little game of poker. Things looked rosy for the Mulligan boys, who chuckled as they thought how soon they were making a beginning, and what a magnificent yarn they would have to tell about how they rooked a priest on the way down.

Nothing sensational resulted from the first few deals, and the priest began to ask questions.

'Be ye going to the races?'

They said they were.

'Ah! and Oi suppose ye'll be betting wid thim bookmakers on the horses, will yez? They do be terrible knowing men, thim bookmakers, they tell me. I wouldn't bet much if Oi was ye,' he said, with an affable smile. 'If ye go bettin' ye will be took in wid thim bookmakers.'

The boys listened with a bored air and reckoned that by the time they parted the priest would have learnt that they were well able to look after themselves. They went steadily on with the game, and the priest and the young squatter won slightly; this was part of the plan to lead them on to plunge. They neared the station where the priest was to get out. He had won rather more than they liked, so the signal was passed round to 'put the cross on'. Poker is a game at which a man need not risk much unless he feels inclined, and on this deal the priest stood out. Consequently, when they drew up at his station he was still a few pounds in.

'Bedad,' he said, 'Oi don't loike goin' away wid yer money. Oi'll go on to the next station so as ye can have revinge.' Then he sat down again, and play went on in earnest.

The man of religion seemed to have the Devil's own luck. When he was dealt a good hand he invariably backed it well, and if he had a bad one he would not risk anything. The sports grew painfully anxious as they saw him getting further and further ahead of them, prattling away all the time like a big schoolboy. The squatter was the biggest loser so far, but the priest was the only winner. All the others were out of pocket. His reverence played with great dash, and seemed to know a lot about the game, so that on arrival at the second station he was a good round sum in pocket.

He rose to leave them with many expressions of regret, and laughingly promised full revenge next time. Just as he was opening the carriage door, one of the Mulligan fraternity said in a stage whisper: 'He's a blanky sink-pocket. If he can come this far, let him come on to Sydney and play for double the stakes.' Like a shot the priest turned on him.

'Bedad, an' if that's yer talk, Oi'll play ye fer double stakes from here to the other side of glory. Do yez think men are mice because they eat cheese? It isn't one of the Ryans would be fearing to give any man his revinge!'

He snorted defiance at them, grabbed his cards and waded in. The others felt that a crisis was at hand and settled down to play in a dead silence. But the priest kept on winning steadily, and the 'old man' of the Mulligan push saw that something decisive must be done, and decided on a big plunge to get all the money back on one hand. By a dexterous manipulation of the cards he dealt himself four kings, almost the best hand at poker. Then he began with assumed hesitation to bet on his hand, raising the stake little by little.

'Sure ye're trying to bluff, so ye are!' said the priest, and immediately raised it.

The others had dropped out of the game and watched with painful interest the stake grow and grow. The Mulligan fraternity felt a cheerful certainty that the 'old man' had made things safe, and regarded themselves as mercifully delivered from an unpleasant situation.

The priest went on doggedly raising the stake in response to his antagonist's challenges until it had attained huge dimensions.

'Sure that's high enough,' said he, putting into the pool sufficient to entitle him to see his opponent's hand.

The 'old man' with great gravity laid down his four kings, whereat the Mulligan boys let a big sigh of relief escape them.

Then the priest laid down four aces and scooped the pool.

The sportsmen of Mulligan's never quite knew how they got out to Randwick. They borrowed a bit of money in Sydney, and found themselves in the saddling paddock in a half-dazed condition, trying to realise what had happened to them. During the afternoon they were up at the end of the lawn near the Leger stand and could hear the babel of tongues, small bookmakers, thimble riggers, confidence men, and so on, plying their trades outside. In the tumult of voices they heard one that sounded familiar. Soon suspicion grew into certainty, and they knew that it was the voice of 'Father' Ryan. They walked to the fence and looked over. This is what he was saying: 'Pop it down, gents! Pop it down! If you don't put down a brick you can't pick up a castle! I'll bet no one here can pick the knave of hearts out of these three cards. I'll bet half-a-sovereign no one here can find the knave!'

Then the crowd parted a little, and through the opening they could see him distinctly, doing a great business and showing wonderful dexterity with the pasteboard.

There is still enough money in Sydney to make it worth while for another detachment to come down from Mulligan's; but the next lot will hesitate about playing poker with priests in the train.

# Our New Horse

## A.B. ('Banjo') Paterson

The boys had come back from the races
All silent and down on their luck;
They'd backed 'em, straight out and for places,
But never a winner they struck.
They lost their good money on Slogan,
And fell, most uncommonly flat,
When Partner, the pride of the Bogan,
Was beaten by Aristocrat.

And one said, 'I move that instanter
We sell out our horses and quit,
The brutes ought to win in a canter,
Such trials they do when they're fit.
The last one they ran was a snorter—
A gallop to gladden one's heart—
Two-twelve for a mile and a quarter,
And finished as straight as a dart.

'And then when I think that they're ready
To win me a nice little swag,
They are licked like the veriest neddy—
They're licked from the fall of the flag.
The mare held her own to the stable,
She died out to nothing at that,
And Partner he never seemed able
To pace it with Aristocrat.

'And times have been bad, and the seasons
Don't promise to be of the best;
In short, boys, there's plenty of reasons
For giving the racing a rest.

The mare can be kept on the station—
Her breeding is good as can be—
But Partner, his next destination
Is rather a trouble to me.

'We can't sell him here, for they know him
As well as the clerk of the course;
He's raced and won races till, blow him,
He's done as a handicap horse.
A jady, uncertain performer,
They weight him right out of the hunt,
And clap it on warmer and warmer
Whenever he gets near the front.

'It's no use to paint him or dot him
Or put any "fake" on his brand,
For bushmen are smart, and they'd spot him
In any sale-yard in the land.
The folk about here could all tell him,
Could swear to each separate hair;
Let us send him to Sydney and sell him,
There's plenty of Jugginses there.

'We'll call him a maiden, and treat 'em
To trials that will open their eyes,
We'll run their best horses and beat 'em,
And then won't they think him a prize.
I pity the fellow that buys him,
He'll find in a very short space,
No matter how highly he tries him,
The beggar won't *race* in a race.'

★

Next week, under 'Seller and Buyer',
Appeared in the *Daily Gazette*:

'A racehorse for sale, and a flyer;
Has never been started as yet;
A trial will show what his pace is;
The buyer can get him in light,
And win all the handicap races.
Apply here before Wednesday night.'

He sold for a hundred and thirty,
Because of a gallop he had
One morning with Bluefish and Bertie,
And donkey-licked both of 'em bad.
And when the old horse had departed,
The life on the station grew tame;
The race-track was dull and deserted,
The boys had gone back on the game.

\*

The winter rolled by, and the station
Was green with the garland of spring,
A spirit of glad exultation
Awoke in each animate thing.
And all the old love, the old longing,
Broke out in the breasts of the boys,
The visions of racing came thronging
With all its delirious joys.

The rushing of floods in their courses,
The rattle of rain on the roofs
Recalled the fierce rush of the horses,
The thunder of galloping hoofs.
And soon one broke out: 'I can suffer
No longer the life of a slug,
The man that don't race is a duffer,
Let's have one more run for the mug.

'Why, everything races, no matter
Whatever its method may be:
The waterfowl hold a regatta;
The 'possums run heats up a tree;
The emus are constantly sprinting
A handicap out on the plain;
It seems like all nature was hinting,
'Tis time to be at it again.

'The cockatoo parrots are talking
Of races to far away lands;
The native companions are walking
A go-as-you-please on the sands;
The little foals gallop for pastime;
The wallabies race down the gap;
Let's try it once more for the last time,
Bring out the old jacket and cap.

'And now for a horse; we might try one
Of those that are bred on the place,
But I think it better to buy one,
A horse that has proved he can race.
Let us send down to Sydney to Skinner,
A thorough good judge who can ride,
And ask him to buy us a spinner
To clean out the whole countryside.'

They wrote him a letter as follows:
'We want you to buy us a horse;
He must have the speed to catch swallows,
And stamina with it of course.
The price ain't a thing that'll grieve us,
It's getting a bad 'un annoys
The undersigned blokes, and believe us,
We're yours to a cinder, "the boys".'

He answered: 'I've bought you a hummer,
A horse that has never been raced;
I saw him run over the Drummer,
He held him outclassed and outpaced.
His breeding's not known, but they state he
Is born of a thoroughbred strain,
I paid them a hundred and eighty,
And started the horse in the train.'

They met him—alas, that these verses
Aren't up to the subject's demands—
Can't set forth their eloquent curses,
*For Partner was back on their hands.*
They went in to meet him in gladness,
They opened his box with delight—
A silent procession of sadness
They crept to the station at night.

And life has grown dull on the station,
The boys are all silent and slow;
Their work is a daily vexation,
And sport is unknown to them now.
Whenever they think how they stranded,
They squeal just like guinea-pigs squeal;
They bit their own hook, and were landed
With fifty pounds loss on the deal.

# My racing problems No. 2: The fatted napes

## C.J. DENNIS

THOSE THOUGHTFUL PEOPLE, to whom the matter is of interest, will remember that, on a recent day, I submitted to my friend, Percy Podgrass, the well-known scientific dilettante, a rather baffling racing problem upon which I had stumbled almost by accident. Since its publication, I learn, the matter has aroused intense interest amongst those more highly cultured members of the sporting fraternity to whom abstract questions are far more exciting than any sordid consideration of concrete gain acquired by wagering on sporting events.

The number of such people may not be large, but their enthusiasm is flattering.

My problem, it will be remembered, is, or rather was, this: 'Why is it that a large proportion of chronic racecourse gamblers, of a certain type, have abnormally fat necks while the residue of their number have napes abnormally thin?'

Percy has now been concentrating on the problem for some 48 hours—allowing time off for sleep, meals, snacks, spots, golf, bridge, face massage and so forth. Today, he came to me with shining eyes and what I believe to be, not only a feasible, but a highly ingenious and probable solution.

Its announcement will, I make bold to say, create a worldwide sensation among biologists, zoologists, psychologists and other apologists for the existence of humanity wherever it is discussed.

And this is what my pal Percy propounds:

Certain animals (he explains), inured by their environment or habitat (nice word) to alternating periods of plenty and poverty, have been, after aeons of patient evolution, equipped by wise Nature with a remarkable gift. This is the ability to store, in convenient portions of their bodies, during periods of plenty, a certain fatty substance of high nutritive value. Upon this substance they are later able to draw when a sudden scarcity of their natural sustenance forces them, as it were, to go on the dole.

It is Percy's considered opinion that the chronic gamblers in question have now definitely joined the ranks of these mammals, so highly favoured by Nature. The fat-naped ones (he declares) are those at present at or near a peak of prosperity. Those with dwindling necks are enduring the temporary privations of a 'tough spin' or a 'rotten trot' because of a too sanguine predilection for 'hairy goats'.

Further (as Percy points out), by staggering or alternating these periods, all-wise Nature saves these too acquisitive punters from themselves. For, if they had their own passionate desire, and the heyday of prosperity were unwisely prolonged, their necks would explode.

The solution (Percy tells me) came to him in his bath, almost miraculously. Using the loofah briskly, he was humming the words of an old gambler's song, when a certain couplet struck him like a blow. All lovers of literature will remember the significant lines—'One day you're a great big winner; Next day you ain't got no dinner.'

And there, as Percy says, he had it in a nutshell, Q.E.D., or is it *ipsy dixit*?

But I was still not wholly convinced.

Always meticulously careful to submit scientific theories to the most rigid tests, and to clear up every lurking doubt, I cited a case.

Many years ago, I told him, I myself had a rather inexplicable racing win, involving quite a large sum, yet my neck remained thin—or, as vulgar friends have it, scraggy.

Percy said the thing bore its own solution on the face of it. The fatty substance had been secreted, he maintained, not perhaps, in the neck, but a little higher up; and it has never since been dissipated.

Podgrass is a man I usually admire greatly; but there are moments when I suspect Percy of persiflage.

# The Urging of Uncle

**C.J. Dennis**

No; I ain't got a talent for races.
I ain't no frequenter of courses;
But I've lately been watchin' the paces
Of some of these promisin' 'orses.
Huh! promise? if 'orses 'ave uses,
'Tain't bringin' no joy to the faces
Of uncles wot 'arks to abuses
From nieces wot follers the races.

It's this 'ow. A friend of my niece's
Is friends with a friend wot rejoices
In knowin' a cove wot increases
'Is wealth thro' 'is wise racin' choices.
So we gits the good oil. But reverses
Leaves me with three thruppeny pieces,
While riches pours into the purses
Of friends of friends' friends of me niece's.

Now, I ain't a great reader of faces
Nor wise to the wiles of the courses;
But when I gits out to the races
I meets a nice feller wot forces
Acquaintance, an' w'ispers advices
Concernin' dead certainties w'ich is
All startin' at much better prices
Than wot my niece tips. So I switches.

Now, I ain't so much 'urt that our riches
Is down to three thruppeny pieces
Because from sure winners I switches;
It's them narsty remarks of my niece's.

'Ot anger within 'er it surges,
She sez, at an uncle wot places
'Is faith in a feller wot urges ...
No; I ain't got much talent for races.

# The whisperer

## A.B. ('BANJO') PATERSON

A WHISPERER IS A man who makes a living, often a very good living, by giving tips for races.

The well-dressed stranger or countryman who goes to a race meeting, as he leans over the rails and studies the horses, will find an affable stranger alongside him and they drift into conversation. The affable stranger says, 'That's a good sort of a horse,' and the ice is broken and before long the countryman is 'told the tale'.

Now, the tale has many versions, and it all depends on the listener which version is brought forward. The crudest plot that finds patrons is the old, old friend-of-the-owner story. In this drama the whisperer represents himself as a great friend of the owner of a certain horse, and if necessary he produces a confederate to represent the owner. The whisperer and confederate talk in a light-hearted way of putting a hundred each on, and they agree that they will do it if the price is good enough, but if they cannot get a fair price they will wait for another day.

The stranger thinks he ought not to miss such a chance as this, and carelessly suggests that he would like to be allowed to put a tenner on with their money. They demur and say that they have a good deal of other money to put on for friends and if they tried to put too much on, it might spoil the price. However, as being entreated to do so, they take the stranger's tenner as a great favour and that is the last he sees of it or them.

This is a simple way to get money, but it has its drawbacks. If the stranger is an absolute novice, he may be persuaded to back a horse with no possible chance, and then the gang never lose sight of him and they try to get another tenner out of him for the next race.

If he looks like a man that knows anything at all, they have to suggest backing a horse with some sort of a chance, and if that horse happens to win, they have to leave the course hurriedly, because it is a very awkward thing to have an infuriated countryman looking for you with a racecourse detective when you depend on your wits for a living.

So the friend-of-the-owner story is only tried on novices and as a last resource, for it can only be worked on a very raw fool and raw fools as a rule have not enough money to be worth robbing. Also it is a breach of the law, and the true artist in whispering can 'find 'em' without that.

The higher-grade class of narrative depends for its success not on the tale but on the way it is told. The artistic practitioner goes to the races and picks out by some unerring instinct the right 'mark'. He may select a countryman or a sailor or a stuck-up—anyone that looks as if he had money and was ready for a gamble. The whisperer tells a tale suited to his more educated client.

This time the tale is that he has a friend in a racing stable (which is quite true), that White Cockade is favourite but has not been backed by its stable and will not try to win, and that he knows a horse that is on the whole 'an absolute cert if they spur it'. He can find out all about it from his friend in the racing stable. Will the client have £20 on it if he can find out that it is all right? The client, anxious to be up to date, says he will.

Off goes the whisperer and comes back very mysterious. 'Good thing! Paleface second favourite at 6 to 1. Better have twenty on it. The favourite is as dead as mutton!'

He hypnotises the client, who soon gets the suggestion that he must back Paleface, it would be absolutely chucking a chance away not to have a good punt on Paleface, 6 to 1 is a real gift about Paleface; after they have conversed for a while the client would eat a tallow candle and swear it was milk chocolate if the whisperer offered it to him.

It was once said of a really great whisperer that he could talk a punter off a battleship into a canvas dinghy in mid-ocean.

Like horse taming, it is all done with the eye and the voice. Having hooked his fish, the whisperer now pilots him up to a bookmaker and sees the money put on, and they go off to watch the race.

The favourite runs wide at the turn and loses his position and never quite gets into the fighting line, but Paleface hugs the rails and comes away in the straight and wins easily. The whisperer and his client go off together to draw £120 of the best and the whisperer, if he handles his client properly, should get at least £20 for himself out of it. More than that, the client will be good for more betting, certainly until the hundred is gone, and probably a bit more on the top of that.

Some of these whisperers do really well when money is plentiful and sportsmen generous, and they build up quite a connection with country punters. Some of them keep the same clients for years. No one has ever actually heard of a whisperer selling his business or floating it into a company, but that may come later on. They deserve all they make, too. Do you think, oh most astute reader, that you could make a living by going to the racecourse and finding out winners and then inducing perfect strangers to back them and give you a share of the proceeds?

Like most other professions, whispering tends to be overcrowded. Practically every ex-jockey or stablehand with the necessary brains has his little circle of punters, and some of the boys in the stables learn to 'whisper' winners before they can see over the half-door of the stable. It takes a really good judge of racing and of human nature to keep his clientele together for long; and sometimes even the masters of the art make mistakes, as the following absolutely true tale of the trainer and the whisperer will illustrate.

It was when things were dull in Melbourne but booming in Sydney that a crowd of Melbourne followers of racing came up to Sydney on the track of the money. One of the Melbourne visitors was an expert whisperer and he had not long been on the Sydney course before he saw a genuine bushman, bearded, cabbage-tree-hatted, sunburnt and silent.

Bearing down on the 'bushie', he told him the old tale, and said that he had a friend in Layton's stable and that one of Layton's horses was 'a certainty if they backed it'. Layton, it may be mentioned, was a leading Sydney trainer.

After the usual spellbinding oratory on the part of the whisperer, the 'bushie' agreed to put £10 on the horse and went away to see some friends, arranging to meet the whisperer after the race. The horse won all right and the whisperer was at the meeting place bright and early.

He had not long to wait. Up came the bushman, smiling all over, and the whisperer expected a very substantial 'cut' out of the winnings. 'Did you back it?' he said. 'What price did you get?'

'I got fives—£50 to 10.'

'You won fifty, eh? Well, what about a tenner for me, for putting you on to it?'

'Oh, I don't know. Why should I give you a tenner? I'd have backed the horse whether I saw you or not.'

The whisperer tried persuasion and even pathetic appeal: he reduced his claim to 'two quid', but even at that the pastoral individual was adamant. At last the whisperer lost his temper.

'You'd have backed it without me telling you! You, you great yokel! What do you know about racehorses?'

'Well, I ought to know something. My name is Layton. I train that horse. I've just been away for a holiday in the bush. But I'll tell you what I'll do. I'll give you two pounds if you can point me out any man in my stable that told you to back it.'

As he finished speaking, as the novelist says, 'he looked up and found himself alone.'

# How Babs Malone Cut Down the Field

**Barcroft Henry Boake**

Now the squatters and the 'cockies',
Shearers, trainers and their jockeys
Had gathered them together for a meeting on the flat;
They had mustered all their forces,
Owners brought their fastest horses,
Monaro-bred—I couldn't give them greater praise than that.

'Twas a lovely day in Summer—
What the blacksmith called 'a hummer',
The swelling ears of wheat and oats had lost their tender green,
And breezes made them shiver,
Trending westward to the river—
The river of the golden sands, the moaning Eucumbene.

If you cared to take the trouble
You could watch the misty double,
The shadow of the flying clouds that skimmed the Bogong's brow,
Throwing light and shade incessant
On the Bull Peak's ragged crescent,
Upon whose gloomy forehead lay a patch of winter's snow.

Idly watching for the starting
Of the race that he had part in,
Old *Gaylad* stood and champed his bit, his weight about nine stone;
His owner stood beside him,
Who was also going to ride him,
A shearer from Gegederick, whose name was Ned Malone.

But *Gaylad* felt disgusted,
For his joints were fairly rusted,
He longed to feel the pressure of the jockey on his back,

181

And he felt that for a pin he'd
Join his mates, who loudly whinnied
For him to go and meet them at the post upon the track.

From among the waiting cattle
Came the sound of childish prattle,
And the wife brought up their babe to kiss his father for good luck;
Said Malone: 'When I am seated
On old *Gaylad,* and am treated
With fairish play, I'll bet we never finish in the ruck.'

But the babe was not contented,
Though his pinafore was scented
With oranges, and sticky from his lollies, for he cried,
This gallant little laddie,
As he toddled to his daddy,
And raised his arms imploringly—'Please, dad, div Babs a wide.'

The father, how he chuckled
For the pride of it, and buckled
The surcingle, and placed the babe astride the racing pad;
He did it, though he oughtn't,
And by pure good luck he shortened
The stirrups, and adjusted them to suit the tiny lad,

Who was seemingly delighted,
Not a little bit affrighted,
He sat and twined a chubby hand among the horse's mane:
His whip was in the other;
But all suddenly the mother
Shrieked, 'Take him off!' and then 'the field' came thund'ring down
    the plain.

'Twas the Handicap was coming,
And the music of their drumming

Beat dull upon the turf that in its summer coat was dressed,
The racehorse reared and started,
Then the flimsy bridle parted,
And *Gaylad*, bearing featherweight, was striding with the rest.

That scene cannot be painted
How the poor young mother fainted,
How the father drove his spurs into the nearest saddle-horse,
What to do? he had no notion,
For you'd easier turn the ocean
Than stop the Handicap that then was half-way round the course.

On the bookies at their yelling,
On the cheap-jacks at their selling,
On the crowd there fell a silence as the squadron passed the stand;
Gayest colours flashing brightly,
And the baby clinging tightly,
A wisp of *Gaylad*'s mane still twisted in his little hand.

Not a thought had he of falling,
Though his little legs were galling,
And the wind blew out his curls behind him in a golden stream;
Though the motion made him dizzy,
Yet his baby brain was busy,
For hadn't he at length attained the substance of his dream!

He was now a jockey really,
And he saw his duty clearly
To do his best to win and justify his father's pride;
So he clicked his tongue to *Gaylad*,
Whispering softly, 'Get away lad';
The old horse cocked an ear, and put six inches on his stride.

Then, the jockeys who were tailing
Saw the big bay horse come sailing

Through the midst of them with nothing but a baby on his back,
And this startling apparition
Coolly took up its position
With a view of making running on the inside of the track.

Oh, *Gaylad* was a beauty,
For he knew and did his duty;
Though his reins were flying loosely, strange to say he never fell,
But held himself together,
For his weight was but a feather;
Bob Murphy, when he saw him, murmured something like 'Oh, hell!'

But *Gaylad* passed the filly;
Passed Jack Costigan on *Chilli*,
Cut down the coward *Watakip* and challenged *Guelder Rose*;
Here it was he showed his cunning,
Let the mare make all the running,
They turned into the straight stride for stride and nose for nose.

But Babs was just beginning
To have fears about his winning,
In fact, to tell the truth, my hero felt inclined to cry,
For the *Rose* was still in blossom,
And two lengths behind her *Possum*,
And gallant little *Sterling*, slow but sure, were drawing nigh.

Yes! Babsie's heart was failing,
For he felt old *Gaylad* ailing,
Another fifty yards to go, he felt his chance was gone.
Could he do it? much he doubted,
Then the crowd, oh, how they shouted,
For Babs had never dropped his whip, and now he laid it on!

Down the straight the leaders thundered
While people cheered and wondered,
For ne'er before had any seen the equal of that sight
And never will they, maybe,
See a flaxen-haired baby
Flog a racehorse to the winning post with all his tiny might.

But *Gaylad*'s strength is waning,
Gone in fact, beyond regaining,
Poor Babs is flogging helplessly, as pale as any ghost,
But he looks so brave and pretty
That the *Rose*'s jock takes pity,
And, pulling back a trifle, lets the baby pass the post.

What cheering and tin-kettling
Had they after, at the 'settling',
And how they fought to see who'd hold the baby on his lap;
As President Montgom'ry,
With a brimming glass of 'Pomm'ry',
Proposed the health of Babs Malone, who'd won the Handicap.

# PART 3

# The Cup is More Than a Horse Race

# The Cup is more than a horse race

## LES CARLYON

'MORT FROM CHICAGO'—THAT's how he introduced himself to me in an hotel dining room four years ago in Lexington, Kentucky. If the name sounds Runyonesque, Mort wasn't. He was that peculiarly American creature, the urban horse investor. From the big city, he sent his money to Kentucky where thoroughbreds ate it, but in a tax-effective way.

Mort owned pieces of several swish yearlings to be sold in the pavilion across from Blue Grass Airport, where the Arab buyers had already parked in their jets much as we park Commodores. After we had been talking half an hour, Mort suddenly said:'Yeah, I bred a Melbourne Cup winner once.' It was less than a boast—more like you or I confessing to having once kicked a goal for Mount Pleasant seconds.

Years earlier, Mort and his partners had sold a yearling to Sheikh Hamdan Bin Rashid Al Maktoum of Dubai, dreaming the colt would make them famous in the Derby at Epsom, England, or the Arc de Triomphe at Longchamp, France. The colt ran second in a big German race and third in the Rome Derby before being bundled off to Australia. As At Talaq, he won the 1986 Melbourne Cup. Mort felt things could have turned out better.

I told him that while the Cup wasn't as famous as the races he coveted, it was a lung-buster, perhaps the most honest staying race in the world, and never won by a soft horse. Cup day, I told him, was one of the world's great booze-ups, a public holiday no less. Then I hit him with the clincher: kids from Moonee Ponds went along dressed as the Pope. Mort didn't say much. I'm sure he thought it was Mt Pleasant seconds.

It's hard to explain the Cup to an outsider. Most of the turf's fabled events were got up by racing insiders for themselves. The Epsom and Kentucky Derbies are about the supremacy of genes and the buying power of the ruling classes. The public is allowed to join in for the crowd scenes. The best colt of the year usually wins and is hustled off to the breeding shed. Sheikh What's-His-Name doesn't get too excited about the stake money because he's worth a couple of billion anyway. Besides, he spent $20 million on yearlings that year, so he's still behind, but who's counting?

Our Cup is quirky. Got up for people, it is: a cross between a horse race and a folk festival. And it mocks good order because it's a handicap. This gets rid of the preordained factor: just about any runner can win. It's the best sporting idea anyone ever had in this town—if only because racing is international and AFL footy isn't.

And the Cup is folksy. Ray Trinder, the Tasmanian owner who won in 1972, was seen outside the course holding the Cup in a cupboard box and trying to hail a cab. It doesn't go like this at Epsom or Longchamp. In Melbourne, the script is by Shakespeare. The Cup is a saga about horses and the human condition, about lowbrows and highbrows, toffs and villains, irony and rough humour. And the improbable.

In 1987, Harry Lawton had bought Kensei out of a New Zealand paddock for $15,000. Now the chestnut had won the Cup. 'Looked like a yak when I bought him,' said Harry. 'Had a coat about

3 inches long.' Harry used to be a fitter and turner, and played footy for Preston at $4 a game. Rosedale, a bay stallion owned in America by Nelson Bunker Hunt, once thought to be the richest man in the world, ran third to Kensei. 'Tell Bunker I'm sorry I knocked him off,' said Harry. It only goes like this in Australia.

As the Cup field paraded last year, the crowd, as it always does, fell silent. When Fraar, owned by the above-mentioned Sheikh Hamdan, reached the top corner of the yard, a falsetto voice cried out: 'I love you, Fraar.'

Next time around, Michael Jackson cried out even louder. 'I want to marry you, Fraar.'

Only on such a day can a wag from Werribee, or wherever, make thousands laugh. When, around 15 minutes later, Ireland's Vintage Crop came back the winner, a joker in white Arabic robes rose, arms outstretched, to welcome him. Here, having a day out, was Lawrence of Nunawading, or possibly Sheikh Akbar Bin Merv of Wagga. In 1992, maybe the same gent came as Batman. Next Tuesday he could be Roseanne. Only in Australia.

Cup crowds always seem bigger than AFL Grand Final crowds because racegoers need to move around more. Last year I was looking for an old friend, the Irish journalist Robin Park. I couldn't find him. But when Vintage Crop swooped on the leaders, I heard Robin's voice. Somewhere in that throng of 80,000, he was yelling as only a patriot with a bookie's ticket can. I didn't find his body until an hour later. Robin flushed and short in his action, mainly because of all the money he was carrying.

One reason the Cup had endured so well is that it keeps reinventing itself. In the early 1980s, it began to look worn. Too often it was won by mere handicappers, game horses but not the stuff of legend. People said the Cox Plate at Moonee Valley had more class. Without fanfare, the VRC began to handicap the Cup as a 'quality handicap', which favoured good horses. Up popped winners as classy as Empire Rose, Kingston Rule and Let's Elope. Then, last year, the VRC attracted two European runners and took the race to the world.

So it was that in the wind and rain we heard Irish accents at the winner's stall. Back came Vintage Crop, a long chestnut with a sheepskin noseband and a plaited mane. Hauntingly Irish, it was: the light soft and grey, the grass bruised and squelching, the rain incessant.

Back, too, came Mick Kinane, Vintage Crop's jockey, mud spattered across his shoulders, face and crotch. He had struck the chestnut just five times with the whip. He had gone out along its neck, kept his head low, and helped the gelding to the line. Behind him, local jockeys were sitting up, flailing away, and generally demonstrating why Australian jockeys are no longer as popular as they once were in Europe. Vintage Crop changed the nature of the Cup. Kinane's example may yet change the way Australian jockeys ride.

As usual, the return to scale made the running of the bulls at Pamplona, Spain, seem dull. Eventually Rod Johnson, the then VRC chief executive, took Dermot Weld, Vintage Crop's trainer, and some of the print journalists to a bar. Here, we met a chameleon. One moment Weld would talk as clinically as a surgeon, explaining how he had planned the whole thing, which he had. Next, he was a romantic, reciting bush poetry. Can you imagine the winning trainer on Derby day at Epsom holding forth on Michael Magee, who owned a shanty on the outer Barcoo?

They drink at the Cup. Leaving the course in the dark after phoning in your story, you feel like the lone wowser at a Roman orgy. Cans rattle, glass crunches underfoot, tote tickets flutter, car boots gape. The air reeks of stale beer and you have to step around the bodies. Feeling absurdly chaste, one makes it to the street and hails a cab. Except the driver doesn't stop at once; he slows down and peers. 'Why didn't you stop right away?' I ask as we head for town. 'Got to be careful who you pick up here,' he says.

The carousing starts early. Arriving at the Cup one year, the first human I saw on the course was a youth, dead drunk and wearing only shorts, stretched out along the limbs of a shrub near the birdcage entrance, like a South American sloth but with tattoos. Far away a pipe band played 'Scotland the Brave'. There were similar wildlife displays all over the course. The runners were going out for race one.

Long ago before the police brought precision to breathalyser queues, a knight of the realm was leaving the Cup in his Rolls with a crony. Both had enjoyed a top day of betting, drinking and lying. They were waved into the queue to be tested by the new-fangled breathalyser. Both at once tumbled into the back seat.

A policeman strode up. 'Get this car moving . . .' he started. 'What's going on? Who's driving?'

'It's the damned chauffeur,' said Sir M. 'Just got out and ran away when we were signalled to stop. Must have been drinking.'

'Well, one of you move the car,' the policeman demanded. 'You're holding up the line.'

'We can't possibly do that, officer,' said Sir M. 'We're pissed.'

Broadly speaking, four classes of people go to the Cup. A few men come in morning suits and toppers. They are the last surviving members of a class to which they never belonged—the English aristocracy. They look more self-conscious than the working-class kids who come dressed as Madonna. There are the thousands of women who dress so elegantly. You think of the Rome's Via Veneto, then notice the lady is standing next to a drunk in a gorilla suit. And there is the suburban middle class. They stake out patches on the Flemington lawns. Things are so territorial here one thinks of the rookery scene in nature documentaries. Plots are marked out by a tartan rug on one's corner, a Great Western bottle on another. Oh, and there are the racing diehards. They mostly hate Cup day.

The Cup is a reference point. Grand Flaneur, ridden by the crack Tommy Hales, won in 1880, days before they hanged another useful horseman, Edward Kelly, after a $30 trial. By 1895, Grand Flaneur was champion sire and no one knew where Ned's body had been thrown. The wounded from Gallipoli limped around Flemington to see Patrobas win in 1915, the year Australia bought its nationhood with blood. Russia, a chestnut stallion, won in 1946, as the Allies realised they had licked Hitler only to inherit Stalin. Equally poetic, Think Big won in 1975, days before Gough Whitlam was sacked as PM by Sir John Kerr. A few years later at the Cup presentation, Kerr, slurring and looking like something gone to seed, tried to upstage a horse on Cup day.

In the country towns of my youth, the Cup was the reference point. A squint-eyed farmer would say: 'We haven't had a crop as good as this since . . . buggered if I can remember . . . when The Trump won the Cup.'

One of the townsfolk was a defrocked jockey who once rode a double at Flemington. In Cup week people bought him beers and took him seriously. For the rest of the year we treated him for what he truly was: a derelict.

But, in the end, and rightly, we remember only the horses. Who can forget Light Fingers nosing out Ziema in 1965? Light Fingers, the mare, small and finely chiselled. Ziema, the gelding, big and homely. Roy Higgins throwing everything at the little girl, asking her to crash through the wall. Johnny Miller cuddling Ziema, who was inclined to give up if passed. Two bobbing white bridles, two hearts close to bursting.

And what about Empire Rose in the muggy heat of 1988? She was huge like the Himalayas and had a lot of bad disposition. With joints like water melons, she should have broken down, yet she won our hardest race, neck down low, ears laid back threateningly. Laurie Laxon, her trainer, said she won because she had a 'good aggressive attitude'. What Laurie meant was that she hated other horses.

In 1960, the Centenary Cup, 101,000 of us turned up because Tulloch, the best horse most of us will ever see, was going around. That's just what he seemed to do: go around. Neville Sellwood took him via Footscray Tech and he flashed home seventh. Hi Jinx, the winner at 50 to 1, came back in silence. I was young and idolised Tulloch. I couldn't understand what had happened. I have matured a bit since; I think I now understand what happened.

In 1989, a new prince of trainers arrived: Lee Freedman. People will tell you afterwards they knew their horse would win; Lee told anyone who wanted to listen the Saturday before, after Tawrrific had run in the Mackinnon. Freedman stood watching the bay being cooled down. Each time the horse passed, he would say: 'I love him, I love him. He's a toughie, my favourite horse. He can win the Cup.' On Cup day, Freedman, his collar smudged with lipstick, said quietly: 'I told you so'. He was, and is, a man with faith in himself.

In 1976, the year Van Der Hum won in a cloudburst, I stood with my mate Mick from Queensland and watched the field parade. We had a wonderful view because no one else was dumb enough to stand in the rain. After the pneumonia passed, we felt we had matured a lot. In 1985, the two of us again watched the parade and agreed on one thing: What A Nuisance couldn't win because his coat was too dull. He won, and we matured some more. We felt better when we learned Johnny Meagher had trained the horse from a paddock.

Bart Cummings had trained nine Cup winners. His finest performance was perhaps Kingston Rule in 1990. With the look of eagles in his eye and copper lights in his coat, Kingston Rule seemed too pretty, too brittle, to be a contender. Bart made him one.

Kingston Town almost won the Cup in 1982. Tommy Smith, his trainer, and David Hains, his owner, thought he had, then the wrong number went up. The pair came down the steps with the uncomprehending looks of people herded out of a hotel fire at 3 a.m.

Johnny Letts, who won on Piping Lane in 1972, hadn't ridden at Flemington before and asked other riders where he should make his run. 'Go at Chiquita Lodge,' they told him. Letts assumed Chiquita Lodge to be a '30-storey motel' rather than a single-storey stable block at the 1000-metre post. He never saw it. He decided to go when he saw Roy Higgins send Gunsynd forward. Higgins had gone Chiquita Lodge. It only goes like this in Australia.

While I never convinced Mort from Chicago, Mick Kinane a few months ago told an English journalist of his ride down the Damascus road: 'It gets as much hype as the Derby and the Arc put together, and though I never dreamt as a child of winning the race—like I did the Derby—I'd recommend it to anyone.'

So would I.

*30 October 1994*

# Myths and legends, poets and dreamers

## JIM HAYNES

PERHAPS THE TRUE MAGIC of the Cup is that everyone throughout the country has a way of being involved in racing once a year, in some way or another. Every Aussie gets something from the Cup, has a feeling or opinion about it, and has a way of looking at it.

After all the media attention and the build-up, when the human and equine drama and romance has been played out to the minute, the nation waits for what is the most universally anticipated instant in horse-racing each year.

The entire nation stops. All of us—racing fanatics, totally uneducated once-a-year-mug-punters, the party generation swaying drunk in their stilettos and cheap suits, and prudish aunties with two-dollar sweep tickets—wait for the barrier gates to open.

The nation breathes as one.

Then, with a roar from the course that echoes from every television and radio in the land, and a universal gasp from the rest of us, the gates spring open, our hearts stop and ... they're off ...

## The legend of Archer

It is an obvious truism that the Melbourne Cup is 'such stuff as dreams are made on' in the Australian racing world.

That Cup Day and Anzac Day are the most iconic cultural events in our national calendar is self-evident. For better or for worse, these two days are the ones which Australians have taken to their hearts and singled out as special celebrations of our lifestyle, heritage, and national character.

The Cup is surrounded every year by a media frenzy which includes inordinate masses of trivia, history, statistics, tall tales and drama from the past, and a myriad of myths and legends.

Since the Cup was first run in 1861 the Australian public have clamoured to believe the most ridiculous and romantic tales of coincidence, supernatural premonition and divine intervention. Each year brings new examples of heroism and perseverance as horses and jockeys and trainers battle, overcoming seemingly insurmountable odds, to achieve victory.

This all began with the unlikely legend of Archer's long walk to Melbourne to win the first Cup, two years in a row. This 'walk' never happened the first time around, and to suggest that Australia's most successful trainer, Etienne de Mestre, would have sent his valuable Cup winner from the previous year on a second arduous marathon walk is laughable. Yet, many believe it, despite accounts from the time that Archer, like all other normal human beings and horses, made his way to Melbourne by boat.

Newspaper accounts of the day show that Archer left Sydney on 18 September 1861 on the steamer *City of Sydney*, together with two stablemates, Exeter and Inheritor, and arrived at Port Melbourne three days later.

Also on board were Etienne de Mestre, and jockey Johnny 'Cutts', who was, in fact, John 'Cutts' Dillon, one of the most respected jockeys in New South Wales. Despite stories to the contrary, Cutts was not from the Nowra district and never lived there, athough his brother-in-law Walter Bradbury worked for de Mestre, and lived at Terara.

This pretty much puts a hole in the theory, or 'legend', that Johnny Cutts was born and raised in the area around Nowra; supposedly one of many Aboriginal stockmen who replaced the stockmen of European descent when they left to join the goldrushes.

There is even a more ridiculous 'legend' that Archer's strapper, Dave Power, not only walked him to Melbourne, but rode him under Cutts' name in the Cup . . . and was of Aboriginal descent.

Perhaps Power walked Archer to the nearest port of embarkation from his home on the south coast of New South Wales, or perhaps he walked him from the Port Melbourne docks to the hotel stables at South Yarra, where he was trained for the first Cup; but he certainly never walked him to Melbourne from his home near Nowra, nor did he ride him in the Cup.

Archer went by steamboat from Sydney to Melbourne three times to compete in Victorian races, in 1861, 1862 and 1863.

De Mestre's horses usually boarded the steamer at Adam's Wharf near his property at Terara, on the Shoalhaven River. However, floods in 1860 altered the course of the river channels and made navigation dangerous. So, from 1860 to 1863, horses needed to be walked to the wharf at Greenwell Point 13 kilometres to the east. Perhaps this was the origin of the 'walking to Melbourne' legend.

The longest distance Archer ever walked was the 250 km from the end of the railway line at Campelltown to his owners' paddock near Braidwood when he retired from racing in 1864.

Etienne de Mestre, cunning as he was, may have enjoyed spreading the ridiculous rumour about the walk as part of his plan to empty the pockets of Melbourne's bookmakers. It is more obvious, however, that he achieved his goal by keeping the relatively unknown Sydney horse away from prying eyes and training him in what was then known as St Kilda Park, opposite the Botanical Hotel, where he was stabled in South Yarra.

Archer had won his last seven starts in Sydney, but those wins were spread out over a year and the form of the various colonial horses was not well known 'intercolonially'. It was the Cup that would eventually bring Australian champions together from around the continent and give us a real 'Australian racing scene'.

De Mestre single-handedly backed his victorious horse in from 8 to 1 to 6 to 1, with the result that the bookmakers of Melbourne were left reeling and more grist was added to the mill of interstate rivalry, or intercolonial rivalry, as it then was.

Neither the handicapper nor the bookmakers of Melbourne missed Archer the following year. He was given 10 st 2 lb (64.5 kg) to carry and was favourite at 2 to 1. Of course, he added another chapter to Cup history by winning yet again.

In the true spirit of colonial rivalry, Archer was given the massive weight of 11 st 4 lb (72 kg) by the handicapper in 1863. De Mestre had paid the first acceptance fee of 5 sovereigns and was incensed when weights were announced. However, he eventually relented and Archer and another runner from his stable, Haidee, left by steamboat for Melbourne on 16 June.

De Mestre's agents reminded him on 1 July that he needed to send final payment and acceptance that day, so a telegram was sent to the Melbourne office of George Kirk & Co., asking them to accept on his behalf. De Mestre sent the telegram himself, as the due date was a normal working day in New South Wales, and records show it was received at Melbourne Telegraph Office at 1 p.m.

However, Wednesday 1 July was a public holiday in Melbourne, and the telegram was not delivered until 7.30 p.m.

Acceptances closed at 8 p.m. and, when George Kirk handed the telegram to the stewards at the Turf Club the next morning, those honourable sporting men, having found a loophole to stop Archer once and for all, decided it was too late.

This decision caused a furore at the time; even Victorian owners lobbied the club to accept the entry, but to no avail. Mind you, it was highly unlikely that Archer, carrying 11 st 4 (72 kg), could have won anyway, and the Victorian owners doubtless realised this. If he had run it would have been the biggest weight carried in the history of the Melbourne Cup.

All the interstate entrants pulled out in protest and only seven local horses ran in what is considered the worst and weakest Cup in history. It was won, in front of 7000 people, by Banker, carrying 5 st 4 lb (34 kg).

It is both fitting and ironic that the public holiday which enabled this unsportsmanlike decision to be made was Separation Day, the day that Victoria celebrated its official separation from New South Wales in 1851.

Archer was taken by train to Ballarat in August 1863 and ran poorly in a sweepstakes race. He was suffering from fever and an injured fetlock and returned to Sydney to recover and be trained for the Metropolitan Handicap of 1864. He broke down once more on the eve of the race, however, and never raced again.

Although Archer is shown in the record books as being owned by de Mestre, and he raced in the trainer's famous all-black colours, he was actually leased by de Mestre and was always owned by an old school friend of de Mestre's, J.T. Roberts, in partnership with his brother-in-law and two nephews.

Archer was retired to stand at his owners' property, Exeter Farm, near Braidwood, where he was foaled, for a fee of 10 guineas, but his progeny failed to win a stakes race, bearing out, perhaps, de Mestre's opinion that Archer was not among the best horses he had ever trained.

Archer died, aged 16, in 1872. An ornament made from his tail hair, coiled into a horseshoe shape and set in silver and mounted on red satin, can be seen at the Australian Racing Museum in Melbourne.

So, right from its very beginnings, the Cup was shrouded in myths, tall stories and romance.

If looked at devoid of its myths and fairytales, the first Melbourne Cup was a rough-and-tumble affair. One horse bolted off the course during the race, three of the 17 runners fell and two died. Two jockeys were seriously injured and suffered broken bones.

Archer defeated the favourite, and local champion, Mormon, by 6 lengths in the slowest time in Cup history, 3 minutes 52 seconds, in front of the smallest crowd ever, 4000 people.

Archer had previously defeated Mormon over 2½ miles in the Australia Plate at Randwick. So the form was there to see and de

Mestre's betting coup was a real triumph over local pride. An injury to Archer, real or feigned, leading up to the race may have helped the price get out to an appetising 8 to 1 before De Mestre pounced and reduced the odds to 6 to 1.

De Mestre also took home £710 and a handmade gold watch. There was no second prize, so the locals were left empty-handed.

The second year the odds were not as juicy. Archer won by 8 lengths, a feat not equalled until Rain Lover won by the same margin in 1968. His trainer took home £810 and another watch. Mormon again ran second and collected £20.

Etienne de Mestre was a colourful character who became part of Cup legend by training five winners, a record that lasted for 99 years, until Bart Cummings broke it in 1977. The famous trainer was one of ten children of another fascinating character in our history, Prosper de Mestre.

The son of a French officer fleeing the Revolution, Prosper was born at sea on a British ship after his father's death. He was raised and educated in America after his mother remarried and lived and traded in China, India and Mauritius before arriving in Sydney, where his right to trade as a 'foreigner' was challenged and he subsequently became the first person ever to be naturalised as an 'Australian', or at least a British subject in Australia!

Etienne himself had 11 children and developed the land his father was granted at Terara, near Nowra, into a successful training and breeding establishment. Archer's stable is still there. In fact it's a bed and breakfast establishment today and, if you are prepared to believe Cup and local folklore, you can spend a weekend sleeping where Archer was supposedly stabled for most of his racing life.

Maybe you believe he walked to Melbourne, too.

## The tale of Peter St Albans

Other Cup folklore includes the tale of the 12-year-old 'Aboriginal' boy named Peter riding Briseis, the first female horse to win, in 1876.

The story goes that Peter was born on the St Albans stud property near Geelong to an Aboriginal mother; perhaps he was the son of St Albans' owner, Jim Wilson Snr, or his son, also Jim. Another version has the boy being left as a baby on the doorstep of one of St Albans' grooms, Michael Bowden, to be raised by him and his wife.

As he had no 'real' surname, so the story goes, he was given the name of the property and became Peter St Albans, youngest jockey and first Aboriginal rider to win the Cup!

Unfortunately, this wonderful story, like Archer's walk to Melbourne with his Aboriginal 'strapper/jockey', has more holes in it than a Swiss cheese.

Two elements of the story are true. He was known as Peter and he was very young, in fact he was only 12 and, oddly enough, this fact explains the whole wonderful concoction.

Aged only 12, the boy had ridden Briseis, as a two-year-old, to three victories at Randwick earlier in the year, including an incredible win in the Doncaster Handicap where he rode her at 5 st 7 lb (35 kg). However, the VRC rules did not allow jockeys to ride in the Cup until they were aged 13, and Peter was a few days shy of his 13th birthday on Cup Day 1876.

The regular jockey for St Albans' horses was the legendary Tom Hales, who could not make the Cup weight at 6 st 4 lb (39.5 kg). As Briseis won most of her big races as a two- and three-year-old, she was given very light weights to carry, which meant that a good lightweight jockey was required.

Few grown men could ride at those weights, but Peter was an excellent rider who knew the horse as a stable boy at St Albans and had ridden her to victory in three races in Sydney. So, cunning old Jim Wilson came up with the 'cock-and-bull' story of Peter's origins to allow him to ride Briseis in the Cup. He argued to the VRC that both the boy's birth date and parents were unknown, but he was probably older than 13.

'Peter St Albans' was actually born in Geelong on 15 November 1864, and there is a birth certificate to prove it. He was the son of Michael Bowden and his wife and, though christened Michael, he was known as Peter from an early age. There is a painting at the State Library of Victoria by Frederick Woodhouse showing Peter as a youth, looking very white and European, standing alongside Briseis with Tom Hales in the saddle.

Michael 'Peter St Albans' Bowden was a successful jockey for several years around Geelong and also rode successfully interstate until a bad fall at age 19 saw him switch to training. He died in 1900 at the age of 35. The Geelong Thoroughbred Club awards the Peter St Albans Trophy each year to the jockey who rides the most winners at the Geelong track.

Other Cup folklore has William Evans weighing-in unconscious after wasting more than 10 pounds (4.5 kg) in a week to ride the 1907 winner Apologue at 7 st 9 lb (48.5 kg). Evidently the totally exhausted jockey collapsed after the horse passed the post and was placed unconscious on the scales.

Let us hope that Dame Nellie Melba and famous English contralto Dame Clara Butt, whose combined presence on the lawn was the social highlight of Cup Day 1907, were not unduly distressed by witnessing the poor jockey's plight!

## Reckless and Tommy Woodcock—A national love story

The Cup was already well established as the highpoint of Melbourne's social calendar when poor Evans passed out past the post. Indeed, once the race had recovered from the debacle of 1863 and the two rival race clubs of Melbourne combined to form the Victorian Racing Club in 1864, the race quickly developed into far more than a mere rich handicap where horses from all colonies could compete.

The dream of the creators of the race, Captain Standish and the committeemen of the Victoria Turf Club, was to show the Victorian colony's supremacy over New South Wales in all matters, especially sporting matters, by running the richest race on the continent. This was looking like becoming reality as crowd numbers for the event went to 25,000-plus in the first decade of the race's history and had reached a regular 100,000 by the end of the second decade.

Although Melbourne has given way to Sydney as the financial capital of Australia and the most populous city in the 150 years since the Cup was created, it remains the sporting capital of the nation, largely due to the iconic status of the Melbourne Cup.

Racing has always been a focus for literature, art and romance since the earliest times of the sport in Britain. There is something in the nature and history of the sport which brings to the surface the more imaginative and romantic aspects of our humanity. The nobility and beauty of the horse, the drama of the competition, mere men controlling large and powerful animals—all these things inspire awe and wonder.

The whole fickle and glorious nature of the human drama is intensified and crystallised in the sport of thoroughbred racing. What is it that draws us to the sport? The vicarious thrill of the risks involved? The possibility of making and losing fortunes? The snob appeal of the involvement of the nobility? The possibility that the sport may make a prince from a pauper, and vice versa?

Whatever it is, it is typified and made easy for Australians via the Melbourne Cup. Each year all Aussies can get a massive dose of 'whatever it is' in early November and then return to the humdrum of normality. Those of us afflicted by the 'racing bug' habitually raise our eyebrows at this seasonal invasion of the uneducated into our 'world' and enjoy the event as the culmination of the racing season which, for us, lasts 12 months in every year.

The general Australian population of some 22 million can, with the help of the media, enjoy the annual human and equine drama and suspense as the Cup approaches. They are told the usual stories of potential 'rags to riches' battlers, the horses who might compete become characters, and Cup history and mythology is retold to a point that a collective sigh of relief goes up when the gates spring open on that first Tuesday afternoon in November.

After the race comes a week of reflection on the winners and losers. Recent examples of Cup 'drama' being used to create more

Cup folklore and provide millions of words in 'human interest' journalism are the stories of Tommy Woodcock and Reckless in 1977 and the amazing story of Media Puzzle's win in 2001.

Reckless was trained by Tommy Woodcock, who was famous as the strapper of Phar Lap when he won the Melbourne Cup in 1930, and who accompanied Phar Lap to America and was with the great racehorse when he tragically and mysteriously died after winning the Agua Caliente Handicap in world-record time in Mexico.

Reckless, trained by the 73-year-old iconic 'battler', was known as 'the people's horse' by the media due to his lovely nature and the fact that his trainer was much loved for his attachment to, and obvious love for, the iconic Australian champion Phar Lap.

It was a real 'battler's story' as Reckless started 33 times before winning his first race at the age of five.

Woodcock resurrected the horse's career and trained him to run fourth in the Cup of 1976. He then went on to win the Sydney, Adelaide and Brisbane Cups in 1977, a feat never equalled before or since.

All Australia wanted the gentle stallion and his trainer to win the Melbourne Cup in 1977. In scenes never before seen on major racetracks, Tommy Woodcock gave children rides on the stallion's back on racedays before he raced, including Flemington on Cup day!

To so nearly achieve the ultimate dream of winning all major 2-mile events, including the Melbourne Cup, in one year and then fail by a length in running a brave second to Gold and Black was poignant enough. For the most-loved racing character and the most-loved horse in Australia to be the protagonists in the drama had sentiment fairly oozing from the pens of journalists.

It is not in words, however, but in two photographs taken at the time that we see the true appeal of the story. One, taken by *Melbourne Age* photographer Bruce Postle, shows Reckless and Tommy Woodcock lying side by side in the horse's stall the night before the race, with the big stallion nuzzling his smiling trainer. The second, taken minutes after the race, showed horse and man walking out of the saddling paddock as the presentations take place to the winner's connections.

## Media Puzzle and Damien Oliver—by the grace of God

In 2002 the nation was awash with emotion as Damien Oliver, 10 metres past the post seconds after winning the Cup on Media Puzzle, raised his whip and eyes heavenward in memory of his brother Jason, killed earlier in the week while riding in a trial in Perth. Jason was just days away from his 33rd birthday and Damien flew to the funeral the day after winning the Cup.

Oliver had won the Cup previously on Doriemus in 1995 and had dedicated that win to his father Ray, a man he barely knew as he was also killed in a racing accident while riding in the Boulder Cup at Kalgoorlie in 1975 when Damien was just three years old.

The Cup of 2002, like most Cups, had its share of dramatic and history-making elements. Media Puzzle had recovered from a fractured pelvis to win the Cup ahead of his more famous stablemate, Irish champion stayer Vinnie Roe. Media Puzzle's trainer, Irishman Dermot Weld, made history by becoming the only overseas trainer to ever win two Cups. Until that day in 2002 he had been the only overseas trainer to ever win one Cup! He also achieved the difficult feat of training the quinella that year.

All that drama was overshadowed by the human tragedy of the Oliver family's grief and loss. The memorable and inspirational moment that capped off the Cup hype and put the event into perspective came when Damien Oliver, asked what the Cup win meant to him, replied, 'Melbourne Cups don't mean a thing to me anymore. I'd give it back right now to have my brother back.'

## Shadow King

Sentiment plays a big part in the public appeal of the sport of racing, and it is a huge part of what we love about the Cup. This is well demonstrated in the way we have remembered the amazing Cup career of Shadow King, who also happened to be a son of Comedy King, the first imported horse to win the Melbourne Cup.

Shadow King ran in six Melbourne Cups without ever winning, although he was placed in four of them, finishing fourth and sixth in his other two runs.

'As unlucky as Shadow King' was a common saying in Australia in the 1930s and 1940s, and the racing public loved the horse who came to represent the archetypal Aussie battler.

The fact that our premier race is a handicap rather than a true test of 'quality' means that our champions often lose as they battle to overcome the odds and win with the top weight. We love seeing everyone get 'a fair go', but we still love our champions whether they win or lose the Cup. Wakeful, Kingston Town, Gunsynd and Phar Lap in 1931 were cheered from the course, gallant in defeat.

We also love the underdog and that was Shadow King. He should have won in 1933 when he was almost knocked down on the turn and Scobie Breasley managed to get him balanced again but failed by a head to catch Hall Mark.

In a wonderful gesture to the horse who represented the Aussie belief that the main thing was to 'have a go', the VRC allowed him, aged ten and carrying saddlecloth number seven, to lead the field onto the track for the Melbourne Cup of 1935.

The crowd of 110,739 clapped and cheered sentimentally but considered the horse to be merely a colourful footnote to the race that year, until he flew home to narrowly miss a place, finishing fourth at 100 to 1 to prove, once again, that 'having a go' can make dreams *almost* attainable.

In a further addition to Cup history Shadow King was re-trained as a police horse after retiring and performed ceremonial duties at the Melbourne Cup every year until he passed away in 1945.

## Dreaming to win

Dreams and premonitions have long been a part of Cup folk-lore. There are many accounts, mostly unsubstantiated, of people dreaming the winner. Shearers riding miles but arriving too late to place a bet having dreamed the winner in an isolated shearing shed; housewives telling husbands the name of the winner before the race due to women's intuition, a premonition or cryptic dream, only to be ignored or laughed at by the husband until proven right on race day.

The most famous Melbourne Cup dream story is the one concerning Walter Craig, owner of the 1870 winner, Nimblefoot.

Craig was the owner and the licensee of Ballarat's Royal Hotel. He had purchased the hotel in 1857, at the height of the gold boom. It was originally known as Bath's Hotel but, after Alfred Duke of Edinburgh stayed there in 1867, it became known as the Royal.

In the same year legendary horseman and poet, Adam Lindsay Gordon, took over management of the hotel's substantial stables and livery business. Walter Craig and his horses are mentioned several times in Gordon's verse.

In August 1870 Craig dreamed that he saw his horse, Nimblefoot, winning the Melbourne Cup. The horse carried Craig's violet silks but the jockey was wearing a black armband in the dream.

Craig recounted the dream to several people and died within days of the premonition. An account of this strange event did appear in the *Melbourne Age* just prior to the running of the Cup, which lends some credibility at least to this piece of Cup folklore.

Needless to say, the horse subsequently won the Cup with the jockey wearing a black crepe armband to mark the passing of the owner.

Walter Craig's death is the central feature of another piece of Melbourne Cup mythology. It seems that Craig and a group of friends, including well-known bookmaker Joseph Slack, were drinking at Craig's hotel in February 1870 when Craig asked the bookmaker what odds he would give on an AJC Metropolitan Handicap–Melbourne Cup double featuring Croydon and Nimblefoot.

The bookmaker, in a spirit of conviviality, offered to bet £1000 against a round of drinks for the group and Craig duly obliged. Although the double proved successful, Craig died before the result was finalised and, according to the unwritten rules of gentlemanly sportsmanship, death cancels out debts of honour.

Legend has it, however, that Joseph Slack chose to honour the bet made with his friend and paid Craig's widow the £1000. A second account of the story has the bookmaker paying £500 to the widow in order to appear honourable while still acknowledging the accepted rules of sportsmanship surrounding such verbal, or 'handshake', bets.

Stories of 'dreaming the winner' had become such an accepted feature of the annual Cup publicity barrage by 1886 that a young Banjo Paterson was able to use the idea as the basis of a comic poem, 'A Dream of the Melbourne Cup'.

Published in the *Bulletin* just prior to the Cup of that year, the poem has several interesting elements.

For one thing it demonstrates Paterson's parochial support for his home colony of New South Wales and reminds us just how fierce the rivalry was between that state and Victoria.

Paterson, who was a member of the first New South Wales polo team to play against Victoria, sees the race in his dream as a match between the New South Wales champion, Trident, and the great Victorian stayer, Commotion.

When the actual race was run, some weeks after the poem appeared in the *Bulletin,* it was a pyrrhic victory for Paterson's 'dream horse' Trident, who finished fourth, but well ahead of Commotion, who came in 21st in a field of 28 runners.

The result that year would have pleased young Banjo Paterson, however, as the race was won by the New South Wales bred, trained and owned horse, Arsenal.

Even more pleasing to New South Welshmen would have been the fact that Arsenal's previous owner was a Victorian, Mr W. Pearson, who also owned Commotion.

Pearson was a wealthy sportsman who owned a large team of horses in Melbourne and had dreadful luck in attempting to win the Cup. Commotion had finished third behind Martini-Henri in 1883 and second behind Malua in 1884.

Pearson then purchased Arsenal, who was bred at Tocal Stud near Maitland, for 625 guineas. The horse won the VATC Criterion Stakes and performed well in lead-up races to the Cup of 1885, in which the three-year-old was given the featherweight handicap of 6 st 9 lb (42 kg). In spite of all his promise, however, Arsenal ran a shocker in the big race, finishing 31st in a field of 35.

Disgusted with both his poor luck and the horse, Pearson sold Arsenal to Mr W. Gannon, a Sydney racing man, for a mere 375 guineas. Trained by Harry Rayner and ridden by inexperienced jockey W. English, Arsenal won the Cup in 1886, soundly defeating Commotion, carrying the Pearson colours.

Paterson's poem also pokes fun at the typical punter's fear of picking a winner but not being paid. The poet also has some fun with the various old wives' tales concerning which foods give us restless nights and vivid dreams.

The poem was only the third of Paterson's verses to be published in the *Bulletin* and it demonstrates the 22-year-old writer's enthusiasm for racing and his sense of humour, along with more than a hint of the anti-Semitic attitudes of the day.

# A Dream of the Melbourne Cup

## A.B. ('Banjo') Paterson

Bring me a quart of colonial beer
And some doughy damper to make good cheer,
I must make a heavy dinner;
Heavily dine and heavily sup,
Of indigestible things fill up,
Next month they run the Melbourne Cup,
And I have to dream the winner.
Stoke it in, boys! the half-cooked ham,
The rich ragout and the charming cham.,
I've got to mix my liquor;

Give me a gander's gaunt hind leg,
Hard and tough as a wooden peg,
And I'll keep it down with a hard-boiled egg,
'Twill make me dream the quicker.
Now I am full of fearful feed,
Now I may dream a race indeed,
In my restless, troubled slumber;
While the night-mares race through my heated brain
And their devil-riders spur amain,
The tip for the Cup will reward my pain,
And I'll spot the winning number.

Thousands and thousands and thousands more,
Like sands on the white Pacific shore,
The crowding people cluster;
For evermore it's the story old,
While races are bought and backers are sold,
Drawn by the greed of the gain of gold,
In their thousands still they muster.
And the bookies' cries grow fierce and hot,
'I'll lay the Cup! The double, if not!'
'Five monkeys, Little John, sir!'
'Here's fives bar one, I lay, I lay!'
And so they shout through the livelong day,
And stick to the game that is sure to pay,
While fools put money on, sir!
And now in my dream I seem to go
And bet with a 'book' that I seem to know—
A Hebrew money-lender;
A million to five is the price I get—
Not bad! but before I book the bet
The horse's name I clean forget,
Its number and even gender.
Now for the start, and here they come,
And the hoof-strokes roar like a mighty drum

Beat by a hand unsteady;
They come like a rushing, roaring flood,
Hurrah for the speed of the *Chester* blood;
For *Acme* is making the pace so good
There are some of 'em done already.
But round the back she begins to tire,
And a mighty shout goes up, 'Crossfire!'
The magpie jacket's leading;
And *Crossfire* challenges, fierce and bold,
And the lead she'll have and the lead she'll hold,
But at length gives way to the black and gold,
Which away to the front is speeding.
Carry them on and keep it up—
A flying race is the Melbourne Cup,
You must race and stay to win it;
And old *Commotion*, Victoria's pride,
Now takes the lead with his raking stride,
And a mighty roar goes far and wide—
'There's only *Commotion* in it!'
But one draws out from the beaten ruck
And up on the rails by a piece of luck
He comes in a style that's clever;
'It's *Trident! Trident!* Hurrah for Hales!'
'Go at 'em now while their courage fails';
'*Trident! Trident!* for New South Wales!'
'The blue and white for ever!'
Under the whip! with the ears flat back,
Under the whip! though the sinews crack,
No sign of the base white feather;
Stick to it now for your breeding's sake,
Stick to it now though your hearts should break,
While the yells and roars make the grand-stand shake,
They come down the straight together.
*Trident* slowly forges ahead,
The fierce whips cut and the spurs are red,

The pace is undiminished;
Now for the *Panics* that never fail!
But many a backer's face grows pale
As old *Commotion* swings his tail
And swerves—and the Cup is finished.

And now in my dream it all comes back:
I bet my coin on the Sydney crack,
A million I've won, no question!
Give me my money, you hooked-nosed hog
Give me my money, bookmaking dog
But he disappeared in a kind of fog . . .
And I woke with 'the indigestion'.

## Poets, bushies and a fair go

It is obvious that, when Paterson wrote 'A Dream of the Melbourne Cup', the Cup had already developed a special place in our culture and folklore, although as a sporting institution it was a mere 25 years old.

In that relatively short time, the Cup had become a pivotal event in the year's calendar and, for many bushmen as well as residents of other cities, a trip to see the running of the race was the sporting equivalent of a pilgrimage to Rome or a hajj to Mecca for the devoutly religious.

Several years after Paterson's poem was published, Breaker Morant, writing about the joys of the life of drovers and itinerant bushmen, mentions this pilgrimage in a poem titled 'Westward Ho!':

We may not camp to-morrow, for we've many a mile to go,
Ere we turn our horses' heads round to make tracks for down
below.
There's many a water-course to cross, and many a black-soil
plain,
And many a mile of mulga ridge ere we get back again.

That time five moons shall wax and wane we'll finish up the work,
Have the bullocks o'er the border and truck 'em down from
    Bourke,
And when they're sold at Homebush, and the agents settle up,
Sing hey! a spell in Sydney town and Melbourne for the 'Cup'.

Many factors contributed to the Cup becoming such an important event on the national sporting calendar. Among these were the intensity of intercolonial rivalry and the huge popularity of the magazine which published Paterson's verse, the *Bulletin*.

The *Bulletin* began its life in 1880 and celebrated all things Australian, although there was to be no 'Australia' until 1901. This magazine was almost single-handedly responsible for developing the great tradition of Australian rhymed verse that helped to define our national character. Under editor J.F. Archibald's guidance the *Bulletin* developed a voice that has been described as 'offensively Australian' and helped to begin a slow process of change in our national perspective, from unquestioningly pro-British to more proudly 'Australian'.

The Cup, as has been noted earlier, is a distinctly Australian phenomenon. The fact that our greatest race is a handicap, as opposed to the classic British races which are true tests of quality, being weight-for-age events, demonstrates the difference in cultural sensibilities between the 'old country' and the nation which began its European history as a convict settlement.

It is part of our culture to give everyone, and every horse, a 'fair go' and it perhaps accounts for the huge popularity of the Cup among all Australians, even those with no interest at all in the sport of racing.

Paterson and Morant were horsemen and racing men who both rode in races and wrote many poems and stories about the sport, quite a few of which appear in this volume. The Cup, however, has captured the imagination of many poets and writers who were far less well-informed about the 'sport of kings' than were the well-known poets who were also great horsemen, like Paterson, Morant, Adam Lindsay Gordon and Will Ogilvie.

Each year the Cup was celebrated in doggerel by anonymous balladists and in newspaper verses. Most notably C.J. Dennis managed to write witty, wonderful light verse about the Cup every year for the Melbourne *Herald-Sun* from the mid 1920s until his death in 1938. His efforts have their own story elsewhere in this collection.

Most of these celebratory rhymes were written in haste, and in rather clunking couplets, by poets much less talented than C.J. Dennis. The details of the race and the praise of the winner were paramount, rather than the literary quality. One of the few verses of this type which has survived is one that celebrated Carbine's famous Cup win, when he carried the biggest winning weight ever, 10 st 5 lb (66.5 kg), in 1890. Here is an extract:

The race is run, the Cup is won, the great event is o'er.
The grandest horse that strode a course has led them home once
    more.
. . . With lightning speed, each gallant steed along the green
    track tore;
Each jockey knew what he must do to finish in the fore.
But Ramage knew his mount was true, though he had ten-five up,
For Musket's son great deeds had done before that Melbourne
    Cup . . .
Brave horse and man who led the van on that November day!
Your records will be history still when ye have passed away.

There are many of these anonymous, second-rate verses celebrating Cup wins down the years, and more than a few about Phar Lap's win in 1930. This is a snippet from one of the better ones:

With a minimum of effort you would simply bowl along,
With a stride so devastating and an action smooth and strong.
And you vied with the immortals when, on Flemington's green track,
You won the Melbourne Cup with nine stone twelve upon your
    back.

Archer pictured in a newspaper sketch of the day, carrying
Etienne de Mestre's famous all-black colours. (Courtesy of AJC)

The Cup-day crowd watch Bravo win the 1889 Melbourne Cup.
(Courtesy of VRC)

A newspaper artist's impression of the 1891 Cup atmosphere at Flemington. (Courtesy of VRC)

Darby Munro unsaddles Peter Pan after winning the Duke of Gloucester Cup at Flemington, 10 November 1934, four days after winning his second Melbourne Cup. (Courtesy of ARM)

Frank McGrath—the master trainer of great stayers such as Peter Pan, Prince Foote and Amounis. (Courtesy of Newspix)

Comic Court, the 1950 Melbourne Cup winner who was trained by Jim Cummings and strapped by a young Bart Cummings. (Courtesy of ARM)

The heyday of racing—Randwick racecourse in the 1950s when it was quite normal for enormous crowds to attend. (Courtesy of AJC)

Part of the Randwick racecourse betting ring in the 1950s, before the advent of legal off-course betting. (Courtesy of AJC)

Light Fingers, on the outside, defeats stable mate Ziema by a nose in the 1965 Melbourne Cup. (Courtesy of Newspix)

Galilee, ridden by John Miller, wins the 1966 Melbourne Cup—the second in a row for trainer Bart Cummings. (Courtesy of Newspix)

Think Big with Bart Cummings after his first Melbourne Cup victory in 1974. The strapper is a youthful Guy Walter. (Courtesy of Newspix)

Reckless and Tommy Woodcock share a stable bedroom before the 1977 Melbourne Cup. (Courtesy of Bruce Postle/Fairfax Photos)

Two great ladies of the turf. Trainer Sheila Laxon and the champion mare Ethereal, two weeks before the mare's 2001 Melbourne Cup victory. (Courtesy of Colin Murty/ Newspix)

Vintage Crop wins the Melbourne Cup in 1993, the first horse to do so who was owned, trained and bred overseas. (Courtesy of Steve Hart Photographics)

Glen Boss celebrates Makybe Diva's first Melbourne Cup victory on 4 November 2003. (Courtesy of Darren McNamara/Newspix)

A moment in history—Makybe Diva wins her third Melbourne Cup on 1 November 2005. (Courtesy of Kelly Barnes/Newspix)

Damien Oliver looks heavenward after winning the 2002 Melbourne Cup on Media Puzzle. (Courtesy of Richard Cisar-Wright/Newspix)

Bart Cummings shows Viewed the Melbourne Cup, Bart's 12th, after the horse's victory in the big race on 4 November 2008. (Courtesy of David Geraghty/Newspix)

How the hearts of thousands quickened as you cantered back
   old chap,
With your grand head proudly nodding to the crowd that yelled,
   'Phar Lap.'

## The poetry of the Cup

One of the oddest poems ever written about the Cup is an attempt by famous lyric poet, Henry Kendall, to capture the entire running of one particular Melbourne Cup in a style of poetry that seems oddly inappropriate for dramatic story-telling.

This poem differs from most of the verses written about the Cup not only in its more lyrical style, but also because it is by a poet not known as a balladist, bush versifier or racing enthusiast.

Most Cup verse takes the form of plain old doggerel, straight out story-telling, or, in the case of more sophisticated poets like Paterson, Morant and C.J. Dennis, well-informed humour or social commentary.

In his attempt to capture the colour, mood and excitement of the Cup of 1881, Henry Kendall concentrates solely on the actual race. There is no attempt to capture the raceday atmosphere or the general excitement of the event, as Dennis often did. Kendall, instead, waxes lyrical over a horse that was unfancied by racegoers and started at 50 to 1. This horse, Zulu, had evidently been used as a cart horse for part of his life, according, once again, to Melbourne Cup mythology.

Still, Zulu was no doubt a beautiful-looking creature. He was, by all accounts, a small well-formed horse and was certainly jet black, which no doubt accounts for his name. He was also, as Kendall mentions, a grandson of the great colonial sire Sir Hercules who sired Yattendon, The Barb and Zulu's sire The Barbarian, a full brother to The Barb. The Barb won the Cup in 1866 and Yattendon sired Cup winners Chester and Grand Flaneur.

The horses and jockeys mentioned by Kendall in this edited version of the poem are Somnus ridden by Cracknell, which finished 23rd; Santa Claus ridden by Bowes, which finished 30th; and Waterloo ridden by O'Brien, which finished 14th.

Darebin, who had won the VRC Derby in world-record time just days previously, was ridden by Power and finished 18th. This colt was equal favourite with Waxy who finished 4th.

The Czar ridden by Trahan and owned by Mr J. Morrison finished 2nd at 20 to 1, and 'Ivory's marvellous bay' was Sweetmeat, ridden by P. Piggot and owned by Mr T. Ivory. He finished 3rd, having finished 2nd two years before.

The 'marvel that came from the North' was AJC Derby winner, Wheatear, ridden by Ensworth, which fell when a dog ran amongst the horses at the half-mile post.

A feature of the race which does not rate a mention in Kendall's poem is the fact that Dodd, the jockey on Suwarrow, which also fell, died as a result of the fall. Burton rode The Wandering Jew into 16th place and the legendary Tom Hales was 17th on Trump Voss.

Now that we have all the facts and prosaic items dealt with, let us enjoy the lyrical, poetic account of the 1881 Melbourne Cup from the pen of one of the greatest Australian poets, Henry Kendall.

## How the Melbourne Cup Was Won

### Henry Kendall

In the beams of a beautiful day,
Made soft by a breeze from the sea,
The horses were started away,
The fleet-footed thirty and three;

Where beauty, with shining attire,
Shed more than a noon on the land,
Like spirits of thunder and fire
They flashed by the fence and the stand.

And the mouths of pale thousands were hushed
When *Somnus*, a marvel of strength,
Past Bowes like a sudden wind rushed,
And led the bay colt by a length;

But a chestnut came galloping through,
And, down where the river-tide steals,
O'Brien, on brave *Waterloo*,
Dashed up to the big horse's heels.

But Cracknell still kept to the fore,
And first by the water bend wheeled,
When a cry from the stand, and a roar
Ran over green furlongs of field;

Far out by the back of the course—
A demon of muscle and pluck—
Flashed onward, the favourite horse,
With his hoofs flaming clear of the ruck.

But the marvel that came from the North,
With another, was heavily thrown;
And here at the turning flashed forth
To the front a surprising unknown;

By shed and by paddock and gate
The strange, the magnificent black,
Led *Darebin* a length in the straight,
With thirty and one at his back.

But the Derby colt tired at the rails,
And Ivory's marvellous bay
Passed Burton, O'Brien, and Hales,
As fleet as a flash of the day.

But Gough on the African star
Came clear in the front of the field,
Hard followed by Morrison's *Czar*
And the blood unaccustomed to yield.

Yes, first from the turn to the end,
With a boy on him paler than ghost,
The horse that had hardly a friend
Shot flashing like fire by the post.

In a clamour of calls and acclaim,
He landed the money—the horse
With the beautiful African name,
That rang to the back of the course.

Hurrah for the *Hercules* race,
And the terror that came from his stall,
With the bright, the intelligent face,
To show the road home to them all!

Regarded by many as Australia's finest poet, Kendall was a very different type of poet to Paterson, Morant, and the rest of the *Bulletin* versifiers. He was also a very different type of person. He started his working life as a public servant with the Lands Office, but suffered family scandals, bankruptcy and bouts of mental illness. He resigned his position to live in poverty before working in a timber business owned by friends on the mid north coast of New South Wales, around the area of the town which now bears his name. His poetry was critically acclaimed but never made him any money. Towards the end of his life, the premier of New South Wales, Sir Henry Parkes, appointed him Inspector of Forests.

Apart from his obviously well-researched 1881 poem, which demonstrates a good knowledge of the horses involved, Kendall does not appear to have had any deep or lasting interest in horse-racing, as did Paterson, Morant and Gordon. It also seems most unlikely, given the rather sad circumstances of his life, that he ever had any money to bet with.

What we do know is that, as well as knowing an awful lot about trees, Kendall spent much of his working life in the saddle, so we can assume that he was a poet who knew something about horses and he obviously knew a bit about racing.

It is hard to imagine a poet like Lesbia Harford knowing much about horses, however, let alone being a regular follower of racing.

Born in Melbourne in 1891 she suffered from a congenital heart defect and later from tuberculosis. Neither ailment stopped her graduating in law in 1916 from Melbourne University (oddly enough, in the same class as Robert Menzies) at a time when women rarely achieved such things. Lesbia was a free thinker and radical, an active socialist, pacifist and champion of working women. She worked in factories and sweat shops and wrote excellent poetry without ever bothering to have any published. Her short but fascinating life ended when she succumbed to tuberculosis in 1927, aged 36.

Lesbia Harford was certainly a wonderful poet, but hardly the type of person to study a form guide or be seen in a marquee during spring carnival social events.

Nevertheless, she was Melbourne born and bred, and that was enough for her to take the time to write at least one poem about the Melbourne Cup.

## The Melbourne Cup

### Lesbia Harford

I like the riders
Clad in rose and blue;
Their colours glitter
And their horses too.

Swift go the riders
On incarnate speed.
My thought can scarcely
Follow where they lead.

Delicate, strong, long
Lines of colour flow,
And all the people
Tremble as they go.

222

# Bart: The King of Cups

## BRUCE MONTGOMERIE

AUSTRALIA ALMOST LOST LEGENDARY Melbourne Cup trainer Bart Cummings before he ever trained a horse.

When he was 11, in 1939, Bart almost drowned while swimming off the jetty at Adelaide's famous Glenelg Beach.

He was going under for the third time when he was rescued by his 12-year-old schoolmate, Brendan O'Grady, the son of a local barber.

Brendan received a commendation from the Royal Humane Society of Australasia for his heroic action. If it hadn't been for his alertness and bravery, history would have been robbed of an iconic Aussie character—and arguably the greatest racehorse trainer this country has ever produced.

James Bartholomew Cummings became known to us all as 'Bart' because he shared his father's first name and the family used his middle name for convenience.

'J.B.' did it tough in his early days as a trainer and struggled to make a living for himself and his family. His perseverance, patience and uncanny knack of 'knowing good horses when he saw them' eventually made him a legend.

There are three factors which made Bart the 'Cups King', with an unprecedented 12 Melbourne Cup wins over a period of 44 years.

Firstly, there is his understanding of training for stamina. Secondly, his amazing knack of timing horses' campaigns. Lastly, his dedication to the welfare of his horses.

If you count Bart's involvement as strapper of 1950 winner Comic Court, he has been involved in 13 Cup wins over a 60-year period. Now, that's a feat that will surely never be repeated. And, he's not finished . . .

Bart Cummings came from hardy stock. His grandfather, Thomas Cummins, was a ploughman by profession. Born in 1828, Thomas migrated from Ireland to South Australia on the sailing ship *Empanadas* and arrived on Christmas Day 1853.

Thomas Cummins changed his surname to 'Cummings' on arrival and settled in the desolate South Australian hamlet of Eurelia, 280 kilometres north of Adelaide. At least he was now ploughing his own land, although it was rather barren land much of the time.

Bart's father, Jim, was one of six sons Thomas and his wife brought up on the drought-stricken pastoral land in the north of South Australia.

Following two bad years, which included a cyclone, dust storms and thunderstorms, young Jim had had enough of Eurelia and, leaving his parents' farm behind, he braved the unforgiving heat and trekked to Alice Springs to work for his bachelor uncle, James, who needed help running his large station, Granite Downs, at Ellery Creek.

Jim got precious little in return for all the hard work on his uncle's property, but he took to handling and riding horses naturally and was quick to make his name as a rider. Jim also worked as a relief driver on the famous Birdsville mail coach, driving the section between Bloods Creek and Alice Springs.

Jim's first major victory as a jockey came when he won the 1898 Alice Springs Cup on an aged mare named Myrtle, owned and trained by his uncle.

Fed up with conditions on his uncle's property, Jim took up his uncle's offer to take on Myrtle if he won the race. He took Myrtle, a gelding called Radamantos and an old stock horse, and headed south on the long and arduous 1720-kilometre ride back to Adelaide.

This was a truly amazing feat on its own, but two weeks after arriving at Jamestown he had Myrtle fit enough to win the local cup. It was the first official success for Jim Cummings as a trainer— and the beginning of the Cummings training dynasty.

Settling in Glenelg, Jim went on to set a record by training the winners of every classic race in South Australia and training winners in every state except Queensland.

By the time Bart Cummings was born on 4 November 1927 his father was established as South Australia's top trainer. Young Bart worked around the stables and had various jobs away from home while his father allowed him to find his own feet and make his own decisions about life.

As a child Bart fancied himself as a jockey and used to practise his riding skills on Cushla, a brilliant galloper who won nine races for Jim Cummings. She was a docile mare and helped teach the nine-year-old Bart Cummings to ride.

Bart has been allergy-prone since childhood, and has suffered from asthma all his life. When he was 16 an Adelaide specialist diagnosed him as being allergic to horses and chaff. The doctor's advice to stay away from both was advice Bart never heeded.

By 1947, at age 19, he was a registered strapper with the South Australian Jockey Club and worked for his father for £2 a week and his keep.

★

Jim's best racehorse, Comic Court, was to steer Bart Cummings on the path to becoming a trainer.

Bart was Comic Court's usual strapper at race meetings and he often rode him at trackwork.

Comic Court had failed in his first two attempts in the Melbourne Cup, finishing fourth as a three-year-old in the 1948 Melbourne Cup and 20th as 7 to 4 second favourite in 1949.

Experts then considered Comic Court suspect at 2 miles, although he was bred to stay the distance, by Powerscourt out of Witty Maid, who was a grand-daughter of Comedy King. He had multiple St Simon bloodlines on both sides of his pedigree, and the experts were proved wrong when Jim Cummings produced the five-year-old to win the 1950 Melbourne Cup.

Jim had owned Comic Court's sire and dam, Powerscourt and Witty Maid. However, when racing was banned in South Australia during the war, Jim Cummings took up temporary residence in Victoria and sold both of them to the Bowyer brothers, who bred four classic winning horses from them.

Comic Court was foaled in 1945 and given to Jim to train.

The 22-year-old Bart was the strapper for Comic Court's Melbourne Cup win and, as he led the horse back to the winner's stall, he daydreamed for the first time about training his own Melbourne Cup winner.

About this time Jim Cummings was spending more time in Melbourne than Adelaide, and young Bart was often left in charge of his father's home stables. Such responsibility was perfect grooming for the future champion trainer.

Still, Bart Cummings took no steps towards becoming a trainer until a decision by the South Australian Jockey Club forced him to take out a training licence. When his father went to Ireland for six months and wanted to leave Bart in charge of his team, the SAJC told Bart he would have to take out a training licence.

Bart took up training permanently in May 1953. He was given the bottom set of stables at his father's Glenelg complex and a couple of horses, one of which was the Port Adelaide Cup winner, Welloch.

Bart's first city winner was Wells, which won the SAJC Devon Transition Handicap (6 furlongs) at Morphettville on 12 February 1955.

Three years later Stormy Passage gave Bart his first feature win in the city by taking out the 1958 South Australian Derby at Morphettville.

Bart's first weight-for-age winner came in the VATC Underwood Stakes (10 furlongs) at Caulfield when the unfancied Trellios beat the favourite, Lord, by half a length.

The future 'Cups King' had an inauspicious start to his Melbourne Cup career when his first runner, Asian Court, at 40 to 1, finished 12th in 1958.

Bart's first Melbourne Cup success came with a quinella seven years later, at his fourth attempt, in 1965, when one of his favourite horses, Light Fingers, won and another of his runners, Ziema, finished second.

Bart spotted Light Fingers as a yearling at Pirongia Stud in New Zealand. He did not think the foal was much to look at but as she took off across the paddock it was a different story. As soon as he saw her move Bart said he noticed the mighty stride of a natural galloper.

'She had tremendous will to win and would strain every limb in her body to do so,' Bart recalled.

Light Fingers almost missed the Cup in 1965. In the Caulfield Stakes she clipped the heels of Winfreux and almost fell, causing her to rick a muscle in her shoulder. It looked like the end of her spring campaign and she was forced to miss the Caulfield Cup, but the magic of Bart Cummings had her ready to run on the first Tuesday in November.

Bart had three runners in the 1965 Melbourne Cup: the big, tough stayer Ziema, another hardened character The Dip (winner of the AJC Metropolitan Handicap), and Light Fingers. It looked like Ziema would take the Cup until Light Fingers emerged from the pack to challenge. The tiny chestnut mare and the big black gelding went to the line locked together and Light Fingers won by a lip.

Light Fingers was raced on lease by Melbourne grain merchant, Wally Broderick, who owned her older full brother, The Dip. The two were well named, being by the French stallion Le Filou, which translates as 'pickpocket'. 'Dip' is an old Aussie slang term for just that, a pickpocket. Light Fingers's name was clever and an obvious choice as a full sister to The Dip.

Light Fingers was originally named Close Embrace by her owners, the Dawson family. This name came from her female lineage; her dam, grand-dam and great-grand-dam raced as Cuddlesome, Fondle and Caress. Wally Broderick preferred the name to come from the sire's side to match her full brother, and re-registered her before she raced in his famous colours of white with royal blue spots and cap.

Bart then went on to chalk up three Melbourne Cups in a row, with Galilee and Light Fingers adding another quinella in the 1966 race and Red Handed winning in 1967.

Bart's second quinella in the race saw the owners of the unlucky Ziema, the Baileys, win with Galilee; while it was Wally Broderick's turn to finish second, again with little Light Fingers.

Galilee was an astute buy 12 months before Bart's first Cup win with Light Fingers. His success on the track is an example of Bart's eagle eye and training ability.

Galilee threw his offside front leg out at a 45-degree angle, which produced an awkward, almost laughable, gait; but Bart noticed that Galilee was not knock-kneed but pigeon-toed, and that he actually put his hooves down perfectly. Good training and shoeing could overcome the condition. The Baileys trusted Bart and consequently won the Melbourne Cup in 1966 after going within a whisker the year before with Ziema.

★

In the spring of 1966 Galilee had an arthritic condition, and as the rumour spread he drifted from 6 to 1 to 14 to 1 for the Caulfield Cup. However, there was no indication of soreness when Galilee unleashed his withering finish to beat Gala Crest by a length and a half to give Bart his first Caulfield Cup victory.

Bart attacked the 1966 Melbourne Cup with two starters: Galilee and Light Fingers. Bart brought Light Fingers to Melbourne rather short of condition, with only four lead-up runs in which she had been second twice and third once.

Once again history was made when Bart became the first trainer to quinella the Melbourne Cup twice. With little more than a furlong to run Light Fingers stormed to the front. For a moment it seemed she would triumph until Bart's better-conditioned runner, Galilee, breezed past her for an easy 2-length win.

Galilee was a champion. He became the first racehorse since Even Stevens in 1962 to win the Caulfield–Melbourne Cup double and was recognised as the best horse in Australia since Tulloch.

'Not only is Cummings the man of the moment but also at least the racing man of the decade,' one newspaper claimed. 'His Cups win climaxed a run of successes, as no other Australian horse trainer has known.'

Cummings's success in major races surpassed even that of Sydney's Tommy Smith, who had broken almost every training record.

Racing historians were astounded at Bart's feat of claiming the Caulfield, Melbourne and Sydney Cups with Galilee. In more than a century no trainer had prepared one horse to win that hat-trick.

Bart's most astonishing, and highly profitable, 1966–67 season, with a small but strong team of horses, set a Commonwealth training record—winning $358,918 in stakes money.

Bart finished the season with seven cups to his credit. He had quinellaed the Melbourne and Adelaide Cups, and won the Caulfield, Sandown, Sydney, Brisbane and Queens Cups. It was one of the most sensational training performances in Australian racing history, a record that may never be equalled.

No man had trained three Cup winners on the trot. But soon

after Galilee won the 1966 Melbourne Cup Bart forecast he had another 'good thing'. He announced that Red Handed would win the 1967 Melbourne Cup.

Again Bart's expert knowledge of horses stood him in good stead when he had settled for an 'ugly duckling' chestnut colt by Le Filou, lot 202 at the 1963 New Zealand yearling sales.

Bart had tried to prepare Red Handed for Galilee's 1966 Melbourne Cup but then, as a four-year-old, he fell in the Geelong Cup in October, breaking a bone in the near hock, which ruled him out of the Cup. It was only with careful nursing and skilled veterinary care that the chestnut stayer was brought back to racing ten months later.

Red Handed was a frail-looking, plain customer.

Few people noticed that Red Handed almost fell in the straight the first time around in the 1967 Melbourne Cup while travelling wide and looking for a position. He was well back in the field for most of the race but hit the front 400 metres from home. With 100 metres to go he seemed beaten when Red Crest passed him and forged clear. However, Red Handed fought back, drew closer with each stride and went on to win by a neck.

Bart had become the first trainer in the 107-year history of the Melbourne Cup to train three successive winners of the race. The normally unflappable, deadpan trainer admitted Galilee had given him a big thrill when he won in 1966, but said the pleasure was far greater when Red Handed completed the hat-trick. It was also the first time Bart's stable colours—the now-famous green and gold diagonal stripes with a white cap—had been carried to Melbourne Cup Victory.

Bart's third Melbourne Cup had come along just when some people were saying his luck had run out and he owed his success in 1965 and 1966 to two horses 'anyone could have trained'.

Red Handed's win was a typical example of Bart's earnest pursuit of perfection—patience and care, attention to detail, homework and hard work have always been essential to the Bart Cummings style of training.

Bart claims he does not believe in luck, but he admitted he gave Red Handed a helping hand by using Light Fingers's bridle on him in the 1967 Melbourne Cup.

By Melbourne Cup time the following spring Bart had trained plenty of winners, but his four runners in the Flemington marathon were all beaten out of the placings. It was the first time in four years he had failed to get a winner or a placed horse.

'I don't suppose a man can go on expecting to train the Melbourne Cup winner year after year,' he philosophised laconically.

Bart opened a permanent stable in Melbourne during 1968 with enough space for 60 boxes. Since 1965 he had been making two raids a year on Melbourne's rich purses, and the new set-up was his first step in his plan to become the first trainer to operate self-contained stables in three capital cities: Adelaide, Melbourne and Sydney.

By the late 1960s Bart was getting among the big prize money just as he planned. He was soon to feature in one of the most stunning incidents in the history of the turf in Australia.

Leading up to the 1969 Melbourne Cup Bart had four acceptors in the big race: Big Philou, Swift General, General Command and The Sharper. The first of a series of sensations occurred when Big Philou was beaten into second place by Nausori in the Caulfield Cup. Cummings entered a protest against Nausori, which was upheld. For only the second time in the history of the Caulfield Cup, the result was altered by the stewards to place Big Philou first.

Big Philou was to be withdrawn suddenly, just 45 minutes before the start of the 1969 Melbourne Cup. Bart noticed the horse scouring profusely in his stall and advised the stewards that the horse was distressed. It was one of the most sensational dramas in Cup history.

Big Philou had been nobbled, and the repercussions dragged on for more than a year. After receiving the result of the urine samples and droppings taken from Big Philou, it was discovered that the gelding had been administered a drug called Danthron.

Bart did not know how Big Philou had been 'got at'. VRC stewards swabbed 14 of Bart's horses between November 1969 and August 1970 but all swabs returned negative findings.

In 1974 Bart was involved in a battle with Tommy Smith to become the first Australian to train horses to win more than 1 million dollars in stakes money before the season ended on 31 July.

On 17 June Bart pipped Tommy to reach the million-dollar mark. Bart picked up $200 in the first race at Caulfield when Lady Antoinette finished fourth, and even though Hello Honey was unlucky to finish second in the Birthday Handicap at Warwick Farm, the $1200 prize money she won did the trick. His runners went on to earn $12,250 in four starts—Eagle Farm, Warwick Farm, Caulfield and Victoria Park—that day, giving him a total of $1,011,252 for the season.

Bart had few better years than 1974. His stable took $272,360 over four days at the Melbourne Cup Carnival at Flemington, winning a staggering $432,430 from the time the Carnival opened with the Caulfield Guineas on October 12. His nine winners and a dead heat in the four days of the Melbourne Cup meeting were a training record for Victoria.

In 1974 Bart spearheaded his effort to win his first Melbourne Cup since 1967 with the great mare Leilani and the aptly named Think Big.

Leilani was easily his highest stakes-winner, with $143,550 from wins in the Toorak Handicap, Caulfield Cup, Mackinnon Stakes and Queens Cup. Astonishingly, Bart was to quinella the 1974 Melbourne Cup with horses he had cleverly acquired in 1972.

The trainer with a special eye for stayers had taken a chance at the New Zealand sales on a good-looking yearling and made the successful $10,000 bid. This on-the-spot decision was to prove as astute as his choice of Light Fingers, Galilee and Red Handed in previous years.

On Bart's arrival back in Australia, a Malaysian banker and property developer, Dato Tan Chin Nam, from Kuala Lumpur, asked him to buy a horse, preferably a stayer, and Bart suggested Think

Big. At the same time as he bought Think Big he liked the look of a filly by Oncidium from the good race mare Lei. Bart snapped her up on lease and registered her as Leilani.

Leilani became the 11th mare in history to win the Caulfield Cup, giving Bart his third victory in the race. Her Caulfield Cup win had been so convincing that she became a short-priced favourite to win the 1974 Melbourne Cup.

On the other hand, Think Big's 1974 Melbourne Cup campaign was unimpressive. He finished last in the AJC Metropolitan at Randwick on 7 October, failed in the Coongy Handicap at Caulfield on 16 October on a heavy track and was eighth in the Moonee Valley Cup on 26 October.

It rained heavily on the morning of the Melbourne Cup, but the track was still officially 'good' and Leilani was made 7 to 2 favourite.

Leilani loomed into contention in the straight and appeared to have the Melbourne Cup in her keeping until Think Big wound up and charged home to win by three-quarters of a length. Think Big had given the trainer his fourth Melbourne Cup, and with Leilani's second placing he had managed to quinella the race for the third time.

In May 1975 Bart shifted to new AJC stables at Randwick Racecourse and named the yard 'Leilani Lodge'. In June that year he chalked up his 13th Derby victory when Bottled Sunshine won the Queensland Derby.

During the 1974–75 season horses trained by Bart earned $1,399,182 in five states, creating another Australian record. The Cummings magic carried on into the 1975–76 season, and Bart approached the 1975 Melbourne Cup with three chances: Holiday Waggon, Leica Lover and Think Big.

Bart was confident of winning his fifth Melbourne Cup with either Leica Lover or Think Big. Think Big had again been unimpressive in lead-up races, beating only one horse home in the Mackinnon Stakes.

With 100 metres to go in the Cup Think Big grabbed the lead and the only challenge came from his stablemate, Holiday

Waggon, who tried hard before finishing three-quarters of a length away second. Think Big knew only one thing—how to stay. It was another Melbourne Cup quinella and Bart's fifth Melbourne Cup, making him the first man to achieve five Cup wins in the 20th century.

Think Big never won another race in 19 starts. Bart was preparing the six-year-old for a tilt at the 1976 Melbourne Cup when the gelding broke down and was retired.

Bart had 30 horses entered for the 1976 Melbourne Cup, but his only runner come post time was Gold And Black. All eyes were on Bart's runner but a freak deluge—5 inches (12 cm) of rain accompanied by lightning and thunder just 30 minutes before the start of the Cup—had punters rushing to back the New Zealand mudlark, Van Der Hum, into 9 to 2 favouritism.

Van Der Hum surged through the slush to score by 2 lengths from Gold And Black.

In 1977 Bart's chances of winning the Melbourne Cup were boosted when Gold And Black zoomed home for a half-length second in the Mackinnon Stakes.

The galloper was in line to become the first racehorse in the 20th century to win a Melbourne Cup after being runner-up the previous year. Punters were not convinced and allowed Gold And Black to drift to 11 to 2 in the betting.

Gold And Black and Reckless, trained by Phar Lap's legendary strapper Tommy Woodcock, were destined to fight out the 1977 Melbourne Cup, with Gold And Black finishing just the stronger.

In claiming the race Bart had become the first trainer in history to prepare six Melbourne Cup winners.

He had now won six Melbourne Cups and also had five seconds, two fourths, a fifth and two sixths from the 32 runners he had started in 15 Melbourne Cups since 1958. No wonder he was being called the Cups King.

Bart's four starters in 1978—Panamint, Vive Velours, Belmura Lad and Stormy Rex—did nothing to add to the legend, with Panamint at tenth the closest of the four at the finish.

In 1979 it was an older horse with leg problems, the 1977 Melbourne Cup placegetter, Hyperno, that was to add the next chapter to the legend.

The Cups King was at first reluctant to take on the horse, reasoning that it was hard enough to win races with sound horses, let alone with unsound ones. But Bart's methods suited Hyperno, who responded to the trainer's patient care even though his legs swelled badly after running in the Toorak Handicap of 1978.

On the Tuesday before the 1979 Melbourne Cup, Bart trialled the problem horse in blinkers and the gallop pleased him enough to believe he had another Cup winner. Hyperno went on to give the maestro his seventh Melbourne Cup. Hyperno's win also put paid to any suggestions that Bart had lost his touch.

Bart quinellaed the 1980 Caulfield Cup with Ming Dynasty and Hyperno but failed to get a placegetter in the Melbourne Cup, with Ming Dynasty finishing 17th.

Bart was awarded an Order of Australia for his services to horseracing in 1982, an honour for both him and his industry. It seemed that springtime in Melbourne belonged to Bart Cummings. His record of seven Melbourne Cups seemed destined to remain intact for years to come.

Between 1979 and 1986, however, Bart's Cups fortunes slumped and his only placing was Mr Jazz—third in 1983.

Bart finished the 1985–86 season 11th on the Sydney trainers' list, the lowest he had been since opening his Sydney stable, and the 'knockers' were out again. 'They' said he was not putting enough effort into his horses and he was washed up as a trainer.

Unbelievably, in 1989, Bart found himself faced with a debt of more than $22 million when an ambitious syndication scheme he had hoped to get off the ground that year failed during an economic recession and he was left to pay for more than 80 yearlings.

Despite all his problems Bart won the 1989–90 Sydney trainers' premiership—his first in that city—and finished the season with six Group 1 wins, second to Colin Hayes with 13. However, Bart did not have a runner in the 1989 Melbourne Cup.

When 1990 rolled around, Bart had not prepared a winner of the Melbourne Cup for a decade, since Hyperno in 1979.

Bart put that decade of Melbourne Cup failures behind him in decisive fashion when he trained the 7 to 1 favourite, Kingston Rule, to win in 1990, and made it two in a row when Let's Elope won in 1991, with Shiva's Revenge finishing second to give him his fifth quinella in the race.

Let's Elope was the first mare to take the Caulfield–Melbourne Cups double since Rivette in 1939. Let's Elope was a duffer on rain-affected ground and, luckily for Bart, the spring of 1991 and the autumn of 1992 were seasons of fine, dry weather. The mare began a seven-race winning streak with the Turnbull Stakes in October, taking both Cups, and the Mackinnon, and returned in the new year to take the Orr Stakes, St George Stakes and Australian Cup, in course record time.

Bart had achieved what no other trainer had done. He had now won eight Melbourne Cups. Was there any stopping him from continuing to dominate the legendary staying event? He was certainly making it his race. Surely at his age he could not win another one!

Then, in 1996, along came a mighty stayer named Saintly. Darren Beadman wore the now-famous Dato Tan Chin Nam colours—black and white check with yellow sleeves—that day in November. It seems the born-again jockey sang a few hymns to the aptly named Saintly as they left the rest of the Melbourne Cup field in their wake. That was Cup number ten.

A new method of discovering ulcers in horses helped Western Australian galloper Rogan Josh to win the Melbourne Cup in 1999, giving J.B. Cummings his 11th Melbourne Cup winner in the process.

Bart was the first to use a video gastro-endoscope machine which offered a way of checking for ulcers in a horse's stomach. He used the process to sort out the health problems suffered by Rogan Josh and guided the gelding to a famous Cup victory.

In racing, fortunes are bound to fluctuate over time and even champion trainers have lean spells. Bart's top race wins dried up during the 2000–01 season in what was the start one of his worst losing patches.

The Cups King went 12 months without a Group 1 winner and did not even have a runner in the 2000 Melbourne Cup. He had six Melbourne Cup hopes—Crown Mahal, Matriculate, Philidor, Indian Ridge, Darne Cath and Ringleader—start in the Saab Quality in an effort to qualify one or two of them in the 2000 Melbourne Cup through a win or second placing, but they all failed to run a place. The closest he came to having a runner in the Cup that year was with Philidor, who had qualified 36th, and Matriculate, who had been 27th in order of entry in the race.

Going into his 2002 Melbourne Cup campaign, Bart had only one Group 1 victory for the season.

The fickle punters were quick to write Cummings off, suggesting that he had passed his best and age was catching up with him. He failed to have a placegetter in the Melbourne Cup between 2001 and 2007. Despite Bart's apparent rise to glory again with Rogan Josh in 1999 it wasn't proving to be another golden era.

It was during the 2002 Melbourne Spring Carnival that Bart claimed all the overseas gallopers coming to Australia were making it difficult for local trainers to get a start in the Melbourne Cup. These comments were misconstrued as sour grapes in some quarters. What Bart really feared was that Australasian breeders and owners were not bothering to breed good stayers and keep them in training.

Bart was thankful for more support from his old friend, Dato Tan, when the 2008 Melbourne Cup approached. The two were now 'old men', and many saw both as dinosaurs of the turf. But Dato Tan owned the middle-distance galloper Viewed and Bart saw the chance to make him a Cup horse.

How could you bet on Viewed? He came into the race with a reputation as a wet tracker and the form in his four starts leading up to the Melbourne Cup read eighth of 15 at Flemington, seventh of 13, tenth of 17 in the Caulfield Cup, and last of 11 in the LKS Mackinnon Stakes.

Viewed went out at 40 to 1 and was supported by only the most loyal followers of J.B. Cummings. He hit the front at the 350-metre mark in the Melbourne Cup and was 2 lengths clear with 200 metres to run. When he began to tire with 100 metres to go, his 21-year-old jockey, Blake Shinn, thought he had gone too early.

Shinn said he could hear the Luca Cumani–trained Bauer closing in. Many thought the grey import had snatched victory but Bauer died slightly on his run as he closed rapidly and just failed to run out the final few metres to the finishing post.

The crowd roared as the English invader drew closer and the gap narrowed. For Bart it was an odd déjà vu, almost a carbon copy of the 1965 Melbourne Cup when his first Cup winner, Light Fingers, won by the narrowest of margins from stablemate Ziema. This time, however, the rival was an overseas horse, not a stablemate.

This made victory all that much sweeter for the two old friends, Dato Tan Chin Nam and Bart Cummings, both in their 80s.

After Viewed and Bauer crossed the line together and the agonising wait was over, the photo finish gave Viewed the race by a whisker.

The Cup eluded Bart in 2009, although he dominated the Spring Carnivals across Australia with an amazing run of wins in Group 1 races; including the Cox Plate and the AJC Derby, to take his tally of Group 1 wins to 257, more than double that of second-placed contemporary trainer Lee Freedman.

Bart has nothing else to achieve. He was inducted into the Sport Australia Hall of Fame in 1991, was an inaugural inductee into the Australian Racing Hall of Fame and has since been elevated to the status of Legend—and the only other Legend is Phar Lap.

Bart had his face placed on a postage stamp in 2007 and shared the *Weekend Australian's* 2008 'Australian of the Year' Honour with the 99-year-old Dame Elizabeth Murdoch.

The only active racing trainer to be given life membership by the Victorian Racing Club, Bart claims he has no plans to retire at age 82.

Since taking out his trainer's licence in Adelaide in 1953, J.B. Cummings has revolutionised Australian racing with his complete dominance of Australia's most famous race.

Bart's record of Melbourne Cup wins is similar to Don Bradman's amazing batting record. Neither are ever likely to be broken—unless Bart wins the race again.

Italian-born Luca Cumani, one of Britain's leading trainers, and the man whose horse Bart's nosed out in the Cup of 2009, paid his rival the ultimate compliment after the race: 'His record is amazing because I know how hard it is to win a Melbourne Cup. He is a special man . . . He is the greatest trainer in the world.'

## Bart's Melbourne Cup record

- 81 runners, 12 winners, 9 placegetters
- 15 per cent strike rate win, 11 per cent strike rate place, 26 per cent strike rate win/place
- 5 quinellas

# Here's a stayer: The magic of Peter Pan

## JIM HAYNES

'HERE'S A STAYER!'

These were the words Frank McGrath said to his stable foreman when he first set eyes on the flashy chestnut Peter Pan.

It was a summer's day in 1932 when Peter Pan arrived at Frank McGrath's stables near Randwick racetrack. The leggy chestnut with the silver mane and tail was already well into his two-year-old season when he arrived at the stables of the man renowned as a trainer of stayers.

McGrath had trained Prince Foote to win the Melbourne Cup in 1909 and Peter Pan's owner, Rodney Dangar, thought the astute and patient trainer would be just the man to get the best out of his beautiful colt.

Dangar was a patient man himself. He had left Peter Pan to gallop and grow in the paddock, at his family property near Singleton, New South Wales, well past the time when most promising thoroughbreds would be shipped off to training stables. He was happy to send his staying prospect to a trainer of the old school, a man who had won his only Melbourne Cup more than two decades before.

Peter Pan was the result of one of those 'happy chance' matings, a friendly gesture that was actually a last-minute afterthought on the part of Dangar's neighbour Percy Brown.

Brown had booked five mares to go to the imported stallion Pantheon. Pantheon had been imported from Britain to race in Australia and was a very good stayer. His eight wins included the Rosehill Cup, the CB Fisher Plate and two AJC Randwick Plates over 2 miles. He started favourite at 9 to 4 in the 1926 Melbourne Cup and finished third, ridden by the famous Jim Pike. He was placed a further 18 times, giving him a good record for a stayer of 27 wins and placings from 34 starts.

Percy Brown had negotiated a good discount deal to send five mares to Pantheon in his first season at stud. However, when the time came to despatch the mares, he only had four available, so he crossed the road and asked his neighbour if he had a mare to make up the number.

Dangar had an unraced mare named Alwina, whose sire St Alwyne had also sired Melbourne Cup winners Poitrel and Night Watch. He'd bought the mare from the famous Arrowfield Stud for £210 and had no immediate plans for her when Percy Brown called in. He pointed to her in the paddock and said, 'Take that one'.

So, without any real planning, two great staying bloodlines converged to produce a horse that many believe was certainly the prettiest horse to ever win a Melbourne Cup.

Frank McGrath was impressed by the colt's good looks too, but he was more impressed by his solid proportions and strong, clean-cut stayer's legs. He began training him as a stayer and didn't even start him in a race until four months later, in May 1932. The fact that the chestnut was unplaced in a two-year-old handicap at Randwick didn't seem to bother McGrath one bit. He immediately sent him for a spell, and that was Peter Pan's entire two-year-old campaign—one race, unplaced.

The horse managed to run a nail through a hoof and McGrath had to help him overcome an infection and nurse him back to fitness before he could return to training in the spring. This delayed plans a little but didn't stop Peter Pan being the well-backed favourite at 5 to 2 in only his second start in a race, first-up, over a mile in a novice handicap at Warwick Farm.

It was stable money that brought the price in to 5 to 2; the colt had run sensational times at trackwork and Frank McGrath said he thought he had 'the best thing ever on a racetrack'.

What the astute trainer had forgotten was that Peter Pan had only ever raced once in a field of horses and once in front of a crowd. This almost brought the well-laid plan undone, as the colt stopped racing whenever the other horses got close around him. In desperation jockey Andy Knox took him to the outside, only to have the inquisitive colt turn and stare at the yelling crowd.

Knox eventually managed to straighten the flashy youngster and he raced home to dead-heat for first with the runaway leader, Babili. This at least saved the stable from embarrassment, not to mention the trainer's bank balance.

It is remarkable to realise that Peter Pan's next start in a race, his third in the Rosehill Stakes over a mile, saw the raw young colt pitted against the Melbourne Cup winner Nightmarch, the Sydney Cup winner Johnny Jason, and Veilmond, the winner of the ARJ and VRC St Legers.

Peter Pan may have been a raw young colt, but he was good enough to defeat the Melbourne Cup winner by half a length, with the Sydney Cup winner behind them in third place.

Two weeks later, in only his fourth start in a race, Peter Pan contested the AJC Derby. Ridden for the first time by Jim Pike, who had ridden his father into third place in the Melbourne Cup six years earlier, Peter Pan won, easing down by a length and a half. Behind him were such good horses as the Chelmsford Stakes winner, and famed stayer in later life, Gaine Carrington, the AJC and VRC Sires' Produce winner Kuvera, and Oro, who would later win a Metropolitan Handicap.

By now Frank McGrath was not the only one looking at the pretty horse and thinking, 'Here's a stayer'. Peter Pan was backed in at 7 to 2 to win the Caulfield Cup at his fifth start.

Andy Knox was back in the saddle at Caulfield, as Jim Pike could not ride at the three-year-old's handicap weight of 46.5 kg. It was to be Knox's last ride on Peter Pan.

The golden horse with the silver mane and tail was still 'a big baby' in racing parlance and, displaying his often wayward behaviour once again, he missed the start badly. Andy Knox then raced him wide down the straight the first time round in order to catch the field and find a position, but the early sprint unsettled the horse and he pulled throughout the race and ran out of steam to finish fourth behind Rogilla, on raw talent, despite a dreadful run and a less than memorable ride.

It was a poor enough ride for Frank McGrath to sack Andy Knox and engage lightweight Melbourne jockey Bill Duncan to ride the horse in the Melbourne Stakes over 2000 metres on Derby Day.

Peter Pan had not been entered for the VRC Derby, so the Melbourne Stakes (now Mackinnon Stakes) was more or less a consolation prize for Frank McGrath. Missing the Derby was a regrettable oversight, but defeating Caulfield Cup winner Rogilla by a length to win the 10-furlong Melbourne Stakes race against all ages was certainly some 'consolation' for losing the Caulfield Cup a few weeks earlier.

It may have been a consolation, but it was also an impressive enough win for the betting public to send the Sydney colt out as 4 to 1 favourite for the Melbourne Cup, at his sixth start in a race.

But it wasn't only the racing crowd who were impressed by the horse. The flashy three-year-old chestnut was all the rage. He had captured the public imagination and was a popular favourite for the Cup. In fact his popularity rivalled that of Phar Lap, who had been favourite for the Cup for each of the previous three years, and it was as if the sporting public needed another hero to worship after Phar Lap's tragic demise in April that year. Australia was still in the grip of the Depression and people needed dreams and distractions; the golden colt with the film star looks and the silver mane was something to talk about, an equine Prince Charming with talent to match his looks.

Peter Pan was so popular that C.J. Dennis wrote a poem about the public's unerring faith in his ability to win the Cup. It was a parody of Adam Lindsay Gordon's famous verse 'How We Beat the Favourite'. Written in the same style and rhyme scheme it was called 'How We Backed The Favourite'. The poem begins:

'Sure thing,' said the grocer, 'as far as I know, sir,
This horse, Peter Pan, is the safest of certs.'

It goes on to tell how the general public all believed in Peter Pan, including 'the butcher . . . the baker, the barman, bookmaker, the old lady char and the saveloy man'.

Finally Dennis sees Peter Pan in the flesh and is convinced:

I went to the races, and I watched all their faces.
I saw Peter Pan's; there was little he lacked.
And as he seemed willing, I plancked on my shilling
And triumphed! And that's how the favourite was backed.

The public may have had faith in Peter Pan, but his Melbourne Cup victory as a three-year-old was as dramatic and fraught with possible disaster as any before or since.

At around the 5-furlong mark, the colt was 'pole-axed' when crowding on the outside led to a chain reaction, which caused him to stumble and fall. As he fell he was again hit as a second wave of interference swept through the field. This caused his stablemate, Denis Boy, to barrel into Peter Pan and, strange as it seems, this second impact pushed him back onto his feet and certainly prevented a bad fall.

Frank McGrath was so certain his horse had fallen that he lowered his field glasses in disgust. He later said, 'I saw his head go down and then there was a blank space where Peter Pan had been racing.' It wasn't until he heard the course broadcaster call his name in the straight that the trainer realised Peter Pan was still running.

Having recovered his momentum, the tough colt outstayed the field to win by a neck from Yarramba, ridden by sacked jockey Andy Knox. The perennial old Cup campaigner Shadow King was third and Denis Boy ran fourth.

The outpouring of joy from the crowd was incredible: hats flew into the air, men cheered and women shrieked. Everyone loved the happy ending to the Melbourne Cup—won by the people's horse with the fairytale name and the movie-star looks.

It was the sheer determination and patient care of two great men of the turf that won the day for Peter Pan in reality. Many good judges believe that no other jockey except the under-rated Bill Duncan could have kept the big colt on his feet that day; Duncan was a quiet man and a great jockey in an era of great jockeys.

Frank McGrath had not only nursed Peter Pan through a serious hoof infection, he had also shown patience and good judgement to get the horse to win a Melbourne Cup at his sixth race start. It is an indication of McGrath's patience and love of the horses in his care that Denis Boy, his other runner that day and the horse that helped keep Peter Pan upright, had actually been nursed back to racing fitness by McGrath after breaking a knee bone. McGrath persevered and had the horse's leg in a sling until the bone healed. He then trained Denis Boy to win the 1932 AJC Metropolitan Handicap and run fourth behind his more illustrious stablemate in the Melbourne Cup. This would be outstanding management today, let alone in McGrath's era.

The McGrath stable certainly had its share of drama when it came to Melbourne Cups. In 1940 an attempt was made to shoot his Cup favourite—the Cox Plate and Mackinnon winner Beau Vite—in his stall at Glenhuntly. The marksman managed to shoot another of McGrath's horses, El Golea, by mistake. Beau Vite ran fourth behind Old Rowley in the Cup that year and El Golea recovered to run third in the Mackinnon in 1941 and third in the Caulfield Cup in 1942.

Frank McGrath knew horses. He had been a good jockey and was a survivor of the infamous Caulfield Cup race fall of 1885, when 16 horses fell in a field of 41 and one jockey was killed and many injured. As a trainer he understood how to condition a horse and how to place horses to best advantage, but more than that, he was a trainer who cared for his horses. A trainer of the old school in many ways, Frank McGrath was 'modern' in the sense that he always put the horse's welfare first, and his plans were always long-term plans.

The Melbourne Cup victory earned Peter Pan a four-month holiday in the spelling paddock. McGrath wanted him primed for the autumn racing in Sydney. He then came out and won first-up at a mile at Randwick, once again defeating Rogilla.

At his next start his reputation for clumsiness and getting into trouble in races was given a boost when he became tangled in the starting tapes when favourite for the Rawson Stakes at Rosehill, and tailed the field home at 3 to 1 on.

Peter Pan was the big drawcard at the Sydney Autumn Carnival of 1933 and he took out three races in eight days: the St Leger, Cumberland Stakes and AJC Plate. The three-year-old was then handicapped at 9 st (57 kg), 12 pounds (5.4 kg) over weight for age, in the Sydney Cup—the same weight Carbine had carried, as a three-year-old, in 1889.

Frank McGrath told the handicapper times had changed since 1889 and no horse should be given such a weight at three years of age over 2 miles. He then protested in the most effective way possible by simply scratching his horse from the Sydney Cup and putting him aside to prepare for the Melbourne Cup of 1933.

Sadly, however, Peter Pan was to be absent from racetracks for 12 months. He had been handicapped at 9 st 7 lb (60.5 kg) for the Melbourne Cup of 1933 and McGrath thought that this was fair, being 7 pounds (3.2 kg) over weight for age for a four-year-old. However, when he returned from the spelling paddock he was found to be suffering from rheumatism in his shoulders. He was treated and left to recover naturally in the paddock, but he missed an entire year of racing—the bulk of his four-year-old season, normally a career 'prime time' for racehorses.

The golden horse of the previous Sydney Autumn Carnival resumed racing in March 1934 and took a while to get back to his peak. Unplaced over a mile at Randwick on 3 March, he improved to run a good second to old rival Rogilla two weeks later at Rosehill, but was unplaced a week later behind the mighty New Zealand mare Silver Scorn in the Chipping Norton Stakes at Warwick Farm.

Silver Scorn had won 12 races from 13 starts at three and was hot favourite for the AJC Autumn Plate a week after her Chipping Norton victory.

It seemed that Peter Pan had turned the corner, however, and was finding his old form under McGrath's patient training. He trounced Silver Scorn by 2½ lengths in the Autumn Plate and followed up that win with another in the 2-mile Cumberland Plate only four days later.

Just three days after that, Peter Pan was again the punter's favourite as Jim Pike took him out onto the track to run against a classy field, including his old foe Rogilla, in the 2400-metre Kings Cup.

Once again the big chestnut had another of his 'blond moments'. Nicknamed the 'Blond Bombshell', after sultry movie star Jean Harlow, Peter Pan was possibly the most beautiful horse that ever became a champion in Australia, but at times it was almost as if he had a touch of Three Stooges mayhem in his make-up.

Racing neck and neck with Rogilla, Peter Pan suddenly seemed to resent his old rival's persistence. Travelling flat-out, Peter Pan turned his head to bite Rogilla as they neared the winning post, and the terrified Rogilla stuck out his head to avoid the stallion's attack, and won the race by a head!

It certainly appeared that the great stayer had recovered from his crippling rheumatism, even if his manners had not been improved by the lengthy spell. That Autumn campaign had been his worst ever—six starts for two wins, two seconds and two unplaced runs—but Frank McGrath was satisfied the horse was back to his old self, and promptly spelled him to await the Spring Carnivals.

Perhaps the 'Blond Bombshell' knew the score between himself and his rival when he delivered the 'lovebite' to Rogilla. The tactic certainly cost Peter Pan victory in the Kings Cup and it didn't scare off Rogilla effectively either; Peter Pan finished second to him again when he resumed racing in the Chelmsford Stakes in the spring of 1934. So, unfortunately for our chestnut hero, it was not a case of 'once bitten, twice shy'.

Frank McGrath then made a tactical move that confounded the critics. He entered Peter Pan in a 7-furlong sprint race, against the mighty Chatham, at the Victoria Park racetrack. Victoria Park is now a housing estate beside busy Southern Cross Drive near Moore Park, but it was once a beautiful showpiece proprietory racecourse owned by racing entrepreneur Joynton-Smith, and rivalled Randwick as Sydney's premier racetrack in its heyday.

A huge crowd flocked to see the 'Blond Bombshell' race against Chatham, who was the sprint and middle-distance champion of his era and started at 4 to 1 on.

But the canny McGrath had evidently seen something in his horse's behaviour that made him believe he could go against all racing commonsense and bring a stayer back from 9 furlongs to 7 at his second start in a campaign. As usual Frank McGrath's intuition was spot on—Peter Pan defeated the mighty sprinter and set a course record for 7 furlongs at Victoria Park.

Ten days later, Peter Pan was sent out favourite at odds-on in the AJC Spring Stakes at a mile and a half, only to be beaten by a head by his old nemesis Rogilla. This time Rogilla won fair and square, without the aid of a bite from the Blond Bombshell. That made it four times in a row that Peter Pan had finished second to Rogilla; perhaps the record-breaking sprint at Victoria Park had taken the edge off him.

Rogilla and the Blond Bombshell had now clashed ten times, with Rogilla winning on six occasions. Rogilla was a champion himself, a horse who won 26 races, including the Caulfield and Sydney Cups. He was never able to beat Peter Pan again, however, losing every one of his final seven clashes against the champion chestnut.

The Craven Plate over 10 furlongs looked like another match

race between Peter Pan and Rogilla. This time it was Chatham's time to turn the tables on Peter Pan. As Peter Pan, at 10 to 9, and Rogilla, at 6 to 4, engaged in their usual head-to-head struggle down the straight, Chatham, at 8 to 1, swept past them to win by a length.

The three clashed again, with Melbourne Cup winner of 1933, Hall Mark, in the Melbourne Stakes on the first day of the Spring Carnival at Flemington. Peter Pan carried 9 st 2 lb (58.5 kg) and ran his classy rivals off their legs to win easily.

Peter Pan had been alloted 9 st 10 lb (61.5 kg) for the Melbourne Cup, certainly a champion's weight. However, his win on the Saturday had convinced McGrath that the mighty horse was ready for another Cup win and the public were behind him also, making him equal early favourite at 5 to 1 despite his big weight. Then the weather conspired against the great horse.

The day before the Cup was run Melbourne turned on one of its worst rainstorms: it poured and poured all day and Cup Day saw grey skies and more rain on its way. The track was a swamp, all form was 'out the window' and Peter Pan, still suffering from his perennial rheumatism which always worsened in wet weather, and carrying over 61 kg, looked like a dead duck. Even the mug punters deserted the champion. He drifted alarmingly in the betting, out to 14 to 1.

With Jim Pike suspended, McGrath engaged Darby Munro to ride his champion in Melbourne. 'Demon' Darby was usually Rogilla's regular rider but he had ridden Peter Pan before and won on him in Sydney and in the Melbourne Stakes.

The Cup field was as good as you could imagine that year. It included the previous year's winner Hall Mark, Rogilla, dual Derby winner Theo, the great staying mare Sarcherie, and the winners of the Moonee Valley, Australian and Sydney Cups. The rain had made the surface a swamp and the result would surely be no more than a lottery of luck.

It was a gloomy scene in the saddling paddock, literally and metaphorically, as Frank McGrath legged Darby Munro onto the rheumatic five-year-old's back. All the trainer could think to say to the crack jockey as they looked at the bog track, made worse than ever by a day's racing, was, 'Don't worry, they all have to go through it.' They both knew the truth, however—they all didn't have to carry 9 stone 10! Perhaps the Blond Bombshell was truly a 'dead duck'.

As it transpired, however, Peter Pan turned out to be what racing people call 'a real duck'.

In what was a daring decision, Munro decided it was better for the champion stayer to run further on firmer ground than plough through puddles with 61.5 kg. He kept Peter Pan out wide all the way down the straight the first time and all around the course in the 2-mile marathon. At the turn he took the lead and raced away, still well off the fence, to defeat Sarcherie by 3 lengths slowing down, with La Trobe third.

Munro's daring ride had managed to keep Rodney Dangar's orange and green hooped silks cleaner than most, and he now had £5200 in prize money to help pay the cleaning bills.

Had Munro's bold move failed he would no doubt have copped a lot of criticism. As it turned out, the tactic paid off and Peter Pan did the rest, running as some said 'an extra furlong or two'. He was going so well in the running that Munro later told McGrath and others, 'I was sure we would win with half a mile to go.'

So Peter Pan went into the record books as only the second horse to win two Melbourne Cups, after Archer in 1861 and 1862.

As he seemed quite well after his marathon run in the mud on the Tuesday, Frank McGrath sent him around again on the Saturday, in the 14-furlong Duke of Gloucester Cup. Ridden again by Darby Munro, and carrying topweight of 9 st 7 lb (60.5 kg), he easily defeated Sydney Cup winner Broad Arrow.

All Sydney was waiting to see their glamorous history-making champion, so the horse was rushed back to Sydney to run in the Duke of Gloucester Plate 12 days later. He finished a tired sixth behind Oro and was sent for another of those therapeutic long spells his trainer was so keen on. No horse ever deserved a holiday more.

It is part of Cup mythology that horses who win the great race often achieve little else. This is true to an extent, moreso in the modern era when horses are more likely to be trained for one result only. It is also true that many horses who win the Cup are not true stayers, and the effort and training that goes into a Cup win leaves them with little left to win with again.

Peter Pan, however, makes a mockery of the myth.

His autumn campaign of 1935 saw the great horse, with Jim Pike back in the saddle, win five races from five starts. And they were not just any old races.

Conditioned and trained to perfection by the ever-astute Frank McGrath, Peter Pan won the Randwick Stakes, Rawson Stakes, Autumn Plate, All-Aged Stakes and Jubilee Cup in succession, between late March and early May.

Spelled again, he returned in the spring, as a six-year-old stallion, to take out another three from three: the Hill Stakes, Spring Stakes and Craven Plate. In the last two races his old foe Rogilla, unbitten and now a light of former days, finished third and fourth, respectively.

Peter Pan, too, was looking like a horse nearing the end of his career. In spite of being undefeated in his past eight starts, the chestnut warrior was suffering constantly from rheumatism and only McGrath's special care, patience and knowledge of the horse was keeping him fit. No trainer ever placed a horse to better advantage than Frank McGrath did with Peter Pan as a six-year-old.

The trainer suggested to Rodney Dangar that another Melbourne Cup campaign was beyond the champion. There were even rumours about the horse's health and McGrath, a trainer who always placed his horses' welfare above all else, had to suffer the ignominy of having the RSPCA visit his stables to inspect the popular hero. They found him to be in excellent condition, fit and happy and extremely well cared for.

What more was there for the champion to achieve? He was the best stayer ever to race in the modern era, he was as popular as Phar Lap had been, and he had done something no stayer had managed to do since 1862. He was the glamour horse with the quirky personality and the film star looks and he brightened up the mood of a nation during the Great Depression.

Dangar, however, was loath to scratch the horse from the Cup, as many people had invested money on the popular champion. In a compromise decision McGrath trained him for just two runs in Melbourne: the Melbourne Stakes and the Melbourne Cup.

Public sentiment saw the great stayer sent out an odds-on favourite in the Melbourne Stakes, but he finished unplaced and three days later, carrying a crippling 10 st 6 lb (66 kg), he ran in the Cup at 8 to 1, with many people backing him out of sentiment and respect, rather than commonsense.

Peter Pan finished a creditable 14th behind Marabou in the 1935 Cup. He possibly could have finished closer if ridden out hard in the straight but Jim Pike, who loved the horse as much as anyone, eased him down when he realised he had no chance of winning.

After a summer spell the champion looked as good as ever and it was decided to try one more campaign in the autumn of 1936. After an unplaced first-up run in the Randwick Stakes, the old Peter Pan emerged briefly and he ran a good second in the Rawson Stakes, and a creditable third to Sarcherie in the Autumn Plate at Randwick.

Frank McGrath knew the horse well enough to tell Rodney Dangar that enough was enough, and Peter Pan retired in April 1936 to prepare for a stud career.

He proved a reasonably successful sire, with Peter, from his first crop, winning the Williamstown Cup and Eclipse Stakes and a later son, Precept, winning the Victoria Derby.

Always his own worst enemy, the great stallion was prone to fits of madcap behaviour and coltish frolicking. In March 1941 he slipped over during one of these displays of hijinks and broke a leg so badly that he had to be confined in an attempt to heal the break. Sadly his high-spirited temperament was not amenable to confinement and the break was so bad that, after all efforts to save him had failed, he was put down.

There is a large photograph at Randwick of Peter Pan, entering the birdcage after one of his famous Randwick victories in 1934. It is located in the walkway between the Members' Stand and the betting ring and you pass it as you make your way back to the ring after each race.

We don't have many real staying races these days; it's all about what Banjo Paterson called 'your six-furlong vermin that scamper half-a-mile with a feather-weight up'. Staying these days is an art left mostly to dour old has-beens and overseas imports.

Often, after I have backed some poor excuse for a stayer in some weak midweek staying race, I walk back to the ring despondent and pause in front of the photo of the beautiful chestnut.

To anyone unlucky enough to be with me at the races that day I say, 'Hey, come here a minute and look at this horse in the photo—here's a stayer.'

# Cup casualties

## C.J. DENNIS

'A MAN CAN NEVER TELL.' This, I find, is a favourite phrase in the mouths of Australian sportsmen who 'follow the game' more or less as a regular habit. It indicates a mildly philosophic mental attitude that is commendable, and a state of fitting humility before the gods. A man—a mere man—never can tell.

I commend the sentence now to the notice of those countless thousands of amateur sportsmen who, shortly after the publication of these words, will be suffering all the slings and arrows of a faith betrayed, and bearing fardels of confidence misplaced.

I refer to those myriads who backed a loser in the race for the Melbourne Cup.

But who would fardels bear when the slogan of the true sport is available to all as a solace and a shield against the barbs of vain regret? 'A man can never tell.'

Yet those doleful losers, even at the moment, possibly, when these lines swim into their ken, are already imagining vain things and painting in absurdly glowing colours ridiculous pictures of vanished might-have-beens.

But, believe me, a man never can tell. And to such jaded Jonahs as these—also the joyless Jeremiahs and lamenting Lears—I here offer these few soothing bromides to lay, as unction, to their aching souls. (I am not sure that this is the orthodox manner of applying bromides, but it really doesn't matter much.)

Yes, my fellows in adversity. The phrase betrays me; for I fear greatly that I, too, will very soon be counted amongst you. I have risked my paltry all upon the chances of a horse named James Aitch because he seemed to offer the richest rewards. But even at this stage strange misgivings begin to assail me. But let us to our cases.

Take that of my friend, Selwyn X. Shad, who won £300 in Manfred's year. The efficient chief accountant of a prosperous city firm, Selwyn had long nursed in secret the desire to possess a business of his own. That £300 helped him to realise his ambition, and he rejoiced. At the end of two years, Selwyn (a far better servant than master, as events proved) failed in business, and now, after humbling himself greatly, fills a minor position at reduced salary with his old firm. Whereas, if he had not backed the winner—But, of course, you apprehend.

Behold my bosom pal, Peter A. Fittlebrush, painfully propelling homeward his fevered feet after losing his last lone sixpence at a bygone Cup meeting.

Upon his painful pilgrimage he enters a secluded suburban street. A gaily garbed little girl dandles a doll by the edge of the road. Suddenly a baker's careering cart dashes dangerously around a corner, swerves and side-slips straight upon the beautiful babe. Urged by an inflexible will, Peter propels fevered feet aforesaid with sudden speed, snatches, in the nick of time, the babe from beneath those horrible hooves.

From where a palatial pile stands in its own gorgeous grounds near by, sounds first a woman's shriek, then a strong man's hoarse cry of horror. The mother and father rush into the street to receive from Peter's trembling hands their cherished child—unscathed. Peter, whose only good suit, foul with the gutter's grime, is ruined beyond repair, is urged to come within. Here a touching scene ensues. The beauteous babe throws adoring arms about Peter's neck and cries that her preserver must never leave her.

Who today does not know the magic name of Peter A. Fittlebrush, the marmalade magnate, who once saved from dreadful death the youngest daughter, and subsequently wedded the eldest daughter, of the millionaire manufacturer whose right-hand man and partner he is today? Yet, had he backed but one winner ... Need I elaborate?

But, as I write, the Melbourne Cup is yet to be run and won; and still I toy with the lingering hope that perhaps this James Aitch may—Ah well; a man really never can tell.

*Note: James Aitch finished last of the 18 runners in the 1933 Melbourne Cup won by Hall Mark.*

# The bard of Cup week: C.J. Dennis

## JIM HAYNES

NO WRITER HAS EVER captured the flavour of the Melbourne Spring Racing Carnival like C.J. Dennis, who wrote a poem every day for the Melbourne *Herald-Sun* from the mid-1920s until his death in 1938.

Dennis found new angles and perspectives time and again as he celebrated the wonderful 'Aussieness' of 'Cup Week'. His ability to find such variety for his racing verses provides proof for the old adage that racing reflects life itself and is truly the 'sport of Kings and deadbeats'.

When his daily newspaper verses are tallied along with his famous *Sentimental Bloke, Ginger Mick* and *Digger Smith* volumes, his many poems for children and the poems he wrote about the birds that frequented his garden at Toolangi, Dennis's total of rhymed-verse poems comes to well over two thousand, and I have yet to find a poor one.

'Den', as he was known both to his work colleagues and readers during his time at the *Herald-Sun*, was the poet who best captured the common Australian character and lifestyle. He was an unpretentious observer and chronicler of the average Aussie.

The people who inhabit Dennis's poems are real men and women. Unlike Paterson, who wrote about 'larger-than-life characters' and unusual, memorable events, Dennis wrote about 'people' and everyday things.

Although he was, like Henry Lawson, involved in Labor politics early in his life, Dennis's verse exhibits none of Lawson's polemic and social reform agenda. Where Lawson's verse reveals a striving for 'something better' and a sense of loss, Dennis is always happy with life 'as it is'.

Although both Lawson and Dennis struggled at times with the demon drink, their lives could not have been more different in terms of outlook and philosophy. While Lawson was a tortured soul and a 'sad case' in his later years, Dennis appears to have found peace of mind at Toolangi with his wife and his garden, and it shows in his verse.

There *are* stories of Dennis's wife holding his head under the garden tap in order to get him to work on his *Herald-Sun* poem, but his daily contribution always made the train and the quality of verse he could produce on demand is astounding.

Dennis not only wrote sometimes hilarious, sometimes touching, celebratory verse about current events, he often did so within hours of the event and the poem would appear in the *Herald-Sun* the following day. What astonishes me is that it is damn fine verse, too!

Dennis celebrated such momentous events as Bert Hinkler's landing at Darwin, the death of Nellie Melba and Phar Lap's Cup victory, and when it came to Cup Week in Melbourne, Dennis was in his element. Each year he would produce at least one, often two, poems celebrating the social phenomenon of the Spring Carnival.

His keen observation was always directed at the real people for whom Cup Week came as a blessed relief from the rat race and everyday grind, especially in the years of the Great Depression.

In the year of Phar Lap's victory, 1930, Dennis produced one of his funnest Spring Carnival poems. Entitled 'The Barber's Story', it is written from the point of view of a barber who, the day after the Cup, attempts to make conversation with a surly customer who has, rather obviously, backed the second favourite, Tregilla.

Blithely unaware of the reason for his customer's surly mood, the barber goes on and on about how wonderful Phar Lap's victory was: '"Champeen", I sez to him. "Wonderful popular . . ."'

He then compounds the error by commenting, 'But that Tregilla run bad in the Cup.'

Even when his customer vents his frustration with an outburst in which Tregilla is declared a 'Cabhorse!', the barber remains totally insensitive to his customer's state of mind and puts his mood down to the fact that he is a 'real disagreeable sort of a bloke':

> 'Tregilla!?' 'e sez to me, glarin' real murderous.
> 'Tregilla!!?' 'e barks at me. 'That 'airy goat!'
> Surly, 'e seemed to me, man couldn't talk to 'im . . .
> 'Hair-cut?' I sez to 'im. 'No!' 'e sez . . . 'Throat!'

It was a favourite device of Dennis's to find some aspect of Aussie life outside racing and fasten on that as his focus for the Cup each year. In 1931 he delighted in the news that the Australian Naval Squadron just 'happened' to be stationed in Melbourne during Cup Week.

Typically, Dennis saw no harm in this amazing 'coincidence' and celebrated the Aussie predeliction for making the most of the situation and putting 'pleasure' before 'business' when it suited and if at all possible.

He wrote a rollicking sea shanty in 1931 in praise of our brave sailors, which was, in fact, another poetic celebration of what Mark Twain described as 'The Australasian National Day'. Dennis prefaced this verse with the tongue-in-cheek comment that, 'through the usual coincidence many ships, including the Australian Naval Squadron, have reached Melbourne just prior to Cup Week'.

# Sailing Orders

## C.J. Dennis

Up the hook, the bosun said;
(Ho, me hearties, ho!)
There's heavy weather on ahead
(Tumble up, below!)

There's dirty weather coming down,
Our course is set for Melbourne town
And a queer thing that should be!
So show a leg and tumble up,

And pick your fancy for the Cup
With the good ship running free.
Funny thing, the boatman said,
(Ho, me hearties, ho!)

But when November looms ahead
(Tumble up, below!)
To Melbourne Port the orders say,
And nothing's left but to obey,

For the likes of you and me.
And what's a sailor to do,
When duty calls, but see it through,
With the good ship running free?

If I should win, the boatman said;
(Ho, me hearties, ho!)
I'll buy myself a feather bed
(Tumble up, below!)

And never put to sea again.
Yet luck ain't kind to sailor men,
But I'll get my fun, said he.
And every man shall have his lass,

And make his bet and drink a glass,
To a good horse running free, said he,
And that's the life for me!

Two years later the poet turned his attention to the phenomenon of radio, which was profoundly changing the Australian lifestyle.

In a nation as large and sparsely populated as Australia the coming of 'the wireless' meant quite dramatic changes to everyday life. Australia became a nation of 'listeners' able, for the first time, to communicate quickly and share in world events as they happened.

This phenomenon only enhanced the importance of 'The Cup' as an essential part of Aussie culture. Dennis realised the impact this was having and, in one of his 'Cup Week' poems of 1933, he celebrated this new way of being involved in the thrill and excitement of 'The Cup'.

## The Listening Week

### C.J. Dennis

This is the listening week of the year—
Listening-in.
A-cock and alert is the national ear—
Listening-in.
All over the land in the country towns,
From the back of the Leeuwin to Darling Downs,
Layers of 'quids' or the odd half-crowns,
They are listening-in.

On the far-flung farms they are round each set,
Listening-in.
The work and the worry they all forget,
Listening-in.
Wherever an aerial soars in space
To the Cup, or the Oaks or the Steeplechase,
To the roar of the ring and the lure of the race
They are listening-in.
In the far outback there are sun-tanned men,
Listening-in.
Where the woolshed stands by the drafting pen—
Listening-in.
Old Dad's come in from the Ninety Mile;
He scored on the Cup and he wears a smile,
And he 'reckons this game is well worth while',
So he's listening-in.
To the edge of the desert the sound-waves go;
And, listening-in,
Ned of the Overland, Saltbush Joe,
Listening-in,
Recall the giants of years long past,
And the loneliness of these spaces vast;
But they reckon that life's worth living at last
With this listening-in.

Although he often wrote about the 'mug punters', Dennis rarely concerned himself with the feats of the horses themselves, or the jockeys, trainers or owners. He was able to convey the effects of Cup Week on all and sundry. In 1932 he even wrote about the effect of the Spring Carnival obsession on himself, and other poets.

# Galloping Horses

## C.J. Dennis

Oh, this is the week when no rhymster may rhyme
On the joy of the bush or the ills of the time,
Nor pour out his soul in delectable rhythm
Of women and wine and the lure they have with 'em,
Nor pen philosophic (if foolish) discourses,
Because of the fury of galloping horses.
Galloping, galloping thro' the refrain—
The lure and the lilt of it beat on the brain.
Strive as you may for Arcadian Themes,
The silks and the saddles will weave thro' your dreams.
Surging, and urging the visions aside
For a lyrical lay of equestrian pride,
For the roar of the race and the call of the courses,
And galloping, galloping, galloping horses.
This is the week for the apotheosis
Of Horse in his glory, from tail to proboscis.
That curious quadruped, proud and aloof,
That holds all the land under thrall of his hoof.
All creeds and conditions, all factions and forces,
All, all must give way to the galloping horses.
Galloping, galloping—sinner and saint
March to the metre, releasing restraint.
If it isn't the Cup it's the Oaks or the Steeple
That wraps in its magic the minds of the people.
Whether they seek it for profit or pleasure,
They all, willy-nilly, must dance to the measure.
The mood of the moment in all men endorses
The glamorous game and the galloping horses—
Galloping horses—jockeys and courses—
They gallop, we gallop with galloping horses.

Dennis used the fervour and excitement of Cup Week to celebrate all aspects of the Aussie character and human nature. Even the less admirable machinations of married middle-class couples were grist to the mill of his perceptive and humorous verses.

One of Dennis's favourite writing styles was the 'one-sided conversation' in which the reader is presented with only one voice in a conversation and the humour comes, in part, from guessing the obvious 'other side' of the dialogue.

In several Cup Week poems Dennis used this device to great effect to illustrate, and comment on, the never-ending 'cold war' of Machiavellian plotting, game-playing and deceit that is a part of the age-old battle of the sexes in middle-class marriages.

In 'Listen, Elaine' the husband is slowly stripped of his Cup Day punting money by a wife keen on using The Cup as the excuse to obtain an entire new wardrobe. The only voice we hear is that of the husband, firstly making unsuccessful attempts to keep his wife in her old dress:

> 'If you just wore . . . Now, just a minute, please . . .
> That pinkish frock . . . No, wait! Let me explain.
> That pinkish frock with spots . . . You wouldn't *freeze*!
> You've got your furs. Aw, listen, please, Elaine!'

Of course, the punter's need for betting money is of no concern to a fashion-conscious wife. As many of us can attest, wives often obstinately fail to understand the real purpose of race meetings.

Dennis hilariously captures the dilemma of the doomed husband whose 'logic', we all know from experience, will inevitably fail to impress. We are moved to laughter by the all-too-familiar pleas of a fellow sufferer when the husband tries appeasement:

> 'Now, look. We've twenty pounds. Don't let us quarrel.
> Surely we can be sane and quite grown-up.
> If you take most of that, what of the 'moral'

That Percy Podgrass gave us for the Cup?
. . . *Of course he's sure to win.*

As the 'battle' proceeds to its inevitable conclusion—victory for the wife—we share the catch-22 frustration of the husband who knows that the only way he will get to the Cup is by being 'conned' out of his stake money:

'Of course, I wouldn't have my wife look *shabby*.
Take what you need. We'll make a smaller bet . . .
Eight . . . ten . . . twelve quid! Whew! Not much left for betting.
Still, just a flutter and expenses . . . *What?*
Listen, Elaine. What could I be *forgetting?*
Hat? Stockings? Shoes to match? . . . Here . . . Take the lot!'

Ouch! I can still feel the pain of the defeated husband 80 years after that piece was written. Some things don't change.

Dennis proved to be a man ahead of his time in his efforts to maintain gender balance and show the wickedness of husbands and the lengths to which they go to deceive their wives. Infidelity takes many forms, especially in Cup Week when there is a chance to get to 'the races' and waste the housekeeping money 'on the punt'.

Here is another one-sided conversation, which Dennis wrote in 1933, in which the husband attempts to escape his family obligations and get to the Cup meeting. Of course, Cup Day is a public holiday in Victoria and one might expect a family man to take the opportunity to spend time with his wife and children once in a busy year.

With spring in the air and the prospect of a day away from housework with hubby to help with the children, a devoted wife is perfectly entitled to expect that a family picnic is 'just the thing'.

The husband, however, has other selfish and devious plans . . .

# Why a Picnic Jane?

## C.J. Dennis

But, why a picnic, Jane? We went last year,
And missed the Cup; and you know how you grieved
Because we lost . . . Oh! Yes, you did, my dear.
I had the tip, but I was not believed.

It's just sheer nonsense to deny it all.
And when he won, you said, if you recall,
You'd never miss a chance like that again.
Well, cut the Cup. But why a picnic, Jane?

You know how I hate picnics, sticky things,
The grizzling children and the dusty road,
The flies and all those crawlywigs with stings—
My dear, I am not selfish! But that load

Of baskets . . . Eh? Back him at starting price?
That's an idea. And then I could remain
To take you and the children? Hmm'yes. Quite nice.
Jolly, of course. But, why a picnic, Jane?

Wait! Have you thought of burglars? There you are!
The empty house. Remember that last case
Near here? . . . Bright thought, my dear! You take the car.
You've solved it. I'll stay at home and mind the place.

Lonely? Not I. You take the car, of course.
I've a good book; I'll be all right alone.
That's settled then . . . And now, about the horse.
Wait here, and while I think of it, I'll phone.

"Lo! That you, Sam? All set! I can't talk loud.
'Lo! Can you hear me? Listen, lad. It's on.
Tomorrow, yes. Count me in the crowd.
Your car . . . about eleven. They'll be gone.

Great stunt, that picnic! If we make the pace
We ought to get there for the second race.'
Well, Jane, that's all fixed up. I've backed our horse.
Eh? Help cut sandwiches? Why, dear, of course.

It wasn't in Dennis's nature to question or analyse the morality of racing or the social behaviour it generated. He was always less concerned with the heroic deeds of the winners and the jockeys than he was with the everyday thoughts and schemes and disappointments of the nameless normal battlers, office workers, tradesmen and pretentious middle-class pretenders who adored his writing in their daily paper.

'Den' always pitched his writing in the common ruck; he was never concerned with attempting to be more 'informed' than all the other 'mug punters'.

In one Cup Week poem, titled the 'Pondering Punter', he considers all the elements of the form guide and, after expressing the typical 'mug punter's' confusion, concludes: 'I give up . . . has anybody got a pin?'

Dennis loved the confusion and enthusiasm of Cup Week; for him, *not* picking the winner was far more 'Australian' than some tall tale of good luck or a dream which led to a fortune.

This is illustrated in many poems he wrote in Cup Week over the years. It was always the human spectacle and human behaviour that fascinated C.J. Dennis.

In the year of Peter Pan's second Cup win Dennis wrote a wonderful parody of Adam Lindsay Gordon's famous racing poem, 'How We Beat The Favourite'.

Dennis's poem was called 'How We Backed the Favourite'.

While Gordon's poem is a heroic tale of a titanic struggle which celebrates the nobility and bravery of the racehorse, Dennis's poem typically concentrates on the confidence shown by the everyday 'mug punters' in the Cup favourite, Peter Pan.

Banjo Paterson also famously parodied Gordon's poem with a tall tale with a twist, called 'How The Favourite Beat Us', in which a racehorse owner inadvertently signals a jockey to win a race by brushing away a mosquito and subsequently loses his fortune.

There are no heroic struggles and no tall tales of lost fortunes in Dennis's poem, simply the everyday hopes of the 'one shilling' punters. Dennis sees the horse himself as merely another player in the whole drama and excitement of a week, which gives our humdrum, mundane lives a yearly highlight.

Having been told that Peter Pan *will* win, the poet goes to see the horse and make up his own mind:

I saw Peter Pan; there was nothing he lacked.

And, as he looked willing, I plonked down my shilling

And triumphed, and that's how the favourite was backed.

Now, Peter Pan—the flashy chestnut with the flaxen mane and tail—was arguably the most beautiful horse to ever win the Cup. His bravery in recovering from illness to win two Melbourne Cups is the stuff of legend in Australian turf history. C.J. Dennis sums up the horse in the mundane and prosaic phrase 'there was nothing he lacked'. You can't get more Aussie than that!

Similarly, when Trivalve won in 1927, Dennis wrote 'A Post Cup Tale' in which a poor mug punter tells us how he 'switched' at the last minute from his own original choice for the Cup, the eventual winner Trivalve, to some other horse due to the 'urging' of a mate. There is no real concern with the wonderful three-year-old AJC Derby winner who valiantly and famously won the Cup against older, more seasoned stayers. Instead we have an amazingly accurate and timeless portrayal of the punter's eternal frustration with picking winners and *not* backing them; as the protagonist tells us, over and over again, 'I had the money *in me 'and*, just making for the bookie's stand'.

The wonderful thing about Dennis's poem about Trivalve's Cup win is that it has outlived any other poems written about Cup winners in various years because it contains a greater human story and captures an elemental truth about all punters, anytime, anywhere.

There is one poem which illustrates Dennis's ability to capture the everyday human element of the Cup not only dramatically, but with great understanding and humour. In 'An Anticipatory Picture', written in Cup Week 1931, he gives us all the excitement of the race and concludes with a blank space in which we can live out our own Cup dream.

## An Anticipatory Picture

**C.J. Dennis**

The scene upon the frock-flecked lawn
Is, as you please, a picture fair,
Or just a hunk of human brawn,
With blobs of faces here and there.

Stilled are the clamours of the Ring;
The famous race is on at last;
All eyes are on the lengthening string
Of brilliant jackets moving fast.

Torn, trampled tickets mark the birth
Of broken hopes all now would mend,
As quickening hoof-beats spurn the earth,
And the field thunders to the bend.

All men are equal for the nonce,
Bound by an urgency intense,
And eager questionings win response
From strangers tiptoe with suspense.

'What's that in front?' All faces yearn
Toward the track in serried rows.
The field comes round the homeward turn,
As, wave on wave, the murmuring grows,

Waxes and swells from out that host
Till pandemonium begins,
And flecks of colour pass the post
To mighty cries of '(_____*) wins'.
[* N.B.—Write your own ticket.]

# Queens of the Cup

## JIM HAYNES

MANY WOULD ARGUE THAT Makybe Diva, three times Melbourne Cup winner, is the greatest staying mare of the modern era. Others would say that she was one of the greatest stayers ever—regardless of age, era or gender.

Makybe Diva was bred and born in Britain and so was always six months out of sync to her Australian rivals. This made it near impossible to train her for classic two- and three-year-old races, as she was six months younger than all Australian horses of the same official age.

After she was born, Makybe Diva was offered for sale at the famous Tatts Newmarket sales but, luckily for Tony Santic, she was passed in and so was shipped out to Australia with her mother, Tugela, who had been bought in foal to Desert King by Santic, an Aussie who migrated from Croatia as a child and made his money in the tuna fishing industry in South Australia before moving full-time into the thoroughbred industry.

Santic had Tugela taken to Dick Fowlston's Britton House Stud in Somerset before being sent on to Australia, and Makybe Diva was born there on 21 March 1999.

The filly's name was derived from the first two letters of the names of five women who worked in Santic's office and she raced in his now famous colours, a combination of the Croatian and Australian flags. Apart from two starts in Japan, she did all her racing in Australia.

With two lines back to Northern Dancer on her sire side and Northern Dancer and Nasrullah twice on her dam side, Makybe Diva was line-bred to stay all day and had plenty of Carbine blood.

She was broken in and conditioned in two spells at Scone with legendary horseman Greg Bennett.

Like all the thousands of horses he has educated, Bennett taught her 'to be a horse' before she became a racehorse. 'I think there's more to life than running around a racetrack,' Bennett often said.

Makybe Diva stood out as special when it became obvious she could carry Bennett's 85 kg up 'Heartbreak Hill', the rough rise at the back of his Scone property, and not be even be blowing. Plenty of horses don't even get halfway, according to Bennett.

Bennett, a tough man who admitted he cried when the great mare won the Cox Plate, remembered she was 'very smooth to ride'.

'You could almost sit on her back,' he said, 'canter along, roll a smoke and drink a cup of tea at the same time.'

As she never started in the classic races at two and three, it is hard to line up a comparison between the tough bay mare and other great staying fillies and mares. She started once at three and finished fourth. She then went on a winning spree and won six in a row, starting with a maiden at Wangaratta and concluding with wins in the Werribee Cup and Queen Elizabeth Stakes of 2002. Although classed as a four-year-old mare, Makybe was actually a three-year-old filly when she won those major races. The win in the Queen Elizabeth Stakes qualified her for the Melbourne Cup the following year and meant that her trainer, David Hall, could plan a light autumn and toughen the horse up slowly for her first attempt at the Melbourne Cup.

After two unplaced runs in the autumn she was rested for her spring campaign of 2003. She returned to run a series of fourth placings, culminating in the Caulfield Cup, and then took out her first Melbourne Cup by a length and a half carrying 51 kg.

This pattern was repeated in the autumn of 2004. Trained by Lee Freedman, after David Hall left to train in Hong Kong, she ran unplaced in the Chester Manifold Stakes and Australian Cup, third in the Carlyon Cup, and then went to Sydney where she finished third in the Ranvet and the BMW before winning the Sydney Cup.

In the spring the familiar pattern emerged again, with the mare running four times before winning the Melbourne Cup for two unplaced runs and two seconds, notably a close second, from barrier 18, to Elvstroem in the Caulfield Cup.

She returned for the most successful autumn campaign of her career in 2005. After an unplaced run in the CF Orr Stakes, she was a close second to Elvstroem in the St George Stakes, before winning the Australian Cup in record time. She then won the BMW in Sydney in a remarkable fashion, coming from the tail of the field to make up 10 lengths and run down Gai Waterhouse's old warhorse Grand Armee. The Diva was sent to Japan and ran seventh in two international races over 2000 metres and 3200 metres, carrying 56 kg and 59 kg.

After her disappointing overseas campaign it appeared she was being weighted out of handicaps and had perhaps reached the twilight of her great career, but the best was yet to come.

In her final campaign, the spring of 2005, the great mare won the Memsie first up; then ran second, beaten a nose by a great middle-distance horse in Lad of The Manor, in the Feehan Stakes.

She then won the Turnbull Stakes and showed her class by winning the WS Cox Plate, coming six wide around the field on the turn to win running away from Lotteria and two-time winner Fields of Omagh.

From that moment on, all talk was about the great mare winning her third Melbourne Cup. If she did, she would become the only horse in history to win three Cups; and only four others had ever won it twice! She would also have to smash her own weight-carrying record of 55.5 kg for a winning mare by lumping top weight of 58 kg, and she would have to do it from barrier 14.

The nation was in a state of expectation and every aspect of the great mare's life was examined in detail. Her relationship with jockey Glen Boss, who first rode her in the 2003 Caulfield Cup and was to be her jockey for 18 of her subsequent 24 starts, was told from all angles by the media. The fairytale of the migrant fisherman made good and the great mare bred to northern hemisphere time became the main media story of the spring in Australia in 2005. The whole nation was 'Makybe Diva mad' as the Cup approached and it seemed the entire population had backed the great mare.

Of course, we all know that she did it, with relative ease, ridden perfectly by Glen Boss, and was then immediately retired to Tony Santic's stud, appropriately named after her, where a life-size statue of the great horse stands at the gate. There are also statues of her at Flemington and in Tony Santic's home town of Port Lincoln.

In a great piece of tactical riding, Glen Boss had the Diva on the rails as they came down the straight the first time and he 'put her to sleep' and then brought her into the race five deep at the turn. The euphoria that gripped the nation as Makybe Diva hit the lead and then dug deep under her record weight to race into immortality by over a length would be hard for anyone not versed in the history of the Cup to understand.

Australia had found a new idol and a new legend was born; one broadcaster called it 'the greatest Melbourne Cup win of all time' as she passed the post.

Her first foal, a colt by Epsom Derby winner Galileo, sold for $1.5 million at the Inglis Easter Yearling Sales in 2009 and her second, a filly by Kentucky Derby winner Fusaichi Pegasus, fetched $1.2 million the following year.

Makybe Diva's career differed from that of some other great race mares in that she was always conditioned in shorter races for her victories in longer races. This makes her win and place rates look poor in comparison to some other great mares, like Wakeful and Sunline. The Diva started 36 times for 15 wins, four seconds, three thirds, six fourths, and eight other unplaced runs. So, while Sunline and Wakeful have win rates of 69 per cent and 61 per cent respectively, Makybe Diva's win rate was 41.5 per cent and her place rate 69 per cent, compared to 94 per cent and 93 per cent for Sunline and Wakeful.

Of course, when you make history by winning three Melbourne Cups, such statistics become meaningless and, as has been stated several times in this collection, comparing champions of different eras is mere folly, but we all do it anyway!

The nature of racing and weight allocation has changed dramatically in the 200-year history of Australian racing. The nature of the Melbourne Cup, too, has changed throughout its history.

Three fillies and eleven mares have won the Melbourne Cup and several others probably deserved to win it.

Of the three three-year-old fillies that won the Cup, one was great, one was pretty good, and the third was good enough.

Sister Olive had won only once before taking out the big race, in the Maribyrnong Trial as a two-year-old. She had run well for a fourth in the Caulfield Cup and carried a light weight, as you would expect for a horse with few credentials. She was good enough to defeat John Wren's good stayer The Rover, three Sydney Cup winners in Eurythmic, David and Kennequhair, a WS Cox Plate winner, Violoncello, and a Caulfield Cup winner in Purser, so she took some good scalps on that day in November 1921.

Auraria, the Cup winner of 1895, was a good filly that won the South Australian Derby and ran third in the VRC Derby behind Carbine's best son, Wallace. She then won the Cup at 33 to 1 and won the Oaks two days later. She was a daughter of the great stayer Trenton and therefore a grand-daughter of Carbine's sire, Musket. She also carried the blood of the great imported stallion Fisherman on both sides. Her full brother, Aurum, was a champion on the track and at stud in England, but could not emulate his sister, although he ran third in the Cup carrying a record weight for a three-year-old in 1897.

The greatest three-year-old filly to win the Cup was Briseis, the first of her sex to win the race, in 1876, and she was probably the best three-year-old filly ever to start in the race.

At two Briseis, a daughter of imported stallion Tim Whiffler, went to Sydney and won the Doncaster Handicap, a flying handicap, and the All-Aged Stakes, at weight for age, in a week. She then set a record that has never been broken by winning the VRC Derby, Melbourne Cup and Oaks, all within six days. In the Derby she took 1.75 seconds off the race record and ran the second-fastest time ever recorded for the distance, in the world.

Sadly Briseis died in a freak accident in the breeding barn. Hobbled for her first mating, to King of The Ring, she reared up, slipped over and fractured her skull, and it was left to her full sister, Idalia, to carry the bloodline successfully into the future.

The first tough staying mare to win the Cup was the 1904 winner Acrasia. She was aged seven and had run fourth in the Cup two years before. Her sire was Gozo, who also sired full brothers Gaulus and The Grafter to win the Cup in 1897 and 1898.

Acrasia was owned by colourful Sydney bookmaker Humphrey Oxenham, who bred her from his Sydney Cup-winning mare Cerise and Blue. He famously lost her to Lord Cardigan's owner, John Mayo, in a card game on the eve of the Caulfield Cup and bought her back for £2000. Lord Cardigan, carrying 6 st 8 lb (41.5 kg), had defeated the mighty Wakeful, carrying 10 st (63.5 kg), in the Melbourne Cup the previous year.

The tables were turned by the fair sex in 1904 with Lord Cardigan, carrying 9 st 6 lb (60 kg), chasing home Acrasia, carrying 7 st 6 lb (47 kg). The tough mare equalled Carbine's race record, but sadly, Lord Cardigan ruptured himself in his effort to catch her with his big weight and died several days later.

After Acrasia's win there was a gap of 17 years before another female horse, the filly Sister Olive, won the great race in 1921. Then there was an even longer gap of 18 years before Rivette came along to make history in 1939.

Rivette had an interesting pedigree: she had the great sire Isonomy on both sides through her two grand-dams, and her dam,

Riv, was a grand-daughter of Carbine's Epsom Derby-winning son Spearmint. Isonomy started 14 times for ten wins, two seconds and a third, and his wins included two Ascot Gold Cups, in 1879 and 1880. He then became a highly influential sire.

Rivette was bred, owned and trained by an amazing man, Harry Bamber. Oddly enough, the only other Cup winner to be bred, owned and trained by one man was the first female winner, the black filly Briseis, who was owned, trained and bred by Jim Wilson, of the famous St Albans Stud near Geelong.

Harry Bamber was the archetypal 'battling trainer'. He was a blacksmith by trade and served in the Light Horse in World War I. As a dairy farmer on a soldier-settler block he studied veterinary science, and he and his brother and a friend bought Rivette's dam for 200 guineas at auction. She was originally named Riverside and raced as a '14.2 pony', winning many races on the unregistered tracks.

Bamber thought the little mare was good enough to race against thoroughbreds. She had the required pedigree, although she was not in the studbook, so he raced her at Sandown and she duly won. At registered meetings she raced as Riv, since the name Riverside was not available.

The Depression forced the Bamber brothers off their farm, and Harry milked cows to pay the agistment for his mare and her foals, the second of which was Rivette.

Bamber then acquired stables at Mordialloc, and his training techniques were considered quirky. He walked his horses and didn't over-train them, but kept them in work far longer than other trainers. In fact he trained much more like a 'pony' trainer than a thoroughbred trainer.

Rivette did not start at two as she was injured while training on the road. She had her first win at Packenham late in her three-year-old season and was being prepared for the Caulfield–Melbourne Cups double of 1938 when she cut herself badly while rolling on the beach and had to be spelled.

The following year she was in training from February right

through to the Melbourne Cup. She started ten times in welters and handicaps and never missed a place. When the pressure was on she responded and, on that odd preparation, easily won both the Caulfield and Melbourne Cups, making history by being the first mare, and only the third horse, to do so. Had she not completely missed the start in the Moonee Valley Gold Cup, in which she finished third within a length of the winner Gilltown, she would undoubtedly have made more history by being the first horse to win all three Cups.

At the Melbourne Cup presentation ceremony she kicked the holy grail out of Harry Bamber's hands, but he didn't mind one bit. 'She set me up for life,' the battling trainer said.

Rivette had a career severely interrupted by injury, but she was a good hard racehorse who made history in winning the Cups double in the early, dark days of World War II. Her offspring were not registered, as she was not eligible for the studbook.

Racing was severely interrupted in the eastern states during the war, and completely banned in South Australia, which certainly affected the career of Rainbird, the next mare to win the Cup, just after the war ended in 1945.

Rainbird was owned by South Australian racing identity C.H. Reid, whose brother had bred the mare. Rainbird's dam, Sequoia, was a daughter of the great Australian champion Heroic, and she was by the imported stallion The Buzzard, who also sired the 1940 Cup winner, Old Rowley. The Buzzard was a son of Epsom Derby winner Spion Kop, who was himself a son of an Epsom Derby winner Spearmint, who was by Carbine. It is an amusing reflection on Australian prudery that The Buzzard raced, quite successfully, in Britain as The Bastard. His name was changed when he came to Australia.

When racing was closed down in South Australia in 1942, Rainbird's trainer, Sam Evans, moved to Victoria where he trained the filly to win the Wakeful Stakes of 1944 and run an unlucky second in The Oaks.

Rainbird went home to win the 1945 South Australian St Leger, the first since 1941, and her training schedule was again interrupted by lack of shipping at the end of the war. Most trading vessels had been taken over by the navy and took ages to return to normal duties, which meant Rainbird did not arrive back in Melbourne until late September. Although 'under done' she ran a good second in the Caulfield Cup.

She then ran unplaced on a heavy track in the Moonee Valley Gold Cup, and Evans thought that the only thing that could prevent her winning the Melbourne Cup was rain. Like the later great champion Rain Lover, Rainbird was, ironically, a duffer in the wet! The weather stayed fine for the big race, however, and she won the Cup easily by 2½ lengths.

Rainbird went on to win the Port Adelaide Cup and ran second in the Sydney Cup, before heading to the breeding barn where she was a great success. Her daughter Raindear won the South Australian Oaks, and her descendants include the great sire Centaine, the good staying mare Allez Wonder, and many others.

The well-named mare Evening Peal won the Cup a decade after Rainbird, in 1956. She was by the great sire Delville Wood out of Mission Chimes, and had the Spearmint/Carbine/Musket bloodline on both sides of her pedigree.

She was a bonny mare who won 11 races from 51 starts. Her wins included the Wakeful Stakes and the VRC, Queensland and AJC Oaks (then known as the Adrian Knox Stakes). She often raced against mighty horses like Redcraze and Rising Fast and carried a record-winning weight for a female of 8 st (50.5 kg) to beat Redcraze, carrying 10 st 3 lb (65 kg), by a neck in record time in the Melbourne Cup of 1956.

The New Zealand mare Hi-Jinx had one of the least distinguished records of any Melbourne Cup winner. She started three times only in Australia, running unplaced in the Caulfield Cup and a good second in the Moonee Valley Cup before winning the historic 100th Melbourne Cup at 50 to 1.

There was great hype around the 100th Cup and record prize money. Hi-Jinx's win was an anticlimax for the crowd, who had hoped to see the mighty Tulloch carry 10 st 1 lb (64 kg) to victory.

Tulloch, who had returned to racing after two years spent over-coming a crippling illness, ran seventh; it was the only time he was unplaced in 51 starts.

Hi-Jinx, a plain mare described as the ugliest horse in the race by one unkind journalist, returned to one of the mildest receptions in Cup history. She had the breeding to win, however, being bred at the famous Trelawney Stud in New Zealand from a Foxbridge mare, Lady's Bridge. Trelawney Stud had produced three previous Melbourne Cup winners—Hiraji, Foxzami and MacDougal—all from mares by the great sire Foxbridge. Hi-Jinx cost 500 guineas as a yearling, and took out the largest prize ever offered for a race in Australia when she won $40,000 for her Cup victory.

The brave little chestnut mare Light Fingers was spotted as a yearling in New Zealand by Bart Cummings and raced on lease in the white with royal blue spots and cap of Wally Broderick, a Melbourne grain merchant who owned her older full brother, The Dip, also trained by Bart.

The two were well named, being by the French stallion Le Filou, which translates as 'pickpocket', out of a New Zealand mare Cuddlesome. In fact, Light Fingers was originally named Close Embrace by her breeders, the Dawson family, but Broderick wanted a name from the sire's side to match her full brother, so he changed her name before she raced.

Changing a horse's registered name is supposed to be unlucky, but Broderick and Bart struck it lucky with Light Fingers. She was an out-and-out champion, considered 'the best since Wakeful' by older racing men. She started four times at two for three wins and a second, beaten a head. In her three-year-old season she started 12 times for seven wins, two seconds and two thirds; the wins included the VRC Wakeful, Manifold and Oaks Stakes, the Sandown Guin-eas, and the AJC Princess Handicap and Oaks.

Light Fingers suffered a serious virus attack, which delayed her return to racing in the spring of 1965. She also was plagued by back problems and missed the Caulfield Cup after she won but pulled a shoulder muscle in the Craiglee Stakes. She went into the Melbourne Cup on the limited preparation of just five starts.

In one of the greatest Cup finishes of all time the tiny chestnut mare defeated her huge black stablemate, Ziema, by a lip to give Bart his first Cup win and his first Cup quinella.

Her bad back worsened after her four-year-old season, which meant Bart needed all his skill and care to keep her racing. She went into the 1966 Cup carrying a massive weight, on an even lighter preparation than 1965, just four starts; Bart's better-conditioned champion, Galilee, defeated her by 2 lengths even though she ran a great race, hitting the front halfway down the straight and hanging on for a gallant second to give Bart his second Cup quinella in a row.

The racing public loved the little mare and sent her out at 10 to 9 for her final victory in the Sandown Cup, carrying 9 st (57 kg) on a bog track. Light Fingers's record overall was 33 starts for 15 wins, eight seconds and five thirds.

It was to be another 23 years before a female would win another Melbourne Cup, but mares won two out of four Cups between 1988 and 1991—who could forget those two mighty chestnuts, Empire Rose and Let's Elope?

Although bred on different lines, Empire Rose and Let's Elope were similar in many ways. Both were bred and owned in New Zealand, both were huge chestnut mares (Empire Rose only just fitted in the barrier stalls and Let's Elope was not much smaller), and both were mighty tough stayers.

Empire Rose was by the great Sir Tristram out of a Sovereign Edition mare and won good races on both sides of the Tasman, including the New Zealand Cup and Trentham Stakes in New Zealand, and Australia's Mackinnon and Melbourne Cup of 1988.

Her record in the Melbourne Cup is getting towards the 'Shadow King' level. She started four times in the great race for a fifth in 1986, a second in 1987, a win in 1988, and a final unplaced run as a seven-year-old, behind Tawriffic, in 1989.

Although her overall record of nine wins and eight placings from 48 starts is not equal to that of some other great staying mares,

Laurie Laxon's efforts to condition the huge mare to win major races and race on well into her seven-year-old season is remarkable. He was helped in his training by wife Sheila, who rode Empire Rose in her trackwork and would later become the first female trainer to win a Melbourne Cup, appropriately with a mare.

Having watched the huge chestnut mare go around in four Melbourne Cups, the racing public could have been forgiven for thinking she had returned, in different racing colours, two years after her final run in 1989, when Let's Elope took out the Cup.

Let's Elope was by the American stallion Nassipour out of a New Zealand-bred mare by the good English sire Battle-Waggon. In spite of the multinational nature of her pedigree, a look at her breeding confirms that she had three crosses to Nearco, two via Nasrullah and one via Dante, and also had Bois Roussel on her sire side, which means she had an abundance of Carbine blood.

Let's Elope did not start at two, but showed some promise at three while racing in New Zealand. She won her first start and then struggled to win again until taking out a Group 3 event and being sold. Her new owners transferred her to Bart Cummings in Australia, and the 'Cups King' conditioned her for a spring campaign in Melbourne, in 1991, as a four-year-old.

Although she was a duffer in the wet, she showed good staying ability in her first three starts for Bart. Then the weather cleared and the mighty mare went on a winning rampage.

Let's Elope won four races in a row in the spring: the Turnbull Stakes, the Mackinnon and the Melbourne–Caulfield Cups double—the first mare since Rivette to do so.

She then returned in the autumn to win three in a row: the Orr Stakes, St George Stakes and Australian Cup.

Injury and controversy plagued Let's Elope for the rest of her career. A damaged fetlock kept her out of racing until she returned to defeat the champion Better Loosen Up in a match race at five. She was then relegated from close second to fifth for causing interference to that same horse in the 1992 WS Cox Plate, won by Super Impose.

She bled in the Japan Cup and again while racing in the USA, where she was twice first past the post but was again relegated for interference, this time from first to third in a Group 1 race.

The second bleeding attack and a fractured cannon bone forced her into retirement in 1993. She produced the good stayer Ustinov from a mating to Seeking The Gold but, despite her matings with the best US sires, her other progeny did not do well on the track.

In 1998 another two great New Zealand mares fought out a memorable Melbourne Cup finish when Jezabeel, winner of the Auckland Cup and a daughter of that great producer of stayers, Sir Tristram's son Zabeel, defeated another daughter of Zabeel, Champagne, in an unforgettable finish.

Jezabeel was typical of the dour Zabeel offspring who took time to mature and race into condition; she won seven of her 26 starts and was placed another five times.

Jezabeel had Northern Dancer blood via her sire's dam, Lady Giselle, and Nasrullah on her dam side, so she fits the 'Cup-winning' pattern of Carbine blood on both sides.

Having helped husband Laurie to win the Cup with Empire Rose in 1988, Sheila Laxon returned in triumph as a trainer in her own right to take the Cups double with Ethereal in 2001.

Owned and bred by the Vela brothers at Pencarrow Stud, Ethereal was sired by US Breeders' Cup winner, Rhythm, the champion US two-year-old of 1989 and a son of the hugely influential sire Mr Prospector. Completing Ethereal's multinational pedigree was her dam, Romanee Conti, a Hong Kong Cup winner and daughter of Sir Tristram, who carried both Wilkes and Le Filou blood on her dam side.

With a pedigree made to order for a stayer with a turn of foot, Ethereal proved to be just that. She took out four classic races at Group 1 level in winning the Caulfield–Melbourne Cups double, the Queensland Oaks and the Tancred Stakes (now the BMW).

At stud Ethereal produced the handy filly Uberalles, from a mating to Giant's Causeway. Uberalles won at Group 2 level and was third in the New Zealand Derby. Ethereal's other progeny have sold for huge prices, with a colt by Stravinsky fetching $1.3 million at the Karaka sales, but have not excelled as yet on the track.

Two years after Ethereal's Cups double, the history of 'mares and the Melbourne Cup' was to be changed forever when Makybe Diva won the first of her three.

But what of mares who never won the Melbourne Cup? How do Wakeful, Carlita, Desert Gold, Tranquil Star, Flight, Chiquita, Leilani, Surround, Emancipation and Sunline compare to those who did?

Surround, Emancipation and Sunline were great champions, but they were not true stayers, although Surround looked like having the potential to be a great stayer at three. She won the VRC Oaks and Queensland Oaks, but failed in the Brisbane Cup at 3200 metres. After an amazing three-year-old season, in which she started 16 times for 12 wins, she was retired at four, the age at which Makybe Diva won her first race.

Emancipation, for all her brilliance and toughness up to a mile, failed to run beyond 2000 metres. Her tally of Group 1 wins—seven—equals The Diva's, but she was certainly no stayer.

Sunline won almost twice as many times as The Diva at Group 1 level, but she was powerful only over the shorter distances—the longest distance at which she ever competed was 2040 metres—and she was never a candidate for a 2-mile Cup.

Carlita won the VRC Derby and Oaks as well as the Rosehill Guineas and the Craven Plate, and the Kings Plate at weight for age by a massive 25 lengths. She ran third in the Cup of 1915 carrying 8 st 5 lb (53 kg), and sixth—with 9 st 5 lb (59.5 kg), behind Sasanof who was carrying only 6 st 12 lb (43.5 kg)—in 1916.

Desert Gold also raced in World War I and won 19 races in a row. She won 36 times from 59 starts and carried top weight of 9 st 6 lb (60 kg) to finish eighth in the Cup of 1918. It was one of only six unplaced runs in her 59-start career.

Tranquil Star was tough as old boots, starting 111 times and winning two WS Cox Plates, three Mackinnons, and the St George Stakes, Caulfield Stakes, Lloyd Stakes and so on. She carried a record-winning weight for a mare to take out the Caulfield Cup with 8 st 12 lb (56 kg) in 1942, and then carried a whopping 9 st 3 lb (58.5 kg) to run 12th on a bog track behind Colonus, carrying 7 st 2 lb (45 kg), in the Melbourne Cup that year. She even raced on successfully after recovering from breaking her jaw, winning a Memsie Stakes, a William Reid Stakes and her third Mackinnon!

Flight never started in a Melbourne Cup, but could stay. She won the WS Cox Plate, Mackinnon, AJC Oaks, Colin Stephen Stakes and Champagne Stakes, and ran third in a Sydney Cup. At middle distance she was often up against Bernborough, but still ended her career with a respectable record of 24 wins and 28 other placings from 65 starts. Although she was a grand-daughter of Heroic, she was famously bought for just 60 guineas and won more than a thousand times her purchase price in wartime when prize money was very low. Her daughter, appropriately named Flight's Daughter, produced Derby winners Skyline and Sky High, who established a bloodline of world significance when standing at stud in the USA.

The bonny black mare Chiquita won 11 times at three, including the Manifold Stakes, Thousand Guineas, Wakeful Stakes and The VRC Oaks. She found one better in the Jim Cummings-trained Comic Court, however, who defeated her often, including in the Mackinnon Stakes and Melbourne Cup of 1950, where she ran second both times; she also ran second in the Caulfield Cup behind Grey Boots. She had the satisfaction of one win over Comic Court in the Craiglee Stakes over a mile, and their daughter, Comicquita, ran second to Even Stevens in the 1962 Melbourne Cup.

Leilani was a great staying mare, winning six times at Group 1 level in a relatively short career. Her 14 wins, six seconds and six thirds from 28 starts is a great record for a stayer, and her wins included the AJC Oaks, Caulfield Cup, Toorak Handicap, and the Mackinnon, St George, CF Orr and Turnbull Stakes. Bart Cummings's decision not to start her in the Cup with 59 kg means we will never know if she could have been up there with the great mares who won it.

For my money it comes down to Wakeful and Makybe Diva as the two greatest staying mares in our racing history.

Both mares started racing late and missed the classic fillies races for different reasons. Wakeful was amazingly versatile and won the sprint double of the Oakleigh Plate and Newmarket early in her career, at four. Makybe Diva, on the other hand, having never won first-up and never won a race under a mile in distance, came out at seven and won the Memsie Stakes first-up over 1400 metres.

Wakeful won over 4800 metres, a feat not possible in Makybe Diva's day. She also won ten races that would be Group 1 today, compared to Makybe Diva's seven. On the other hand, she started twice in the Melbourne Cup and never won; Makybe Diva won three. Makybe raced a century after Wakeful and much had changed in that time; she never carried the weights Wakeful had to, and her record overall does not match that of Wakeful.

So, it all depends how you look at it and which facts and figures you want to use. The greatest staying mare to ever compete in the Melbourne Cup? Maybe it was Wakeful, or maybe it was Makybe. The greatest mare to win the Cup? Well, history says that it's Makybe Diva . . . and maybe she always will be.

# PART 4

# The Good Old Days

# Azzalin the Dazzlin' Romano

## DAVID HICKIE

ASK ANY OLD-TIME RACEGOER the ownership of the prominent silks 'orange, purple sleeves and black cap' and you'll find most would know them as the colours of Pioneer Concrete boss Sir Tristan Antico.

Ask about their history before that and a few will remember them as the colours carried to fame by the mid 1940s champion Bernborough. It is surprising, however, how few recall their ownership by one of the most colourful characters of Sydney in the 1930s, 40s and 50s—Azzalin Orlando Romano.

Romano, known around town as Azzalin the Dazzlin', was a leading figure in what passed for Sydney's smart set between the wars. His ritzy restaurant, Romano's, had a reputation as the swishest eatery in the city.

Romano's was *the* scene on New Year's Eve and, with the other upmarket restaurant Prince's—run by another horse owner, Jim Bendrodt, in Martin Place—Romano's prided itself as a rendezvous point where the young movers and shakers of the era dined to be seen and preferably photographed for the social pages.

Romano opened his original Romano's cafe at 105 York Street in

1927. In 1938 he acquired additional premises in Castlereagh Street, next to the Prince Edward Theatre and opposite the Hotel Australia, and began Romano's restaurant. He installed an air-conditioning plant, lighting and furnishings, which alone cost £40,000, a tremendous sum in those days.

Things moved slowly for a year or two, but then the war began, bringing a floating population and, of course, the Americans, who guaranteed boom times for restaurants. During the war years, when the restaurant-turned-nightclub became a favourite haunt of American servicemen, everyone stood to attention just before closing time for the playing of the *Star Spangled Banner* and *God Save the King.*

Romano's prospects looked decidedly dim at one point during the boom when the club was declared 'out of bounds' to American servicemen. An Australian publican–punter had flattened an American officer, who had made advances to his girlfriend, by smashing a champagne bottle over the officer's head. But the matter was quickly and discretely resolved, and the ban lifted within a matter of weeks. In the interim Romano's waiters and doormen had merely advised enquiring GIs where to borrow civilian clothes and then ushered them in anyway.

Romano had invested in a farm at Baulkham Hills, northwest of Sydney, to supply his restaurant with vegetables, poultry and pig meat. He kept 6000 fowls on the property. Romano took particular delight in always reminding important visitors and the press, 'I am the pioneer of the first-class restaurant in Australia.'

A magazine of the era summed up:

> Romano's is the nightclub where Sydney's theatre and hotel crowds converge at all hours of the day or night. Romano's restaurant is as spectacular as its owner, a bewildering array of mirrors, blond wood furniture, upholstery in colour something between maroon and burnt orange, concealed lights and high-class dance bands. It is social and near social, expensive and extravagant, the venue of the great and the near great and the would-be great.

The *Sydney Sun* newspaper once noted, 'It became a kind of training ground for generations of Sydney's better-off youngsters.'

Romano also saw himself as a great patron of the theatre and the arts, particularly of the opera, and regularly played host to Toti Del Monte and other stars when they were in Australia. Romano hosted Monte's wedding reception in 1928 with 'thousands of people, champagne and diamonds, and a big gondola of orchids'.

Another celebrated guest was Gracie Fields. 'She came out to sing to the troops during the war,' Romano later recalled, 'and stayed at my house.'

Over the years many famous celebrities dined at Romano's, including Vivien Leigh, who was served by the same waiter who had attended her table in London years before, and knew exactly how she liked her chicken marina. Maurice Chevalier went there every night with his pianist and his wife to drink chianti. 'He was in Sydney 26 days and didn't miss a single meal at my restaurant,' Romano boasted. 'That was the greatest honour anyone ever paid me. Frenchmen know their food.' Bob Hope, Katharine Hepburn and Frank Sinatra went there, too. Prince Philip, then a young naval lieutenant, dined at Romano's regularly during his service with the Royal Navy.

For those in the know, 'going down the mine' meant descending the wide, thickly carpeted staircase past a bust of Napoleon for a night at Romano's. Tony, the headwaiter, immaculate in tails, ushered patrons to their tables; another waiter would present the *carte de jour*; and a third would serve cocktails; a white-aproned attendant would then arrive with bread rolls.

Azzalin Romano was born Orlando Azzalin in Padua in northern Italy and spent his childhood in Verona, where his father was an official in the postal department. Young Orlando wanted to travel the world and, aged ten, he and a 14-year-old companion took a train to Vienna, where he found a job as a pageboy at Vienna's posh Hotel Bristol.

He was paid 15 shillings a week, barely enough to cover his education at the night school from which he eventually matriculated.

Romano later summarised his own success story with the phrase, 'from pageboy to receptionist, to waiter, to cook, to wine butler, to head waiter, to manager, to managing director'.

From the Hotel Bristol he moved about the best hotels and restaurants in Nice, Monte Carlo, Paris and Berlin, and even travelled to the Czar's Russia to become a headwaiter at the Palace.

'I had the pleasure of attending every king of those days,' he later recalled.

His secret, he said, was that he always pursued what he termed 'the experience of the first class'. He explained, 'I wanted only to learn the highest standards in my business. In all my life I have refused to work in cheap places even if it meant taking less money.'

Young Romano had his wish to see the world and, along the way, became fluent in five languages—English, Italian, Spanish, German and French. He also worked on the big European railway trains before eventually heading for England, where his first job involved 18 hours a day as a waiter at the Savoy Hotel, for 5 shillings a week.

Over the next 15 years he climbed the grade, through boarding houses and private hotels, into positions of authority with the Ritz-Carlton Company, the Savoy Company and the Gordon Company. Among the leading hotel restaurants he managed were the Hyde Park Hotel and, in 1922, the Ritz. During those years Romano was also a crack amateur cyclist, winning three gold cups at London's Stamford Bridge track.

It was in England that Romano first learned about racing, but because his job kept him in hotels 16 hours a day he became a punter by betting on the phone. His only ventures to the track were when he waited on the King and Queen during lunch in the Royal Enclosure at Ascot.

While he was headwaiter at the Ritz, Romano found it a major cause of irritation when customers would ask for his name but misunderstand it, mispronounce it or fail to catch it. Then an inspiration came one day as he walked past Romano's Restaurant in London. He immediately changed his name by deed poll. He later explained, 'Romano was so easy to remember. It's just like George in Italian. I have nothing against my original name, a first-class name in Italy, but you have to consider business.'

At an Ascot race meeting while he was in charge of a refreshment marquee for members of the Royal Automobile Club of England, Romano met a Sydney gent named David Stuart Dawson. Dawson persuaded Romano to come to Australia from London, in 1923, to work at a restaurant venture called Ambassadors, which, in its size, aims and expense, was indeed a pioneering step in the Sydney of that time. Several hundred thousand pounds were invested in the lavish establishment, but the response of Sydney's nightlife didn't meet the hopes of its promoters.

The flamboyant Romano quickly became a favourite of the social columns, which took delight in recording the details of his regular sojourns overseas.

For example, in 1934 it was exciting news that Romano, his wife and two children took a six-month trip and motored through England, Scotland, France, Italy and Switzerland. When he returned his opinions were extensively sought: that Vienna was no longer 'the fairyland of Fame', that London was now 'the brightest capital in Europe' and that Paris, in comparison, was 'a dead city'.

The social butterflies were especially interested in his news of 'the latest novelties in cafe entertainment' from the continent, notably that London cabarets were employing more and more American artists and were becoming brighter, and that the latest craze was to have small dancing floors.

Romano would sit in a corner of his club, with characteristic pipe or Havana cigar in hand and a glass of Scotch in front of him, and conduct proceedings. He later installed a portrait of his champion Bernborough in his special corner, and held court below it.

If he was throwing a party of his own, he would adjourn to a private dining room and sing for his guests. As a chorister in his youth, Romano had sung in the High Mass at St Mark's in Venice and at St Anthony's in Padua. During the 1914–18 war he sang at a charity performance in Covent Garden and later he sang at Ambassadors.

'My voice is baritone,' he would declare, 'but I don't know a note of music. My method is to buy a record by a first-class singer, then shut myself in a room and play it over and over again and try to imitate it.'

His favourite song was the prologue from Pagliacci.

During the Depression years Romano and his friends initiated the 'plonk club'. 'In those years,' he later explained, 'there were still a few of us who liked to eat good food and drink fine wines, but we just couldn't afford it. So we decided to keep up appearances, to keep the flag flying. We gave away the fine imported wines and bought plonk.' For 5 shillings a member of the 'plonk club' could have a good meal, half a bottle of plonk and an Australian cigar. Lunch lasted from midday until 4 p.m. and if you were late it meant you must have been doing some business and that meant you shouted for the club.

Romano's, like all nightspots of the era, did a roaring trade in sly grog. In 1935, on one of the rare occasions it encountered any official interference over this matter, a waiter and house manager were each fined £50 for selling sparkling hock at 12 shillings a bottle without a licence.

A police sergeant told the licensing court that the premises were frequented by people of high standing and liquor was sold extensively. He added that the place was run as a cabaret and was always open to the early hours in the morning.

Thereafter, Romano took the necessary precautions and, significantly, Police Commissioner Bill MacKay dined regularly at Romano's restaurant 'on the house'.

However, Romano was personally prosecuted in a Sydney court early in World War II and fined £500 for having presented a false statement of income. In his 1940 annual report, the Commonwealth Taxation Commissioner revealed that, between 1932 and 1938, Romano understated his income by £38,058, adding that this was a case of suspected fraud.

For the most part Romano was always scrupulously careful about his and his establishment's public image. When some influential citizens took a dim view of the high-spirited festivities within his site during the darkest years of World War II, Romano was quick to take on the image of, first and foremost, a man with the national interest at heart. Hence, in April 1943, he announced that his restaurant's famous afternoon tea dance was not to be held in future during working hours 'because of the manpower shortage and in the interests of the war effort'.

During the 1940s the *Adelaide News* said of him, 'This Romano is a personality, handsome, debonair, always immaculately dressed. He has an infectious smile, is a sparkling raconteur and is also a gifted after-dinner speaker. He sings well, and at parties is the life and soul of the company.'

The *Sydney Daily Mirror* tagged him, 'The man who went to Randwick in striped pants and frock coat, spats, grey topper and diamonds.'

Romano had amassed a small fortune from the illegal beer and spirits trade. When matters came to a head during the 1953 Liquor Royal Commission he admitted that he 'carried on for many years' at Romano's Restaurant selling liquor, which he bought on the black market without a permit. He revealed he was also a shareholder and director of the company which owned the notorious Colony Club sly grog den, in the southern suburbs on the Georges River.

Romano's two great passions were restaurants and racehorses and he pursued both with a flair which guaranteed him regular appearances in the headlines. He bought his first horse in 1943 but, within three years, became famous as the owner of Bernborough, 'the Toowoomba Tornado' who won 15 races in succession in 1946 and, according to a newspaper of the time, 'captured the imagination of the racing public as no horse since the fabulous days of Phar Lap'.

Azzalin Romano raced many other top horses over the following seasons. At one point his string totalled 37 thoroughbreds.

In 1946 he paid the top price of 4300 guineas at the annual Easter Yearling Sales for a colt by French sire Le Grand Duc, from a mare called Vocal. The colt was a half-brother to the well-performed Modulation and, after what papers described as a 'brisk bidding duel with Mr A. Basser of Sydney', Romano bought the horse and named it Caruso. It won many good races.

The next year he again paid top price, 3500 guineas, for a bay colt by Midstream from Idle Woods, making it a full brother to Shannon. Romano named the colt Bernbrook and as a three-year-old it won the 1948 Chelmsford Stakes, beating Carbon Copy, Dark Marne and Columnist, and the 1949 Doncaster Handicap at Randwick.

During those years Romano also raced Lady Ajax, Bronze Gold, Grand Romance, Rimini and Haydock, and paid 3500 guineas for a half-brother to On Target and 2700 guineas for a brother of Flying Duke.

In 1950 Romano sold Bernbrook and Caruso to another US millionaire, William Goetz, Louis Meyer's son-in-law. It triggered a sudden announcement by Harry Plant that he had broken off his celebrated relationship with Romano because he had been 'unfairly treated'.

One newspaper of the time noted, 'Romano's zeal to rake in the dollars led to a bitter break with Plant, his trainer, friend and racing counsellor.' Horses trained by Plant for Romano had won a fortune—more than £50,000 in prize money, including more than £26,000 by Bernborough.

Plant, upset that Romano had sold Bernbrook and Caruso while on a trip to the USA, said he had no hint of the plan and declared, 'Romano and I are through for all time'. He also revealed that, after an exchange of letters, Romano, through his lawyer, had ordered Plant to quit the racing stables in Prince Street, Randwick, which Romano owned and Plant occupied and operated in.

Romano, who lived in a £40,000 Killara mansion and also ran a roadhouse near Liverpool on Sydney's western outskirts, continued to race many horses through the 1950s, but had wound down his interest in the sport by the end of the decade. His enthusiasm in culinary entrepreneurial opportunities led to frequent bursts of excitement. At one point in the 1950s he announced a grand plan to establish a chain of luxury restaurants around the capital cities in time for the 1956 Olympic games in Melbourne; the scheme did not eventuate.

With the arrival of the 1960s the old Sydney nightlife scene was changing, and Romano sold his famous restaurant in 1964.

The *Sunday Telegraph* summed it up thus:

The salad days for the former Italian bellhop had been the 30s and 40s, when it was still profitable and desirable to run a grand restaurant. The mood survived into the early 1950s but was gone long before Romano sold out and retired. Napoleon's bust still casts a brave face in the foyer, but the grandeur had withered, the menu that offered 350 splendid dishes had diminished and a swarm of captains and waiters who had smoothly served the tables had shrunk.

After he sold out, Romano's became a discotheque–style nightspot called 'Romano Au Go-Go'.

Romano then left Sydney on a world tour, but in early 1966 he suffered heart problems while travelling in East Africa, and a Ugandan surgeon administered what one newspaper described as 'frequent painkilling injections during a dramatic mercy flight' to the USA, where he underwent emergency surgery.

The three-hour operation, for the removal of an arterial aneurism, involved removal of several inches of weak, ballooning artery and its replacement by a synthetic section made of Dacron.

Romano's English wife, Alice, died in 1971. Their son Renzo had also been a restaurateur in Sydney in the late 1950s before heading for the USA in 1962, where he managed the airport restaurant in Honolulu; later he set out on the American mainland as a professional tennis coach. Romano also had one daughter.

Azzalin Romano lived out his latter years in a flat in exclusive Point Piper, overlooking Sydney Harbour, and died in St Vincent's Hospital in November 1972, aged 78.

# Racing as it was

## A.B. ('BANJO') PATERSON

I FIRST BUTTED INTO the racing game about 60 years ago when I was taken as a small boy to Randwick and saw two three-year-olds, Chester and Cap-a-Pie, run a dead heat in a 3-mile race and they ran the dead heat off the same afternoon.

I suppose you think that trainers ought each to have got six months for training three-year-olds like that, but races were not run from end to end those days. A Cumberland Stakes, 2 miles, in which Carbine beat Lochiel, took over five minutes to run. A trotter could pretty well do that nowadays.

I can just remember James White, a fine big man with a beard and a thorough-going Australian. He believed we could breed first-class horses here and he used Australian sires to an extent that nobody has ever approached since. His great horse Chester was by Yattendon, an Australian-bred horse, and Yattendon was by the Australian Sir Hercules.

Then Chester's son Abercorn was put to the stud, so there were four generations of Australian blood even in those early days. Mr White was like the late John Brown; he believed in breeding and racing his own horses, but he wasn't like John Brown in any other way. He stuck to the one trainer all his life, while John Brown took his whole team away from old Joe Burton simply because Joe told him that one of them was no good

My first experience as an owner came when a country friend sent me down a polo pony, a miniature horse-giantess, thoroughbred, as long as a ship and big everywhere except in height. She could gallop like Eclipse, but was useless for polo, as she needed a 40-acre paddock in which to turn.

Obviously her game was racing, so I leased her to a pony trainer, one Jimmy Gordon, a strong silent man who was, I believe, brother-in-law to William Kelso, the crack trainer of the day. I thought that anything Jimmy didn't know, Kelso would tell him.

Then I moved in one glorious jump right up among the exclusives at the top of the business.

Mainly because I was well known as a writer of racing verse I met and made personal friendships with owners like G.G. Stead, owner of Maxim and many other cracks, G.D. Greenwood (Gloaming), L. McDonald (Wakeful), Sol Green (Comedy King), R.R. Dangar (Peter Pan), W.A. Long (Grand Flaneur) and countless others.

Recognising that I was horse-mad, that great trainer Dick Mason used to make me welcome at his stable and take me along with him when he was saddling Gloaming and others; and here is a queer thing. In all those years I never heard one of those men say that his horse had been pulled by its rider or that he had lost a race through roguery or by interference of bookmakers.

A strange thing, when you come to look at it, for the general idea is that racing is rotten with ramps and roguery.

Some of these men were notoriously mean with presents to riders but they got a square deal just the same. Owners of third-rate horses had plenty to say about the iniquities of riders, but up in the serene air of the classic contenders the subject was never even mentioned.

★

When I first blundered into racing, Mr Henry Dangar was chairman of the Australian Jockey Club, a masterful man. He imported the great St Simon horse Positano—an animal which would never have left England only that he had a will of his own. Mr Dangar entrusted the training of his horse to the capable hands of John Allsopp, one of the old school whose pessimistic outlook on life had earned him the nickname of 'Crying Johnny' of the turf.

Positano had to go to Melbourne to race and Allsopp said that the horse would require a box to himself on the train; if other horses were put in anywhere near him he would spend the trip trying to get at them.

Mr Dangar had never heard of such a proposition, and the trainer was ordered to attend a meeting of the owner and a few of his cronies to give an explanation. 'Johnny' put up such a good 'cry' that he got his own way: nor did he resent being told that the horse's wilfulness must be his fault. Trainers are used to shouldering the blame for everything.

Another English horse which came out here under somewhat similar circumstances was Orzil. He was a really high-class performer in England in the ownership of one of the Brasseys. Mr Pat Osborne, who was later to achieve fame as the owner of Valicare, was visiting England and happened to mention to Brassey that he was looking out for a horse. He could hardly believe his ears when Brassey said that he would give him Orzil. *Give* him, mind you, when the horse was one of the best performers in England.

'He's turned unreliable,' said Brassey, 'but I can't sell him here for fear he might take it into his head to do his best and beat me in a big race. It would make me look a fool. If you take him away out to Australia and guarantee that he never comes back, you can have him for nothing.'

## Randwick real estate

One wonders how long it will be before Sydney reaches out and swallows up Randwick. Possibly, from a town planner's point of view, the racecourse might be allowed to survive indefinitely as a lung of the city, but it seems possible that the trainers and horses may be pushed out, even though Randwick remains.

A trainer needs a large area for his establishment, and, as soon as prosperity returns, the prices and rents will go up, and the trainers will find it hard to stand up against the pressure of population. Already some of them have been driven into suburban backyards, and others are finding it very hard to meet the overheads. Asphalt or cement roads encircle the course on practically every side, and the clatter of a string of horses going out for the exercise at daylight is prolific of strong language among local householders.

No doubt Randwick will last our time, and when it does go the training fraternity will go voluntarily with it. One cannot for long pay Potts Point rents on Randwick profits.

## A £30 purse

Did they ever race £30 at Randwick? 'Too right' they did, according to an old racebook of the year 1866 kindly sent to me by Mr H.L. Harnett, a representative of an old Monaro family. The racebook of those days left a good deal to the imagination. For instance, the names of all horses' sire and dam were not given, but merely the name of the owner and the horse.

By way of compensation, the back of the book contains a number of perforated slips about the size of postage stamps to assist the then popular pastime of getting up a sweeps. Horses were few and prizes paltry, but they managed to provide a four days meeting, with five races on the first, second and fourth days, and four races on the third.

It was in the last race of the meeting, a forced handicap for all winners, optional losers, that the £30 stake made its appearance. The blow was somewhat softened by a sweepstakes of £5 from the eight runners; but the winner had to return 5 sovereigns to the club.

## Riding positions

A thing that made a lot of talk at the time was the change from the old upright seat to the crouch seat. Ted Sloan was doing wonders with the crouch seat and our trainers wanted to try it, but none of them liked to take the plunge. So Tom Payten who trained for all the conservative swells—Sir Adrian Knox, Hon. Agar Wynne, and so on—took it on and he went about it this way.

Payten had a boy named Richardson, 'Dingo' Richardson they called him, and this boy could ride the crouch seat pretty well. So, he had some private trials early in the morning. He made Richardson gallop sitting up and then he made him ride the same horse under the same conditions crouching on his neck.

He told me that the times were at least a second a mile faster with the crouch seat, and he made all his boys get up on their necks. When Tom led, the rest of the trainers soon followed.

The crouch method of riding was invented by the Negro riders in the southern states of America, so Tom Payten said, 'There you are! We've been at it all our lives and it takes a lot of Americans to tell us that a horse carries weight better over his shoulders than over his loins.'

## Use of the whip

There is a story of an English trainer who was putting up an apprentice for his first ride in a race. The youngster, very nervous, came to scale with whip and spurs, but before he weighed out the trainer said to him, 'You had better take off those spurs, my boy; this horse doesn't like them.' Then, as a sort of afterthought, he added, 'Now give me your whip, and you'll be all right.'

This might be regarded by the cynical as a good way of ensuring that the horse did not win; but modern riding has seen less and less use, or misuse, of the whip, and both the crack Australian rider Jim Pike and the crack English rider Gordon Richards are very sparing in the use of the whip. Pike hardly ever brings the whip into play at a finish, and if his horse is beaten he does not add a flogging to the other troubles of the animal. In fact, some grandstand critics have been heard to say that Pike cannot use the whip; but he has proved the fallacy of this opinion on occasions when it was absolutely necessary.

Richards uses a different method from that of Pike, for he flourishes his whip a lot at a finish. An official who interested himself in the matter says that he carefully examined a number of horses that Richards had ridden in what looked like flogging finishes and never found a whip mark on one of them.

Richards found that the mere threat of the whip was enough to get the last ounce out of 99 per cent of horses and that the odd 1 per cent consisted of horses that were slugs by temperament.

In the 'good old days', now passed beyond recall, it was customary to see all the boys go for their whips at the turn, and the poet Gordon, himself a race rider, says:

> Behind, the hoof-thunder is blended
> With the whistling and cracking of whips;

Which makes one wonder why they were such good days, after all—at any rate, for the horses.

## The aeroplane theory

The world moves, but it is a trite saying that some of us move faster than others. New ideas and new theories are constantly introduced, even into the somewhat stereotyped business of racing. For instance, we have had the figure theory and the heart theory, and now we have a new one—the aeroplane theory. This theory relates to 'jockeyship', and is put forward by an amateur aviator, who mixes punting with tailspins and nosedives. Briefly put, his theory is that Pike's wonderful success in the saddle is due to his adoption of the principle of the aeroplane.

'You watch Pike ride,' he said, 'and you will notice that he does not sit like the other riders; he holds his body well clear of the saddle and well clear of the horse's neck, and he keeps his back quite flat and parallel with the ground. Well, what's the result? As he goes along the wind gets under his body and tends to lift him off the saddle; the faster that he goes the less he weighs, and if he could only go fast enough he would weigh nothing at all.'

A somewhat cynical suggestion was made that if Pike could only get fast enough he might even lift the horse off the ground; the theorist, being of a literal turn of mind, did not see any sarcasm in the remark. 'Tell me this,' he said. 'What makes a three-ton airplane with 15 passengers in it rise off the ground? Nothing but the pressure on the air under the upper wing of the machine, and if the pressure of air will lift all that weight, why shouldn't it lift a jockey's body?'

Not having Kingsford Smith at hand as an authority, it was somewhat difficult to combat this novel explanation of Pike's success in the saddle. But if the aeroplane theory should ever meet with popular acceptance, it might be necessary to tie the legs of the lighter boys under the saddle, lest they should disappear altogether.

## Apprentices

Apprentice riders are supposed to be hardened little citizens, above the weakness of displaying any emotion; but, after all, they are only small boys of about 15 or so, prone to the excitability of other small boys of their age

As Kipling says of soldiers, they are 'single men in barracks most uncommonly like you'.

The small apprentice Lightfoot, having ridden his first winner in the two-year-old race at Moorfield, burst into a storm of tears of excitement as he rode back to the weighing yard. It added a human touch to the proceedings.

It is a great thing for a small boy to ride his first winner while still at a weight at which he can get plenty of riding.

This boy Lightfoot is a son of the once well-known rider Joe Lightfoot, a jockey who weighed about as much as a box of matches, but had such wonderful 'hands' that he could hold any horse at any pace in any company. The trouble with Joe Lightfoot was that he had an incurable habit of looking round while leading in a race; in all other respects he was one of the best natural horsemen at his weight ever seen on our turf.

Without knowing anything of the circumstances of the case, one may be permitted to hope that this youngster may turn out as good a horseman as his father without suffering from the looking-round complex.

The handling of racehorses by six-stone-seven boys is one of the wonders of the world. The average grown-up man, though he may figure with distinction on a hack, could not hold a racehorse for half a minute; but these midgets can put him anywhere, and do anything with him, without exerting any physical strength at all. They are the elect out of hundreds that go into apprenticeship, only to find that 95 per cent of them will never make horsemen. It is a case of survival of the fittest, and those that do survive are entitled to all the money they make.

One of W. Kelso's apprentices, on joining the stable, borrowed a book on race riding and started to copy it out in handwriting. It is not known whether he ever finished it—it was a large book—but at any rate he copied out enough of it to make himself a very successful rider, who at the age of 20 was earning more money than most barristers of 50.

The racing business is rather overcrowded just now, but somehow there always seems to be room at the top.

## Stipendiary stewards

So much for straight-going experiences; now for the other side.

I have seen them all, the big punters who bestride this narrow world until one day they are missing; the small battling owners and trainers, living in hopes of finding a big punter who will 'dash it down' for them on a specially prepared horse. Here and in England it is just the same.

Taking it by and large, and expressing it in a comprehensive sort of way, the public got the idea that where there were six races in a day, there were six crimes to be detected, so stipendiary stewards were appointed to control racing.

I seem to have seen the beginnings of a lot of things in my life and among others I saw the beginnings of the stipendiary system.

One of the first men appointed was my lifelong friend, Leslie Rouse, a solicitor by profession and son of Richard Rouse, a grazier and thoroughbred breeder of Mudgee.

Leslie Rouse had an inherited and unequalled knowledge of the thoroughbred horse, had been an amateur rider, and had graduated in bush racing where the prizes are small and the owners and trainers have to be *sans peur* if not *sans reproche* in order to get a living.

Before long there was an outcry that Rouse was catching only the small fry and was letting the big fish escape. He said in reply that it pained him like anything to put out the small and hungry battlers, but as they did such desperate things he had no option.

As he had no legal authority to compel witnesses to appear before him, he had to get his information as best he could.

'The big races are all right,' said Rouse. 'Nobody is going to pull a horse in The Metropolitan to win a race at Menangle; but when I see a horse running three stone above his form and somebody winning a million I always wish that I could catch the man who worked it, but I very seldom can.'

## 'Unwisdom'

I was at a harbour picnic given by New South Wales Premier 'Joe' Carruthers for the great New Zealand owner G.G. Stead, who had been over with his horses the previous year and had simply swept the board. First and second in the Derby, winner of the principal weight-for-age races, he had made turf history.

So, Joe Carruthers, who liked a punt on a good thing, invited me to join a harbour picnic he was giving for G.G. Stead. I did not grasp the idea at first but it soon became obvious that the object of the entertainment was to get Stead to talk about the chances of his colt Huascar, the only animal he had brought over that year.

The affair was a great success, up to a certain point. There was a feast of reason and a flow of champagne. We went around the harbour and visited the beauty spots and the training ships, but not a word about Huascar.

Just as we were getting back to the wharf, Joe came to me and said, 'You know the old sphinx, ask him about Huascar.'

'No,' I said, 'you're the Premier of the State and you're giving the entertainment. You ask him.'

So the question was put, and Stead gave a true sphinx-like answer.

'I've had a lot of experience in racing, Mr Carruthers,' he said, 'and I found one rule that paid me all the time; and that is, when you don't know anything, don't bet.'

Good enough advice perhaps, but not what Joe had expected in return for his champagne.

After parting from our host, Mr Stead and I walked up the street together and he decided to talk.

'If I told him not to back the horse,' he said, 'he would think I was putting him off. If I told him to back it he would not believe that I was giving a good thing away. But I can tell you this colt isn't worth two shillings and I only brought him over to support the meeting as I won such a lot last year. You can tell anybody you like, for none of them will believe you.'

Feeling that I owed Joe something for his harbour picnic, I passed this information on to him.

'Who told you the colt was no good?' he asked.

'Mr Stead told me.'

'Then I don't believe it. Do you mean to tell me that he'd bring a horse all the way from New Zealand if it wasn't a crack? He must think we're simple over here.'

This morbid frame of mind made him back Huascar and the animal, in racing parlance, 'isn't in yet': which only illustrates the 'unwisdom' of telling anybody anything on the turf.

## The Gawk

A good many years ago I was asked to go along with a friend who had a commission to buy a yearling for somebody up-country. I think he took me along to share the blame if he bought a bad one.

We inspected all sorts, big and little, fat and thin, dumpy little fillies and big, awkward, angular colts.

Among the colts, one particular clumsy legs-and-wings youngster attracted our condemnation. To mark him for identification we called him The Gawk. We all agreed that if we bought The Gawk we would deserve to find ourselves in a lunatic asylum looking out, so we decided on a chunky, ready-made filly that looked like racing early.

The filly showed some early promise and then faded away into the backblocks and was never heard of again, while The Gawk, under the name of Bitalli, won the Melbourne Cup.

My friend's principal is still alive and only needs a few stimulants and he will talk for hours about the time he would have won the Melbourne Cup only to entrusting his commission to a couple of blind men.

If there is a moral to this disconnected narrative, it is that it is not as easy to buy a good yearling as one might suppose.

## Honour among thieves

A friend of mine, a respectable grazier and dealer in sheep, asked me to meet him at Wollongong races to talk over a deal in sheep which might do both of us some good. He could not spare the time to come to Sydney. It had to be Wollongong races.

Arrived at Wollongong I was staggered when my friend asked me to put £300 on a horse for him. It was a horse called Valet Boy, a maiden which had never run.

I declined on the grounds that the ring knew very well that I was not a betting man and, if I came along with £300, they would smell danger.

He persisted, but I was obdurate. He and his friends put the £300 on themselves; the horse won, running away, by 6 lengths; and before it had passed the post there were cries of 'I'll bet on the protest!'

Sure enough there was a protest and an investigation by stewards as to the *bona fides* of Valet Boy and I was asked to attend the stipendiary stewards' room as they had been told that I had put the money on.

It turned out that my ultra-respectable grazier had so far slipped from grace as to join up with a lot of bush sharps and they had 'rung in' a well-performed northern horse as a maiden under the name of Valet Boy.

After months of patient enquiry, stewards disqualified the horse trainer and jockey, but they did not get my pastoral friend who was at the back of the whole thing.

Of course, I couldn't talk; there is honour even among thieves.

## What do you know?

Dick Mason used to be a heavy bettor in his younger days and he'd have £1000 on a horse, but he got cautious as he got older.

I met him once at Randwick, when he had just landed with Gloaming and some other horses.

'I've just come here straight off the boat,' he said. 'Do you know anything for this race?'

'Well,' I said, 'I think so-and-so will win.'

'That's no good to me,' he said, 'what anybody thinks. Do you know anything? If you know anything, I'll have a quid on it.'

What he meant by knowing anything was that I should tell him that something had 3 stone in hand and that the others were all running dead.

That's the way fellows get after they have been betting for 40 or 50 years.

## A murmur of discontent

At one hunt meeting in Sydney years ago a horse was being weighed out to run when a bystander remarked casually, 'That's not Murmur at all; that's a horse called Shoo Fly, and he's won races at McGrath's Hill.'

The owner was rounded up and he at once admitted the soft impeachment.

'Murmur went lame,' he said, 'and I wanted to have a run, so I brought this horse.'

He thought that the officials were stupidly particular when they refused to let one horse run under the name of another!

## The picture of misery

As a young man I went up to the Wellington meeting to ride a horse in an amateur hurdle race. This horse had been grievously maltreated, for he had started as many as three times in a day at amateur meetings with huge weights on him, and in his spare time he had been used as galloping companion to a Sydney Cup candidate. He went right off his feed and his owner offered him to me for £25 in full training, but I preferred the personal to the financial risk.

As his trainer refused to have any more to do with him, I handed him over to P. Nolan, who was just starting as a trainer. Nolan got him to face his victuals, and we won a brush hurdle race at Canterbury Park at his first start over jumps; then we took him up to the Bligh meeting at Mudgee. He travelled up all right, in fact he ate all the way up in the train; but as soon as we put him in the loose box at the local hotel he started to shiver all over, while the sweat ran off him and he looked the picture of misery and despair. We thought he was in for an attack of colic. The veterinarian Harry Raynor was called in and after examining him Harry said, 'There's nothing the matter with him; it's just funk. He's remembering something that happened to him the last time he slept in a bush pub stable.'

Sure enough, Harry was right, for the horse won his race with the greatest ease, though he never ate a mouthful at Mudgee; and now, when I hear people say that horses don't remember and don't put two and two together, I recall that poor unfortunate animal shivering in his lonely box and thinking that he was in for another three races in the day with big weights up. There are lot of things that we don't know about horses.

## Those who know . . .

As regards prospects for big races, it may be said that those who know don't talk and those who talk don't know, and this is particularly true of the racing fraternity. Such opinions as are expressed by trainers are mostly guarded and are not marked by enthusiasm.

# The Day That is Dead

## Harry ('Breaker') Morant

Ah, Jack! Time finds us feeble men,
And all too swift our years have flown.
The days are different now to then—
In that time when we rode ten stone.

The minstrel when his mem'ry goes
To old times, tunes a doleful lay—
Comparing modern nags with those
Which Lee once bred down Bathurst way.

The type to-day's a woeful weed,
Which lacks the stoutness, strength and bone
Of horses they were wont to breed
In those days—when we rode ten stone.

But all of us remorseless Fate
O'ertakes, and as the years roll on
Our saddles carry extra weight,
And old age mourns the keenness gone.

The young ones, too—'mong men, I mean—
Watch not the sires from whom they've sprung,
They nowadays are not so keen
As when we—and the world—were young.

They've neither nerve nor seat to suit
The back of Paddy Ryan's roan—
That wall-eyed, vicious, bucking brute
You rode—when you could ride ten stone.

But, Johnny, ere we 'go to grass'—
Ere angel wings are fledged to fly—
With wine we'll fill a bumper glass,
And drink to those good times gone by.

We've *had* our day—'twill not come back!
But, comrade mine, this much you'll own,
'Tis something *to have had it,* Jack—
That time when we could ride ten stone!

# Racing in Australia circa 1895

## NAT GOULD

*The famous English author Nat Gould lived and worked as a racing journalist in Australia for 11 years, from 1884 to 1895. His observations of Australian racing, written more than a hundred years ago, make for fascinating reading.*

## A climate for racing

IN NO PART of the world can be found more enthusiastic followers of the turf than in Australia.

Racing, in my humble opinion, is the most absorbing and interesting of sports. To love horses is an inherent characteristic of Britishers and the bulk of the Colonial people come from good old British stock.

In England the climate is often dead against enjoying racing in the most favourable circumstances, but in Australia there is very little to complain of as regards the weather. Sunny skies in that favoured island are the rule, and it is the exception and not the rule to be let in for a drenching day's sport.

Nine months out of twelve the climate of Australia is all that can be desired, and what more can a man expect?

The racing year commences on 1st August, from which the ages of horses date, so that the three-year-olds running in the AJC Derby in the middle of September* and the VRC Derby in the first week of November, or the last week in October, are much younger than three-year-olds taking part in the English Derby.

So favourable is the climate that flat-racing is going on all year round, and there is no closed time, as in the old country.

Occasionally in the winter months it is necessary to wear a top-coat, but even then the sun is generally warm enough to make it pleasant. The lack of east winds, or frost or snow, make racing a pleasure rather than a burden.

At Christmas it is racing in sunshine to perfection, and the meeting of the AJC at Randwick on Boxing Day may be described as a few hours turned into melting moments.

Many a time, as I watched the race for the Summer Cup at Randwick, has my mind wandered to the old land, and thoughts of the snow and dull leaden sky have almost made me shiver, even with the thermometer at close upon a hundred in the shade.

Christmas in Australia is indeed a contrast to that in England. Boxing Day races in the two hemispheres are also vastly different.

In Australia we have flat-racing amidst glorious sunshine. In England races are held under the National Hunt Rules, probably with a white mantle of snow covering the earth.

There cannot be much pleasure even in backing a winner when your fingers are almost too cold to hold the money, and it must be indeed a dreary occupation to be out 'in the cold' and backing losers with the thermometer down at zero.

If Fortune be cold to us in Australia we have the consolation of knowing that Nature warms towards us.

It must be very depressing to return from a racecourse with empty pockets and a thaw setting in. Men must have strong constitutions to stand the wear and tear of English racing, season after season, and they earn the money they make.

---

*This has long since changed to autumn.

Racing in the Australian Colonies is conducted under the most favourable atmospheric conditions as a rule, and therefore it is all the more delightful and enjoyable.

## Racing men in Australia

I doubt if there can be found as much enthusiasm in a race crowd in any part of the globe as there is in Australia. No matter under what circumstances the racing takes place, the people enjoy it, and even the downfall of favourites has not much effect upon them.

Hundreds of men live 'on the game' and appear to do well at it. How they live is a mystery to most people. They must have money to bet with, and to pay their expenses, and they always have a pound or two to invest upon anything they fancy. These hangers-on of the turf are a nuisance to trainers, for they are constantly badgering them for tips.

Many of them are friends of the jockeys and no doubt obtain information from them; and jockeys are much more ready to talk on an Australian racecourse than they are in England.

On the turf in Australia is an exceedingly pleasant existence. There are the usual ups and downs connected with it, and the same amount of good luck and bad luck.

It is a genuine cosmopolitan crowd on an Australian racecourse. The Governor of the Colony appears to forget his office for the time being and to take a delight in mingling with the people. A racing governor is bound to become popular while a governor who has no fondness for sports of any kind has no hold on the affections of the people.

Lord Carrington was one of the most popular governors New South Wales ever had, and so was Lord Hopetoun in Victoria, and both were real good sportsmen.

Class distinctions are not as marked on colonial racecourses as they are in England. There are no reserves for the Upper Ten, as at Ascot, Goodwood and other places in England. The AJC and VRC have reserves for their members, and there is far more extensive and better accommodation provided for the public in Australia. The accommodation at Flemington and Randwick is far ahead of that on principal English courses.

Racing in the sunny south is far more of a pleasure than a business. Thousands of people are not cooped up in small rings, as though they were so many sheep crowded into a pen. There is plenty of elbow room, even on a Melbourne Cup Day at Flemington there is ample room for the ladies to promenade on the spacious lawn, although there are fifty to eighty thousand people present on the course.

Ten thousand is a small crowd for a great race meeting in Australia, although it does not meet this number at suburban meetings, unless it be an exceptional day.

It is this feeling of freedom and comfort that makes turf life in the colonies so pleasant and enjoyable. There is so much geniality and goodwill about it.

Although men are keen on making money, and occasionally indulge in sharp practices, most owners are not averse to the public knowing what their horses can do and what chances they have of winning.

No owner I ever met likes to be forestalled in the betting market, nor is it natural he should be. It is not in human nature that such should be the case.

Granted the public pay freely toward the race-fund, in the form of gate money, if they bet that is their lookout but they should not forget that keeping racehorses is a very expensive game. Owners of racehorses have a lot to contend with and I think they may be pardoned if occasionally they say bitter things when they find themselves forestalled in the market.

The best part of the day, my opinion, is the early morning, and many a pleasant hour have I spent on the training track watching the horses at work. There are no restrictions placed upon the members of the sporting press watching horses do their gallops.

Formerly at Randwick anyone was allowed on the training track, but now only those persons who have business there are permitted to be present. This is a change for the better.

Every facility is given the representatives of the various news-papers by the racecourse authorities, and with but few exceptions they are treated with courtesy and respect.

The sporting pressmen with whom I associated during my stay in the colonies were a genial, jolly set of men, and thoroughly competent. We had some rare fun as we journeyed to the various meetings, and jokes and anecdotes flew around rapidly. Regular Bohemians they were, and warm-hearted and generous to a degree, always ready and willing to lend a helping hand to a comrade, either in his work or when misfortunes overtook him.

They were men who had many temptations thrown in their way, but kept honest and straight in their careers. Some of the happiest days of my working life have been spent in their society and as comrades the bulk of them were as true as steel.

We had our little differences occasionally and at times the arguments as to the merits of certain horses became heated, but all these disputes ended amicably and the discourse generally ended with, 'Well, what's yours, old man?'

Yes, those were the jolly days, and if any of my old comrades of the Press read this book, I trust that they will allow the writer to class himself as one of them still.

## Jockeys

Australian jockeys have a different style and appearance to the English. They are, as a rule, neat in their dress and it is an exception to see a slovenly jockey.

Good jockeys are few and far between. Many men are able to ride a horse, but this does not constitute a good jockey. Race-riding is an art that few men, and hardly any boys, are proficient in.

At the present time, however, there are some fine riders on the turf in Australia. Such men as John Fielder, the Delaneys, the Goughs, the Cooks, Lewis, Kelso, Parker, Huxley, Harris and Dawes Park are all thoroughly reliable riders. Martin Gallagher is getting on in years, but his hand has lost none of its cunning.

A good yarn is told about Martin Gallagher. At Rosehill he rode a certain horse, and he was called upon to explain its running. The chairman had a horse running in this particular race.

'You could have been much nearer to the winner,' said the chairman.

'Yes,' said Martin, 'but I could not have won.'

'Why did you not ride your horse out?' asked the chairman.

'I got jammed in,' said Martin with a smile, 'one horse kept me in all down the straight; in fact, this horse was "shepherding" me all through the race.'

'And whose horse was that?' indignantly asked the chairman.

'Yours, sir,' was the quiet but very effective reply.

Nothing came of that inquiry.

Jockeys are often accused of pulling horses when they are not at fault. I am sorry to say, however, I have seen horses deliberately stopped.

In the majority of cases the men who instruct the jockeys how to ride races are to blame. If a jockey does not carry out the instructions he receives, he does not get many mounts.

An Australian jockey has not much chance of making a big fortune from riding fees alone; there are exceptions, but not many.

An attempt was made by Mister W.A. Long, one of the members of the AJC Committee, to reduce the jockeys' fee for a losing mount to £1. I wrote strongly against this at the time, and so did others, and eventually the fee was fixed at £2 instead of £3. For a winning mount on the flat a jockey receives £5, and it is considerably more for hurdle and steeplechase riding.

When we consider the small number of mounts a jockey can get in a year, his income cannot be large. Thirty winning mounts is far above the average for a jockey in a season in Australia.

Jockeys are not allowed to bet, but they do bet, and heavily sometimes. It is a bad system, but it will never be avoided so long as a jockey cannot make a good income from riding fees alone. I have known jockeys standing to win large stakes on races. They have told me the amount on several occasions.

It is a pernicious practice for an owner to put a jockey up and give him orders not to win, and yet this is done by men who ought to know better.

I once asked a popular jockey why he did not decline to ride a horse when he was given orders not to win.

'If I did I should never get another mount from him,' he answered, naming a well-known owner. 'Not only that, but he would influence other owners against me.'

Accidents will happen during races, but many could be avoided if mere lads who know no more how to ride a race than they know how to fly, were not put up in the saddle.

These youngsters have no fear because they are unaware of the danger. There are far too many of these apprentices riding in the colonies.

One of the worst accidents I saw was at Randwick, when Alec Robinson was killed by Mister Cooper's Silvermine falling. Poor Robinson was literally smashed all to pieces, and was hardly recognisable when brought into the casualty room.

It is really wonderful how often riders escape. Tom Corrigan and Martin Bourke were killed, one a few days after the other. Corrigan, about the best steeplechase rider in the colonies, was killed by his horse Waiter falling in a steeplechase at Caulfield. A public subscription was raised for his widow, who got a good round sum. The little Irishman was one of the most jovial, goodhearted men I ever met.

Martin Bourke was killed while schooling a horse over hurdles at Flemington. Bourke was the most fearless rider, and the number of falls he had was remarkable. I think he had nearly every bone in his body broken at one time or another.

There are some fair amateur riders in Australia, but not so many as one would expect in such a country. There are hundreds of splendid horsemen in the colonies, and yet very few men capable of riding a decent race in the amateur ranks.

Jockeys have too much spare time on their hands, and this is not a good thing for anyone. I have repeatedly advocated the formation of a jockeys' clubhouse at Randwick, or in the vicinity, where the lads could pass away their spare hours. In such a club they would be free from public house surroundings, and would have their billiards in peace and quietness. Most jockeys are fond of a game of billiards.

It does not look well to see jockeys hanging around the entrance of Tattersalls' club and other places. Very few jockeys in Australia have retaining fees, and are constantly on the lookout for chance mounts.

For a big race leading jockeys will probably be engaged to ride for a stable, and certain jockeys may generally be depended upon to ride for certain owners or stables, but, as I said before, very few have retaining fees.

There is a vast difference in the way races are ridden in Australia to the old country. Waiting tactics are not often resorted to, and it is generally a hot pace the full distance. The severe 2 miles of the Melbourne Cup course is run at full speed, and there is not much chance of waiting on the road. This system of riding is in a great measure due to the time test. If a horse is timed to run 2 miles in say 3.29 or 3.30, then he has to do it in the race if possible. A slow-run race is an exception. I mean, as a rule the horses go at their top, but they may not be fast enough to make good time.

It would surprise many people to see the rate at which horses go over hurdles and steeplechase fences. In a hurdle race horses very often go as fast as they do on the flat. Steeplechasers are often ridden at a breakneck pace, which says more for the pluck than the judgement of the riders.

## Tom Hales

When I first went to Australia Tom Hales was at the height of his fame as a jockey, but of late years he has almost given up riding and is rarely seen in the saddle. His record stands alone, and he has ridden more winners than any other jockey in the colonies. He has won nearly every race of importance on the Australian turf, and his classic wins are too numerous to mention.

As a rider of two-year-olds Hales may be placed on a par with that master of the art, Tom Cannon. Hales has a wonderful sympathy with the horse he rides, and he and his mount appear to understand each other thoroughly. In such races as the Derby, Hales's judgement stands him in good stead, and his knowledge of pace was never better displayed than when he beat Carbine on Ensign in the Derby of 1888.

It was in this type of race for the late James White that Hales scored his biggest wins, and he rode scores of winners for the Newmarket stable.

Tom Hales, in my humble opinion, is one of the best men I ever saw ride a racehorse. He has marvellous hands, a clear, cool head, and is a wonderful judge of pace, a great finisher, and has a good seat. Above all, he is as honest as the day, and there has never been a whisper of suspicion against him during his long career in the saddle.

I have known Hales a long time, and his modest and unassuming manner and thorough straightforwardness have always favourably impressed me. Many happy hours have I spent with him, both on the turf and off, more especially in his beautiful home, Acmeville, at Moonee Ponds, near Melbourne.

Acmeville is a charming residence, luxurious without being ostentatious. Tom Hales at home is the hospitable host and Mrs Hales, a daughter of South Australia's most successful breeder of horses, is a model wife.

Unfortunately Tom Hales is a great sufferer from asthma and is anything but strong. His love of riding, however, is as keen as ever. The last time I was at Acmeville he returned with me to Melbourne in order to go on that night to Caulfield to ride one of his own horses at work next morning.

'I never consider any trouble or inconvenience it may cause me, when there is work to be done,' he said, when I asked him why he left his comfortable home to go out to Caulfield. 'I have always made it a practice through life to be on the spot when I'm wanted. I have done this for the owners I have ridden for, now I am doing it for myself.'

Tom Hales is a wealthy man, and has acquired his money in an honest manner, and has worked very hard for it, I'm afraid to the detriment of his health.

He has a fine stud farm at Halesville, near Albury, in lovely country near the banks of the Murray, and there he is devoting much of his time to the breeding of bloodstock. He purchased Lochiel, the famous son of Prince Charlie, but was induced to part with him, and I think he has regretted the sale ever since.

## Superstitions

The same superstitions exist as in the old land, and racing men are wont to regard certain signs and omens with an amount of awe not understandable to ordinary mortals.

I was seated in a tramcar one morning when a particular friend of mine stepped in and sat down. Suddenly, without a word of warning, he jumped up and rushed out again.

I looked under the seat to see if a dog had been secreted there, and had gone for his calves, but there was nothing to cause alarm in that direction.

Much to my surprise I saw him come in at the other side of the tram and quietly sit down.

'What is the matter?' I asked. 'Too much whiskey last night?'

'No,' he replied, 'it's race day, you know, and I got in the wrong side of the tram. It's unlucky.'

I suggested that getting out again and coming in the other side of the tram did not do away with the fact that he had originally made a mistake. He acknowledged this, but added that repairing the error might lessen the unlucky consequences of the action.

Another friend, who was a 'chief' on one of the Orient Liners, invariably backed a horse whose name suggested something nautical or reminded him of the ship he was on. He backed a horse called Oroya one day, beause it was named after an Orient Liner, and the horse won.

Some men invariably back the first horse they see upon entering the paddock and others back the mount of the jockey whose colours they first come across.

## Women at the races

Women punters abound on the racecourses and the same faces may be seen meeting after meeting. As a rule these punters are middle-aged or elderly women, though there are a few young ones to be found.

It is amusing to watch the tactics of these women. Their faces plainly show the fascination that gambling, not horse-racing, possesses for them. The flushed countenances and restless expression betoken a mind and a system strung to the highest pitch by the pernicious habit they have acquired and which has, alas, thoroughly mastered them.

With a purse clutched tightly in one hand, and either a satchel or umbrella in the other, they push and jostle in the crowded ring, and dart from one bookmaker to the other to see which horses are backed. There is no bashfulness about these dames of the turf and I am afraid some of them forfeit a good deal of what self-respect they have to obtain information.

Some bookmakers, to their credit be it said, have a strong objection to betting with women; and I know more than one man in the ring who declines to bet with them. Others are not so scrupulous, and accept money, no matter from what quarter it comes.

On many occasions I have seen these women, when the race is being run, sitting on a seat in a quiet part of the course, waiting for the winner's number to be hoisted, and taking no interest in the race itself. All they think about is winning money, and for the sport they care very little.

There are thousands of ladies, however, at Flemington and Randwick, on Derby and Cup Days, who visit the racecourse out of pure love of the sport, combined with a natural feminine desire to be seen and to see others.

To the credit of the racecourse secretaries and officials, be it said that they use every endeavour to keep loose women off their courses, and in this they succeed admirably.

## A racecourse demonstration

On racecourses in Australia the public are apt to express their opinions freely when anything suspicious takes place. I shall not forget in a hurry a scene that occurred at Eagle Farm, Brisbane, I think in 1887.

It was when Honest Ned won the Brisbane Cup.

At that time Mr C. Holmes was the starter at the club. There were some hot favourites in the race, such as Touchstone, who had won the Morton Handicap; Lord Headington, winner of the Derby on the first day of the meeting; Pirate, Theorist and several others. Some heavy double event books were then open on the Moreton Handicap and Brisbane Cup.

Honest Ned, owned by Mr D'Arcy, was an outsider.

At the start there was a lot of delay, and at last the horses got off to what appeared to be a false start to the majority of the people. Some of the horses ran the course, and, of this lot, Honest Ned won.

Several of the horses, including most of the heavily backed ones, did not run but remained at the post. The jockeys of these horses declared—two of them to me personally—that the starter called them back.

No notice was taken of the race won by Honest Ned, and the people were waiting for the horses to go back to the post and start again. To the amazement and indignation of the crowd, a rumour quickly went round that it was a start, and Honest Ned had won. The stewards held an inquiry, and the race was given to Honest Ned, the outsider.

I have seen a few exhibitions of feeling on racecourses, but never one to equal that at Eagle Farm when this decision was given. The crowd rushed the grandstand enclosure and commenced to pull down the fencing. For a short time there was a riot, and some of the stewards were greatly perplexed as to what should be done.

The manager of the totalisator took the precaution to retreat with the money to a safe distance until the storm was over. I never saw a racecourse crowd more determined to show how they felt about a race. It was a deplorable blunder on somebody's part, and it would have been better to have run the race over again, but as the starter stated it was a start, the stewards had no option, and awarded the race to Honest Ned.

I met Mr Holmes the morning after as we were crossing the Brisbane River in a ferry boat. He assured me he gave the word to go, and that he was very sorry such a start had taken place. I told him jockeys who remained at the post said he did not say 'go', and that they've heard him call out 'come back'. To this the starter replied that they had made a mistake. It was a lucky race for the ringmen, as Honest Ned got them out of most of their double difficulties.

# Jim Bendrodt

## DAVID HICKIE

WHILE BERNBOROUGH'S OWNER, Azzalin the Dazzlin' Romano, advertised his famous nightspot Romano's restaurant as the swishest eatery in Sydney during the 1930s and 1940s, his great competitor, the equally flash Jim Bendrodt, ran Prince's restaurant on the opposite corner at Martin Place.

James Charles 'Jim' Bendrodt—lumberjack, radio announcer, sailor, soldier, actor, champion athlete, professional dancer and restaurateur—was one of Sydney's most colourful entrepreneurs for 50 years, running dancing halls, skating rinks, nightspots and a string of racehorses.

Jim's father was a Danish sea captain who joined the Hudson Bay Company during its pioneering days around the remote coastal areas of Canada and ferried miners to the northern Arctic during the Yukon goldrushes.

Jim was born in 1896 and raised in the town of Victoria in British Columbia. As a teenager he learned to use his fists around the lumber camps of the Canadian backwoods, and boxed professionally. As a youngster he won titles at boxing, ice-skating and sculling, and played lacrosse at a high level as well as some semi-pro rugby.

Despite his obsession in later years to always appear among the best-dressed men in Sydney, with a red carnation in his buttonhole, he was also renowned for his ability to bounce even the toughest drunks from his nightspots.

In 1913, at age 17, Bendrodt had taken a job shovelling coal in the stokehold of a ship headed for Australia. He landed with a £5 note, one suit, one hat and a pair of boots. Within a fortnight of his arrival he was earning £30 a week as a roller-skating champ. He and partner George Irving performed a duo act described as 'two daring young men with flying legs on roller-skates who entertained patrons of the Tivoli as they raced, tumbled and twisted to a climax like whirling dervishes'.

Bendrodt had held Canadian titles from 3-mile to 24-hour events and the roller-skating craze was just catching on in Sydney. Eventually he was matched against an imported US Champion named Echard in a 24-hour race billed as the 'world championship' at Sydney's Exhibition Building. Bendrodt bet all his savings on himself but lost by a mere 40 yards.

When war broke out in 1914 he was the 198th man to enlist in the initial 1500-man force, which was given 11 days training and sent to annex German New Guinea. He was netting £200 a week from a dance hall, but within a fortnight he was a six-bob-a-day private on a troop ship in the Pacific.

A friend from those days later recalled:

Jim was a dandy—always the best dressed man in town, with that red carnation in his buttonhole. All Jim's mob were shoddily dressed in woeful looking uniforms, made in a hurry for soldiers in a hurry. But not Jim; he'd had his uniform tailor-made, and was a picture of sartorial elegance as he sailed away.

When he returned to Australia in 1915 Bendrodt felt he hadn't yet done enough for the Allies' war effort. He sold everything to buy a first-class passenger ticket on the RMS *Makura*, bound for Vancouver, and sailed off to Canada to join the Royal Flying Corps.

On his return from military service he marched into J.C. Williamson's one day and said he could act. They believed him and he landed small parts in several plays starring Madge Fabian, Lou Kimball and Link Plummer. He later recalled that he was a lousy actor but discovered he was a terrific showman.

He used that showmanship running dance halls in Sydney in the 1920s and 1930s, became a professional dancer and married his partner Peggy Dawes. He also ran a dancing school in Pitt Street. Bendrodt's enterprises included the Palais Royal dance hall at the showground and the Trocadero in George Street. By the late 1930s he'd switched to ice-skating and transformed the Palais Royal into the Ice Palace. He told reporters he had learned to ice-skate on the frozen Canadian lakes in his youth.

He also became a noted campaigner against cruelty to animals, was a prominent and vociferous member of the RSPCA, and bred German Shepherd dogs.

Bendrodt wrote several books about horses and dogs and his short stories regularly featured in major American magazines. Two of his most famous stories concerned horses named Gay Romance, a filly that won him a fortune, and 'Irish Lad', which was in fact the story of his horse Spam who cost backers a fortune when he failed in the Melbourne Cup. Professor Walter Murdoch called Bendrodt 'the Poet Laureate of the horse and dog'.

During World War II Bendrodt began his famous campaign in the press and on radio deploring the slaughter of pet dogs, given up by their owners to be gassed during the days of meat rationing. His plea began; 'Why did you kill him, Mister? Why did you kill your friend?' The response was so amazing that newspapers and radio stations refused to charge him for the advertisements.

Bendrodt soon became a leading owner-trainer of racehorses, with stables at Kensington and a 150-acre model stud, Prince's Farm, at Castlereagh on the banks of the Nepean River, 40 miles west of Sydney.

In line with his obsession with kindness to animals, the facilities at the stud incorporated the ultimate in comfort for his horses, one visitor describing the stud as being 'run on the lines of a first-class hotel for horses', Bendrodt objected to jockeys using whips on horses and other trainers often declared his kindness prevented him from working his horses hard enough to get them into racing condition. They were appalled by his habit of feeding them apples and chocolate.

Bendrodt was particularly criticised for the way he trained War Eagle, whom many experts considered would have been a champion under another trainer. War Eagle won the Lord Mayor's Cup at Rosehill in 1946, and ran placings in the AJC Sires Produce Stakes, Champagne Stakes, Hobartville Stakes and City Tattersall's Cup, but many considered he should have won numerous feature races.

Despite the supposedly easy training workouts, War Eagle held the 10-furlong record at Rosehill for many years. When he died Bendrodt erected a huge cage with eagles in it above the horse's grave at Prince's Farm.

The professionals also ridiculed Bendrodt for his handling of the preparation of War Eagle for the 1945 Melbourne Cup, when the horse finished 19th behind Rainbird. Bendrodt then imported the Irish St Leger winner Spam for the 1946 Cup and backed it to win more than £100,000. Ridden by Billy Cook, Spam finished 12th but Bendrodt always claimed the horse had been flattened by the Australian heat and the hard track.

Bendrodt's introduction to the turf was through a former jockey who worked as a waiter at his dance hall. In 1923 the waiter persuaded him to buy the pony Passella for £100. He kept the mare in a yard behind the dance hall and the waiter trained her in his spare time. The mare had her first start in Bendrodt's colours at Kensington and he bet £400 on her at 2 to 1 with bookie Jack Shaw. Passella, ridden by Bill Cook, dead-heated with another mare, Pretty Sweet, and in those days that meant the pair competed in a run-off an hour later.

Pretty Sweet just beat Passella in a jostling finish but the waiter urged Bendrodt to protest. The complaint was upheld and Passella won.

Bendrodt then bought books, studied breeding and horse care, and began training his own small string of horses.

In 1931, at the height of the Depression, he bought a horse called Firecracker for 60 guineas. Years later a commemorative plaque honouring jockey Bill Cook was unveiled at City Tattersall's Club. It featured three champions: Rainbird, on whom Cook won the 1945 Melbourne Cup; Amounis, on whom he took the 1930 Caulfield Cup; and Carioca, on whom he won 11 races including seven in succession. The plaque also featured the forgotten Firecracker. Below Firecracker were the words: 'the horse that saved the Palais Royal by winning at Menangle in 1931'.

In July 1931 Bendrodt had addressed his 150 employees at the Palais Royal. He had just sufficient cash to pay the £1200 he owed in wages. The Palais would have to close unless the staff adopted his daring plan to win enough to keep it going through the Depression.

Firecracker was entered for a race at Menangle, to be ridden by Bendrodt's friend Bill Cook. The plan was to bet the wages on the horse, with the employees to get double their money if it won and the rest of the winnings to be used to keep the Palais open. The employees agreed, and Bendrodt and eight of the Palais' bouncers drove to Menangle and backed Firecracker from 10 to 1 to 6 to 4, and the horse won by a length from the useful sprinter Gold-digger.

Bendrodt often recalled how he went to the 1937 yearling sales to buy a colt, but peered into a horse's box and fell for the small bay filly inside. He bought her for £450, named her Gay Romance, and later that year she won the Gimcrack Stakes at Randwick.

Bendrodt wagered everything he had on that race and collected a fortune in bets. The winnings helped finance Prince's restaurant, which he opened in Martin Place in 1938 and which soon became the showpiece of his empire.

Prince's was an instant success, but during the war it came in for a lot of criticism from over-patriotic 'blue-noses' who declared no one should enjoy themselves while the troops were away fighting. Bendrodt retorted that Prince's was a valuable recreation spot for troops on leave—they certainly spent a fortune there and made him rich—and the US forces recognised this by placing it at the top of their lists of recommended entertainment establishments.

Bendrodt often claimed that when Mrs Eleanor Roosevelt visited Australia he was the only civilian she sent for—to thank him for helping US troops in their brief spells of leave.

As a punter, Bendrodt often only bet in £5 notes, though every now and then he would 'have a go', but rarely on anyone else's horse. He used to say: 'Punting is one of those things there is no percentage in. I can go broke easier ways than that.'

Nevertheless, he collected £15,000 when Rimfire won the 1948 Melbourne Cup; he explained that he'd selected Rimfire on his breeding three weeks before the Cup and had backed it at 150 to 1.

Other good horses owned by Bendrodt included Snow Star, which won at Canterbury and Randwick in 1948, and Goshawk, one of the first horses to go to the United States from Australia.

One incident which highlighted Bendrodt's great love of horses concerned Tommy Smith's famous first winner, Bragger, a horse that campaigned through the 1940s for Smith and was still racing in top-class races, such as the Newcastle Cameron Handicap and Randwick Tramway handicap, when he was ten years old.

Bragger was returning to Smith's stable after a spell when the float, carrying three horses, caught fire on Parramatta Road near Auburn. Driver Kevin Spain smelled smoke, jumped out and threw open the float doors. The straw was blazing and though he was easily able to lead out two horses, one of which was owned by Bendrodt, Bragger was straddled in fright across a partition and was very badly burned.

Smith fought for weeks to save Bragger and horse-lover Bendrodt enlisted the help of a doctor friend; all three men applied ointments and medicines for the best part of a month, often around the clock, before they finally gave up the hopeless cause and put an end to the horse's suffering.

In 1950, Bendrodt imported the sire Abbots Fell, acknowledged among breeders as the greatest living descendant of Carbine and, at that time, the highest-priced thoroughbred imported into Australia for stud. Bendrodt also imported numerous other horses from England, including the stallion Scarlet Emperor and the broodmare Tollgate.

Jim Bendrodt gave up racing during the 1950s because he said both training horses and selling his stud's produce to other racing men involved 'too much sadness and distress for an animal lover'. He publicly castigated racehorse owners for selling broken-down champions without thought or care as to what may become of them—he himself had refused to sell his beloved War Eagle at the end of his career, despite an offer for the then huge sum of £12,000.

For a time Bendrodt retreated to his old-world cottage in Eastbourne Avenue, Darling Point, where his collection of Royal Meissen porcelain and Bohemian crystal took pride of place. But in the late 1950s he opened a new haunt for the racing fraternity, Caprice Restaurant—opposite Royal Sydney Golf Club and beside the flying-boat base, on the water at Lyne Park, Rose Bay. The restaurant was fitted out at great expense and was described as 'a caravanserai for the connoisseurs of cuisine'.

Bendrodt sold Caprice in 1967. His wife, Peggy, later said, 'He was very upset at having to sell—but he knew his health was becoming worse and he could not continue with the special attention he always gave his patrons.' He took a trip back to Canada in 1968 and, upon his return to Australia, reappeared at the track as a small-time owner-trainer.

Jim Bendrodt died on a Saturday morning in February 1973. Later that afternoon his filly Tropic Star ran third at Randwick at 330 to 1.

# A 'point-to-point'

## A.B. ('BANJO') PATERSON

LAST SATURDAY'S POINT-TO-POINT STEEPLECHASE at Eastwood brought out a field of seven starters, each of whom had his partisans among the crowd of ladies that clustered at the top of the hill.

Eastwood House stands on a round-topped volcanic hill, whose smooth, steep sides are terraced with gardens and shrubberies. The course runs round the foot of the hill and, except for about a quarter of a mile, the horses are in view all the way; but, to keep them in sight, the spectators have to move round the hill, so that on Saturday the amusing spectacle was witnessed of hundreds of fashionably dressed ladies and gentlemen running backwards and forwards on the smooth, green hilltop, shrieking encouragement to the riders, who, far away below them, were toiling gallantly over fences, ditches, avenues, logs, and anything else that came in the road.

The day was fine and clear, the air like wine, and over everything was a scent of grasses and flowers; also there was plenty of excitement, and not a little to laugh at; so what more would anybody want?

To encourage owners to ride their own horses instead of seeking the assistance of the 'professional amateurs', who usually figure in the saddle in such races, it was a condition of the race that any owner riding overweight would be allowed a 1-second start for every pound overweight he carried.

This somewhat novel idea worked fairly well, though the second per pound allowance is not enough. The dauntless seven were lined up by Mister Forward, the starter, with their tails almost touching a big built-up log fence, and then, by the aid of a stopwatch, they were dispatched in a sort of timetable order.

First to go was Andover, a fine big grey horse, about the best specimen of a weight-carrying horse in the lot, but he was very fat, and was carrying more than 15 stone, so that his only chance was for all the others to fall or baulk. He had a 48-second start, and on the word being given he started off on his lonely journey at a good round pace, jumping the first few fences in good style, and disappeared among the timber.

Next to go was Mercadool, another veteran, whose only hope consisted in his being a safe conveyance. He left sharp to time, 17 seconds after Andover. Barney followed 11 seconds later. He is a chestnut horse, and at one time the property of the well-known and well-liked 'Jack' Fitzsimmons, who committed suicide in the gardens. Barney is well known on many showgrounds, but is getting rather past steeplechasing.

Riverstone followed 11 seconds later, a good class of horse, and looking very well. He was ridden by a young gentleman from the old country, whose turnout for neatness and correctness put the rest of the field in the shade; and he rode with pluck, if not with judgement, as will be seen later on.

Tatta, Larry and Sparrow were the scratch horses, i.e. those that carried no overweight, and they left 48 seconds after Andover.

It could hardly be called a race at first. Andover was out of sight, Mercadool just disappearing, and Barney and Riverstone stringing after him like a wild geese, when the scratch horses left; but the water jump altered all that and brought them together in one common bond of disaster.

The spectators on the hill witnessed the start, and then ran round to watch for the first horses to come through the orchard. It seemed a long time. At last Andover appeared, jumping grandly, though it was rumoured that he had already parted once with his rider on the journey, and had been remounted. Be that as it may, he was making no mistake about his fences when he burst in view of the populace. He was followed by Mercadool and Barney, and people held their breath as the trio strung down to the water jump.

This jump is at the foot of the hill, and is of no great width, but the taking off side is higher than the landing side, and the latter was muddy and slippery on Saturday, and not at all an inviting place to jump onto. So, at all events, thought Andover, and on being ridden at it, he dropped dead. He was hurriedly wheeled around, and rushed at it again, but again dropped dead, this time shooting his rider into the wavelets that lapped invitingly below, the rider pulling the bridal off in his fall.

Mercadool and Barney scrambled over more or less ungracefully, and then came Riverstone at full speed. As soon as he saw the water he made up his mind to stop, but the 'new chum' on his back was equally determined to go on, and he rubbed the spurs and whalebone into Riverstone in a style that made the noble animal fling himself in despairing fashion off the bank, much like a suicide jumping off South Head; he landed half in and half out of the water, shooting his rider over his head, while a yell of excitement went up from the spectators on the hilltop.

The rider stuck to the bridle and remounted, but the rein was broken, and the martingale also broke with the result that the saddle slipped back and the horse ran the best part of 2 miles over fences with the loose end of a broken rein flapping round his legs, and his rider most insecurely perched on his hindquarters.

Hardly had he got away again, when the three scratch horses swooped down on the jump. Larry and Tatta baulked, and Sparrow wished to follow their example, but his rider was of the determined order, and he let the old grey have a few rib-roasters that lifted him clean up in the air, only to fall half in and half out of the water as Riverstone had done. And again the shrill feminine yell, 'He's off; he's off', rose from the hilltop.

Sparrow's rider stuck to the bridle grimly, and remounted, and after getting over at the second attempt, the field was pretty well closed up, with the exception of Andover, who, being without a bridle, had run away and was eating grass.

The rest of the race demands little description. Mercadool's rider mistook the course and pulled off at the 'Avenue Double', the red flags on the fence either not being conspicuous enough to catch his eye, or else conveying the impression that they were danger signals. The others rushed the double in style, but the two leaders, Larry and Tatta, baulked in the lane, and would be there yet, only that Sparrow was kept straight and gave them a lead.

Riverstone was in two minds about stopping, but not being used to having a rider sitting on his hips, he thought it better to go on, and he got across somehow, though he practically fell over the second fence. There were 'riders in the stand' watching the race and criticising, who wouldn't have been on the horse for £1000; but his rider still kept on with him, though he was hopelessly in the rear.

From here on, Tatta drew to the front, and it was obvious that, barring a fall, he must win. He is a thoroughbred horse to all appearances and, notwithstanding his great age of 18 years, was in good trim, and 'stood off' his fences and sprang like a stag. Sparrow chased him home pertinaciously, but the grey lost too much ground at the water and at the fences; and the end of the struggle saw old Tatta, very tired, lobbing on in front of Sparrow, with Larry, just in sight, third.

No others finished. There was no time taken.

The usual 'take-down' bookmakers put in an appearance, and laid 6 to 4 against Tatta, and refused to pay when he won, on the grounds that he was the only horse backed, and they had wasted their afternoon for nothing. They were escorted off the premises with threats and bad language; but if the cherry-picking inhabitants of Ryde and Eastwood were half the men that their forefathers used to be, they would have given those bookmakers a wash, if nothing else.

A hurdle race was run after the steeplechase, but the jumps were so flimsy that if a crow sat on them they would fall down, so there was no excitement, except that a big chestnut horse knocked off the top rail with his front legs and got himself tangled up with it, he rolled himself and his rider over and over for a few revolutions. Then the guests drank the health of Mister Eric Terry, the winner of the steeplechase, who rode a good race, and then all and sundry made for home.

# The Cab Horse's Story

## C.J. Dennis

Now, you wouldn't imagine, to look at me,
That I was a racehorse once.
I have done my mile in—let me see—
No matter. I was no dunce.
But you'd not believe me if I told
Of gallops I did in days of old.

I was first in—ah, well! What's the good?
It hurts to recall those days
When I drew from men, as a proud horse should,
Nothing but words of praise:
Oh, the waving hats, and the cheering crowd!
How could a horse help being proud?

My owner was just as proud as I;
I was cuddled and petted and praised.
My fame was great and my price was high,
And every year 'twas raised.
Then I strained a sinew in ninety-nine,
And that's when started my swift decline.

I was turned to grass for a year or so;
Then dragged to an auction sale;
And a country sport gave me a go;
But how could I hope but fail?
'A crock,' said he. And I here began
To learn of the ways of cruel man.

A year I spent as a lady's hack—
I was growing old and spent—
But she said that the riding hurt her back;
So we parted; and I went
For a while—and it nearly broke my heart—
Dragging a greasy butcher's cart.
Then my stifle went. And I, proud horse,

Son of the nobly born,
The haughty king of a city course,
Knew even a butcher's scorn!
So down the ladder I quickly ran;
Till I came to be owned by a bottle man.
And my bed was hard and my food was poor,
And my work was harder still
Dragging a cart from door to door—
The slave of Bottle-oh Bill.
Till even he, for a few mean bob,
Sold me into this hateful job.

As I dozed and dreamed in the ranks one day,
Thinking of good days past,
I heard a voice that I knew cry, 'Hey!
Say, cabby, is this horse fast?'
And he looked at me in a way I know.
'Twas the man I'd loved in the long ago.
'Twas my dear, old master of ninety-nine,
And I waited, fair surprised.
But ne'er by a look and ne'er by sign
Did he show he recognised.

Then I heard his words ('twas my last hard knock):
'Why don't you pole-axe the poor old crock?'
And he turned aside to a low-bred mare
That was foaled on some cockie's farm,
And he drove away. What do I care?
I can come to no more harm.
In a knacker's yard I am worth at least
Some pence for a hungry lion's feast.

# Randwick trainers circa 1895

## NAT GOULD

RANDWICK IS THE HEADQUARTERS of the turf in New South Wales, and I know more of it than any other racing quarter in the Australian colonies.

A quiet, charmingly situated place is the village of Randwick. Built on a rise it commands an extensive view over the racecourse and far away to famous Botany Bay and La Perouse. It also has an outlook over the Centennial Park, and a distant view of the city may be obtained.

Randwick is within easy distance of Sydney, about 4 miles or a shade more from the General Post Office, and the trams run there at frequent intervals.

On Sunday afternoon the Randwick road to Coogee, a small watering place about 6 miles from Sydney, is a sight worth seeing. Hundreds of vehicles of all kinds are out, many of them sulkies with fast trotters in the shafts.

These sulkies are driven at a great pace, and there is a desire on the part of each driver to get in front and head the procession. A spill or two is not much thought of, and a buggy or sulky minus a wheel merely excites derision.

Nothing is more delightful than to pay a visit to some well-appointed racing stable at Randwick and, after inspecting the horses, to have a quiet chat with the trainer in his comfortable house.

Trainers, as a rule, are reserved men, but once you get them started on a favourite topic they are good company and have a large fund of anecdotes and reminiscences to draw on.

One of the principal racing stables is that resided over by Mr Thomas Payten at Newmarket, lower Randwick. These stables were built by the Hon. James White and, in years gone by, Mr White as owner, Mr M. Fennelly as trainer and Tom Hales as jockey, were a formidable trio in Australian racing.

When Mr Fennelly died, Tom Payten took command of the Newmarket horses, and a worthy successor he proved to be.

The success of the famous 'blue and white' on the turf was wonderful; and the stable won almost every race of importance. How many derbies have been won by horses trained here I am afraid to say; but when I first landed in the colonies the AJC and VRC Derby were regarded as standing dishes for one of Mr White's horses. Backers looked forward with confidence to having a plunge on Mr White's Derby colt, and, as a rule, they had occasion to rejoice after the race.

Every classic race of importance fell to the share of Mr White's horses, and the run of successes in these races is phenomenal, but the spell was broken when Mr White decided upon selling the greater number of his horses in training.

Chester was the founder of White's stud, and he was a wonderfully good horse, and Martini–Henri also got some fair stock. Chester, however, must have been Mr White's favourite, and no horse better deserved that honour.

Since Mr White's death Tom Payten has been in sole charge at Newmarket, although the ownership of the horses has changed. Mrs White still keeps up the breeding establishment at Kirkham, and has imported a couple of well-bred English stallions to take the place of the defunct Chester.

Newmarket stables are built on a large space of ground at Lower

Randwick. The trainer's residence is a fine, commodious house, and stands well back from the road in spacious grounds.

The stables are well built, and there is ample room in them. Entering a large covered building, the visitor finds himself in a spacious hall, as it were, at the far end of which are arranged large loose boxes, and above them a wide gallery goes round three sides of the building.

All these boxes are kept in beautiful order, and are airy, and light, and well drained. Everything is neat and clean, as a racing stable should be, and the numerous lads are kept well in hand and are taught their business, and also, what is quite as necessary, obedience.

Tom Payten rules over all with a firm hand, and at the same time, is a just master. Many a happy hour have I passed in these famous stables with the trainer, and have heard him descant with pride upon the various horses as they were led out of their boxes for my inspection.

Some wonderfully good animals have tenanted these boxes. Here I have seen Abercorn, Dreadnought, Cranbrook, Camoola, Carlyon, Titan, Trieste, Autonomy, Stromboli, Prelude, Trident and a host of others of which I am reminded. Thousands of pounds have been spent upon Newmarket, and the money has not been thrown away.

Lower down the road, on the opposite side, stands an unpretentious but cosy-looking house, and at the rear a glimpse can be caught of an extensive range of stables.

This is the abode of Mr John Allsopp, a trainer who has rapidly come to the front during the past ten years. Mr Allsopp is a very different man from Mr Payten, and he has very few equals as a trainer. His stables are built on three sides of a square, with a spacious yard in the centre, and every accommodation for hay and corn, and the various articles of diet racehorses require.

All the boxes at the stable were built on the trainer's own design, and they reflect great credit upon him. Many a good horse has John Allsopp shown me in these boxes. A more devoted man to his work than Allsopp I have never met. He revels in it; and morning, noon and night he can be found on the spot looking after his charges. In great measure I think the secret of his success lies in his constant attention to the horses under his charge.

For a thing to be well done there is nothing like doing it yourself, and Mr Allsopp evidently knows this, and acts accordingly.

The last time I paid him a visit, Paris, now in England, was an inmate of his stables. Paris is about one of the best gallopers I ever saw, and he has won no end of big races with a couple of Caulfield Cups falling to his share.

Cremorne, Trenchant, Sundial, Atlas and others were in the comfortable boxes. One of the best horses Allsopp has had in my time was Gibraltar, and it was most unfortunate when he broke down in Melbourne.

In the dining room at Mr Allsopp's are portraits in oils of most of the good horses he has trained, and he is not a believer in the superstition that after a horse's picture has been painted he never wins a race.

Leaving Mr Allsopp's and crossing the road we come to the stables occupied by Mr H. Raynor, a trainer of the old school.

Harry Raynor's face is familiar at all principal race meetings. He has not what may be called a charming countenance, nor is he much of a ladykiller, but he knows his business thoroughly. He generally appears in the paddock on race days in a slouch hat, and almost invariably carries an umbrella. He looks more like an old bush hand than one of the best trainers at Randwick.

Many a good thing has Harry Raynor been on during his time. He trained for the late Mr W. Gannon up to the time of his death. Mr Gannon was well known as the host of Petty's Hotel in Sydney and at one time acted as starter for the AJC.

Some curious yarns are told about Mr Gannon and his trainer, and one in particular tickled me immensely. It shows how the biter was bitten, in this case with a vengeance.

Mr Gannon owned a horse called Arsenal, a good animal, and Harry Raynor trained it. The horse was much fancied by his owner for the Melbourne Cup and Mr Gannon determined to be in the market in time to get the cream of the betting. He accordingly instructed a well-known betting commissioner at that time to take the long odds to a considerable amount for him.

Instead of doing what he ought in fairness to have done, the commissioner let another big backer and horse owner into the secret. The odds were duly accepted, but the long prices returned to, let us call him 'Mister B', and the shorter odds to the owner, Mr Gannon. Naturally Mr Gannon was riled at not obtaining a longer price, and he determined to get even with Mister B.

Shortly before the Cup was due to be run, Mr Gannon was staying at Menzies Hotel, in Melbourne. Mister B was also there, and the pair were good friends and often dined together.

One evening at dinner Mr Gannon received a telegram. He opened it leisurely, not deeming it of much importance, and read it.

Its contents apparently had an effect on him, for he gave vent to some expressions more powerful than polite.

'What's the matter?' asked Mister B, who was sitting opposite to him, 'anything wrong with the horse?'

Mr Gannon handed the telegram across the table, and when Mister B glanced at it he, too, became very serious.

The telegram was from Harry Raynor, to the effect that Arsenal and 'gone wrong', and it was doubtful if he could start in the Cup.

Mister B thanked Mr Gannon for showing him the telegram, and he intimated his intention of getting rid of the bulk of the money he had taken about the horse, by laying it off. This laying-off business was put into the hands of a commissioner, who commenced operations at once.

As fast as the money was laid off, however, another well-known backer was taking up the wagers in favour of Arsenal. Mister B knew this gentleman, and thinking to warn him against backing a 'dead un', he said, 'It is no business of mine, but are you backing Arsenal for yourself? If so, let someone else have a bit of it. It is my money that is being laid off; the horse has gone wrong.'

'That's strange,' said the backer, who knew nothing of the telegram business.

'Why?' asked Mister B, 'what is strange?'

'Well, I'm backing it for the owner,' was the answer that astounded Mister B, who commenced to smell mischief and went to his commissioner and asked him not to lay off any more Arsenal money.

'I can't,' was the laconic reply, 'I've laid it all off already.'

'And Gannon's got it!' was Mister B's reply.

It was quite true. Mr Gannon had paid the backer in his own coin, and no doubt he chuckled to himself on the success of the telegram.

As a matter of fact, Arsenal did go off his feed before the Melbourne Cup he won, and his clever trainer had an unthankful task in getting him to the post all right.

# A day's racing

## A.B. ('BANJO') PATERSON

WE HAVE COME TO the point where the reader, having followed us thus far, should have learned the rudiments of the noble art of horse-racing. Let us suppose that he finds himself on a racecourse, glasses on shoulder, racebook in his hand, a determined look in his eye and brain waves of information flying about like wireless messages all round him. How is he to start operations? To what shall he apply? Shall he 'follow the money'? Shall he follow a tip? Dare he trust his own judgement? Shall he follow the fortunes of a crude jockey? Truly it is the most hopeless and at the same time fascinating problem that confronts him.

Now is the time to put to the test all that he knows. The programme begins with a maiden race for horses that have never won more than 50 pounds. There are a dozen starters and an unsettled sort of market. The ring are calling one horse as favourite, but possibly it is a favourite that they themselves have appointed to the position, and the alleged money which has made the animal favourite may not be stable money at all.

The 'knowledge boxes' seem to be standing about with a bored air, waiting developments. And now is the time of the bold backer to take a pull at himself to stop and think to concentrate all his talents on the problem before he wastes a shilling.

A maiden plate is always a bad race to bet on. Any old horses that are in the race must of necessity be pretty bad or they would never have reached that age without having won £50. A four- or five-year-old horse that has done any considerable amount of racing and has never managed to land a stake worth £50 is pretty certain to be in the 'latter dead class'. If there are any young untried horses in the race, they may possibly be some good. But the bulk of them are bound to be pretty bad, and of all bad things, a bad horse is about the worst possible to be connected with. So the punter must approach this class of race with much misgiving and should certainly bet light if he bets at all. Still, we go to the racecourse to bet, so here goes to pick the winner of the maiden plate.

First of all let us apply the money test. Is there any horse, whose stable have thought it worthwhile to get a good jockey for him and to back him in earnest with their hard-earned money? Let us see what information on this point the 'knowledge boxes' can give us. Here comes Ike Pickum. He has a small billet somewhere in the city but he attends half the race meetings in the kingdom, wears a diamond pin, bets all the time, and seems to be always better dressed and to have more ready money than most men who work hard and draw double his salary. Ike's opinion ought to be worth having, being a goodhearted fellow as most turf followers are, he will not mind giving us any information that won't interfere with his own plans.

'What are they taking in this, Ike?'

'Well, the ring have Forlorn Hope the favourite at threes but I don't see any of the right people taking it. It may be only the public that are backing him. Better wait a while.'

So far, not much good. Now, if we can, let us get a glance over a bookmaker's shoulder at his book—not a very dignified proceeding, perhaps, but when you are in Rome you must try to do as the Romans—so we sidle up behind a gentleman who is calling 'Three to one on the fee-yuld! Three to one on the fee-yuld!', as if he were a new phonograph with magnifying mouthpiece and all the latest attachments. Let us have a look at his book. Under the heading of Forlorn Hope the entries are fairly thick and about four wagers from the top someone has taken a wager of £200 to £50. Now move on to the next man. In his book also is a wager of the same amount, entered at about the same place in his book. Hah! This looks like business. Now we begin to think that we are on the track of something, and feel like Sherlock Holmes.

Try another man: a bookmaker in a small way this time, whose motto is, 'short prices and civility'. He has a wager entered of £60 to £20, about as big a bet as he cares to lay in one book. Now, what has our inspiration told us? It has told us that someone has been round the ring, putting fairly big wagers on this horse, and in all probability the man that put the money on knew something—or thought he did—because the general public does not invest sums of this size on guesswork. It looks more like the work of a stable commissioner. Of course there is no certainty that it is any such thing, but if you want absolute certainty about turf matters, you won't do much betting. We have at any rate got this far that the horse appears to have been backed by somebody for some real money.

Next comes the question—is the animal's form good enough to give him a good chance of winning? In the case of these maidens, a horse's form is not so very great a guide, as the animal has probably been meeting a lot of bad ones like himself and will be found to have run fairly well when the company was worse than usual. When he met any really decent horses, he, as the French say, *courut obscurement* or, as the Australian translates it, 'run 'orrible'.

While we're thinking out what his form is worth, up comes a friendly trainer and he helps us quite a lot. 'Forlorn Hope,' he says, looking up into the sky apparently for inspiration. 'Well, I know they're backing him, and they've got a good man on him. Of course he's not much good: never was and never will be any relation to a real racehorse: but he's pretty well just now and these are a terrible bad lot.'

'Any of the younger horses got a chance?'

'Well, there's a colt of old Billy Smith's here, Tin Tack they call him, did a real good lop last week; but I don't see my money going in on him. Better stick to the favourite or leave it alone altogether. The others—well, it's a miracle how they can get past the zoo, while there's lions to be fed twice a day,' and with this he sidles off. So now our horse has passed the money test, the form test, the jockey test, and we scurry over to apply the condition test.

A hurried inspection tells us that his condition is good. He has done a lot of racing and is hard and looks fairly competent, though most horses that get beaten often have a worried look when they go out to race; they are so used to getting a good whipping at the end of every strenuous struggle—an experience liable to daunt the stoutest heart. While watching him walk around, we see Tin Tack, a big loose-made, half-ready sort of colt; but somehow there is just that little look of class about him that marks the good one.

The moment for decision is at hand, the hour has arrived, the risk must be faced and we go back to the ring with the bookmakers who have been roaring ever since. There is a steady stream of small punters now putting their pounds on the favourite. They have agreed, if not even as we have, and are satisfied to risk their money. Also an acquaintance in the crowd says he hears the favourite is a certainty—but if you listen to what acquaintances tell you in the crowd, your doom is sealed.

Tin Tack is at sixes with apparently no takers: so, with the feeling of a man saying 'I will' in the marriage service, we take £30 to £10 about Forlorn Hope and climb the stand full of doubt. For it is a queer thing that, no matter what a man backs, he nearly always wishes he had backed something else. Still, all the omens pointed to Forlorn Hope, so let us get up and see it decided.

The field go to the post as we settle ourselves in our seats and the bookmakers crowd round to a position where they can see the race. The roar of their voices reaches us en masse, so to speak, but at last the name Forlorn Hope comes up through the babble of sound like the voice of a tune in a church choir and—heavens, what was that? Fives? Did he say fives Forlorn Hope? He did! There it goes again. 'Five to one Forlorn Hope!' All over the ring now! And we took threes! Gloom, doubt, suspicion, depression all spread themselves round us like a garment. If there is anything in racing that poisons a man's mind, it is taking a short price about a horse and then hearing him go out to a longer price.

Up comes an acquaintance, hot and breathless from climbing the stairs.

'What's Forlorn Hope at down there?'

'Fives now. He was threes. He's lengthening out!'

'What's favourite, then?'

'Tin Tack. Thing of Billy Smith's. They put a lot of money in on it at the last minute! I tried to get onto it, but half of them wouldn't bet me at all and the other half wanted odds. They say it can't lose!'

Horror!

The horses are at the post now and we get our glasses on them, hoping that things may be all right after all. Forlorn Hope looks well and the fact that his price lengthened may merely have been due to the backing of the other. Let us look on the bright side, anyhow. Still—if we had only waited—they're off!

And now you notice an almost invariable thing in a field of bad horses, namely that three-fourths of them never seem to get into the race at all. One would think that being all bad together, they would keep one another company in their misery; but some are grossly unfit, others deadly slow, and others not anxious to distinguish themselves, so the field soon has a long tail to it.

Right in the lead come Forlorn Hope and Tin Tack. Only 6 furlongs, so they are at it hammer and tongs all the way. The older horse has got away a little better than the other and has half a length's lead, but the colt is at his hindquarters and so far there is nothing in it either way. Close by in the press box, one of the reporters with glasses to his eyes is calling the race while his assistant takes down his remarks.

'At the half mile, Forlorn Hope leads by half a length, Tin Tack next going well, then Ruby Star and something in blue, Walrus and Quicklime. Get the distance,' goes on the cold-blooded droning voice. 'Forlorn Hope is done with and Tin Tack comes on with Walrus and something in blue next. What's that in blue, Billy? It'll win all right—Orchid, that's what it is—Orchid and Tin Tack come away together. Orchid going easy, then Quick Lime, Walrus and Forlorn Hope.'

The speaker's voice is drowned in the yells of the crowd as Tin Tack and Orchid settle down to finish.

We have never taken our glasses off the champion Forlorn Hope, hoping vainly that he may make a finishing run and win us our money. But alas, he seems to be tied to the fence while the field like a roaring lion rush past him: his jockey finding that he cannot go the pace with the others has determined that as he cannot be first he is not going to be second or third; so he drops out of it, and finishes flourishing his whip and flogging his boot for the benefit of the handicapper.

Our glory is dust and ashes, our spirit is but a spark, our money is gone; Orchid, whose name we have never even heard called, comes away easily in the last half-dozen strides and wins by a length from Tin Tack. Something has to run third and Ruby Star's apprentice rider, wild with excitement and working overtime with whip and spur, gains the position and earns nothing but the curses of his master and a rise of 3 pounds in the weight for the horse's next appearance.

Orchid! Who would have thought it! We sit dazed while two hard-faced gentlemen pass us on their way down. One says to the other, 'Did you catch that one?'

'Had a seven on it,' is the reply, and they disappear.

Post-mortems are odious, but anyhow let us look into this Orchid business and on what we have done or left undone that we should have missed it. He is a well-bred colt that is trained by one of the old school of trainers, a man who only keeps a few horses and does not have to win a race every five minutes of his life to pay expenses. The horse is ridden by a good jockey and has won several little races at small meetings.

'Was he backed at all?' is the next thing, and we find that his own stable got a good lump of money about him at a long price and then kept their mouths shut. It has been a coup, no doubt, a coup and we were not onto it; that is all that can be said.

How did the two hard-faced gentlemen know it? Well, the only explanation is that they devote all their time and very acute intellects to exactly such problems as these, and they must have got the information and thought it worth following.

Never mind. There are five more races and at least one winner (possibly two in case of a dead heat) in every race. Let us forget our sorrows and be up, and doing somebody.

# Glossary

ALLOWANCES   The permitted weight can be reduced because of the conditions of the race, because an apprentice is riding a horse or because females are racing against males.

APPRENTICE   An apprentice is a future jockey. He or she must be at least 16 years of age. In less important races apprentices receive weight allowances.

BETTING RING   A betting ring is the group of bookmakers taking bets on the race day on the course.

BIRDCAGE   A birdcage is a stable or enclosure where horses are held on race day. Only authorised people are permitted in this area.

BLEED   Horses occasionally bleed at the nose due to rupturing blood vessels. These horses have to be excluded from racing for a time and horses who bleed twice cannot race again.

BLINKERS   Blinkers are side pieces attached to a horse's head to prevent sideways vision. They are used to keep horses focused.

BOG TRACK   If the turf is extremely wet it is described as a bog track. In Australia track conditions are listed as fast (close to perfect), good, dead, slow and heavy (very wet).

**BOOKMAKER**  The bookmaker is the person who sets the odds for a race and takes the bets on it. Skilled bookmakers set their 'book' to win most races.

**BROODMARE**  A broodmare is a female thoroughbred horse used for producing racehorses.

**COLT**  A colt is a male horse that has not been gelded and is less than four years old.

**CRACK**  In horse circles crack means the very best. It can refer to the horse or the jockey.

**CUP**  The Melbourne Cup is the only true cup race, although many cups can be won in racing. It originated in 1861 and was run over 2 miles, now 3200 metres. The Melbourne Cup is a handicap race for all horses and is held on the first Tuesday in November.

**DAM**  A horse's female parent; a grand-dam is the female grand-parent. A horse is said to be 'out of' its dam.

**DEAD HEAT**  The term dead heat is used when two horses cross the finish line together. When races were run in three heats 'dead heats' were re-run.

**DERBY**  The Derby originated in England in 1780, with the first Derby held in Surrey at Epsom Downs. The race was named after the winner of the toss of a coin between the 12th Earl of Derby and Sir Charles Bunbury. Diomed, owned by the steward of the Jockey Club, Sir Charles Bunbury, won the first Derby. Traditionally the Derby is the classic race of the turf, restricted to three-year-old horses and run over 1½ miles.

**FILLY**  A filly is a female horse less than four years old. When a filly becomes a four-year-old it is called a mare. Once a mare gets to stud she becomes a broodmare.

**FIRST-UP**  A horse returning to the races from a spell is said to be first-up. If that horse wins its first race it is referred to as a first-up victory. Some horses are 'first-up' specialists and race well 'fresh'.

**FURLONG**  A furlong is one-eighth of a mile, or 201.168 metres after metric measurements were introduced in Australia on 1 August 1972.

GELDING   A gelding is a male horse whose testicles have been surgically removed. In general geldings are easier to train.

HANDICAP   A handicap is a race where the horses are given advantages or disadvantages in weight to give each entrant an equal chance of winning.

HANDS   The height of a horse is measured in hands; one hand equals 4 inches or 11.6 centimetres. Most thoroughbred horses stand at 15 to 17 hands. A horse is generally taller than 14.5 hands or 58 inches (147 centimetres). Under that it is a 'pony'.

LENGTH   In racing, place and winning margins are measured in lengths. A length is the distance from the nose of a winning horse to its hindquarters. As horses vary in size, so does the length, however the variation is very small. On average a length is slightly greater than 2 metres. Margins of less than a length are a neck, a half-neck, a half-head, a short half-head and a nose.

MAIDEN   A horse that has never won a race; a race for such horses.

OAKS   The Oaks race day originated in England in 1779 and is the female equivalent of the Derby, restricted to three-year-old fillies. It was named after the Surrey residence of the Earl of Derby.

ODDS   The bookmaker sets the odds or probability of a horse winning the race. As the amount of money bet on a horse increases, the odds are reduced as the horse's chances of winning seem to increase.

PLUNGE   A large amount of money suddenly invested on one horse—often in a planned 'coup' in an attempt to get as much money on as possible before the odds are lowered.

ST LEGER   A classic long-distance race.

SHIFT OUT   A horse that 'shifts out' moves away from the fence to a firmer, faster part of the track or to get a clear run. If forced to do so a horse may also shift towards the fence. Horses often drift in or out when tired or whipped, this is referred ro as 'shifting under pressure'.

SIRE   A sire is a horse's male parent; a grandsire is the horse's male grandparent. A horse is said be 'by' the sire.

SPELL   A spell is a break from training and racing where a horse can rest and put on weight in a paddock.

SPRINTER   A sprinter is a horse that races short distances, from 800 to 1400 metres.

STAKES   Stakes are racing events offering large amounts of money for the winner and the placegetters.

STAYER   A stayer is a horse that races long distances of 2000 metres or more. A good stayer is not only able to run the distance but is also fast enough to win.

STEEPLECHASE   A steeplechase is a race over many different and difficult obstacles. Originally it was a cross-country race with a church tower serving as a landmark to guide the riders.

STRAIGHT-OUT BET   A straight-out bet is a bet for a win only. If a field is small or has a short-priced favourite horse the bookmaker takes win bets only. If a horse completely dominates the race the bookmaker will not take any bets.

STRAPPER   A strapper is a stablehand caring for one or several horses on raceday.

STUD   A property specifically set up for breeding horses.

TOUT   Also called 'coat-tugger', 'urger' or 'whisperer', a tout is a person who makes a living selling tips on a racetrack by various methods, often nefarious and unprincipled—a con man.

WASTE   Most jockeys struggle to keep their weight low. They use exercise, fasting and sweating to reduce their weight and these methods are called wasting.

WEIGHT FOR AGE   Weight for age is a method of weight allocation for horses, allowing horses of different ages and gender to compete in the same race under the most equal conditions. Top races use a weight-for-age scale, allowing the best horse to win. The scale was introduced in England in the 18th century and has been modified slightly over the years.

YEARLING   A yearling is a one-year-old horse. To standardise horses' ages every horse in Australia turns one year older on 1 August.

# Acknowledgements

I would like to thank Stuart Neal, Jo Lyons and Siobhan Cantrill at Allen & Unwin for their passion and guidance, Alice Grundy for all the paperwork, and Darian Causby for his cover design. A special thankyou has to go to copyeditor Susin Chow, whose diligence, enthusiasm and suggestions proved that she was the best person we could have found for the job.

Thanks to Les Carlyon, David Hickie, Bruce Montgomerie and Crackers Keenan for their willingness to be part of this collection.

Racing people are generally gracious and helpful but I want to specifically thank Carole in the AJC Library and Sue Hutchinson and Murray Conallin in the AJC office; Lorinda Cramer, Liz Browne and Kathy Peters at the Victorian Racing Museum; and those two master racing photographers, Steve Hart and Ern McQuillan.

Very special thanks to Ellen and Bruce Montgomerie for their assistance and friendship. Thanks also to Dianna Corcoran for helping out with photos, and George and Paul at 2UE for allowing me to talk about racing so often.